LIVING THROUGH CRISES

NEW FRONTIERS OF SOCIAL POLICY

Living through Crises

How the Food, Fuel, and Financial Shocks Affect the Poor

Rasmus Heltberg, Naomi Hossain, and Anna Reva
Editors

THE WORLD BANK
Washington, D.C.

1818 H Street NW
Washington DC 20433
Telephone: 202-473-1000
Internet: www.worldbank.org

1 2 3 4 15 14 13 12

ISBN: 978-0-8213-8940-9
e-ISBN: 978-0-8213-9460-1
DOI: 10.1596/978-0-8213-8940-9

Library of Congress Cataloging-in-Publication data have been requested.

Cover photo: Curt Carnemark, World Bank.

Cover design: Naylor Design, Inc.

In many developing countries, the mixed record of state effectiveness, market imperfections, and persistent structural inequities has undermined the effectiveness of social policy. To overcome these constraints, social policy needs to move beyond conventional social service approaches toward development's goals of equitable opportunity and social justice. This series has been created to promote debate among the development community, policy makers, and academia, and to broaden understanding of social policy challenges in developing country contexts.

The books in the series are linked to the World Bank's Social Development Strategy. The strategy is aimed at empowering people by transforming institutions to make them more inclusive, cohesive, resilient, and accountable. This involves the transformation of subjects and beneficiaries into citizens with rights and responsibilities. Themes in this series include equity and development, assets and livelihoods, citizenship and rights-based social policy, and the social dimensions of infrastructure and climate change.

Titles in the series:

- *Assets, Livelihoods, and Social Policy*
- *Building Equality and Opportunity through Social Guarantees: New Approaches to Public Policy and the Realization of Rights*
- *Delivering Services in Multicultural Societies*
- *Inclusive States: Social Policy and Structural Inequalities*
- *Institutional Pathways to Equity: Addressing Inequality Traps*
- *Living through Crises: How the Food, Fuel, and Financial Shocks Affect the Poor*
- *Social Dimensions of Climate Change: Equity and Vulnerability in a Warming World*

CONTENTS

Tables

In our world of accelerating change, we are ever more globally connected. The most recognized dimensions of connection are those that affect the richer countries and middle classes everywhere. The runaway explosion of information and communication technologies is one dimension. The rich country debt and banking crisis is another. They conspicuously affect the rich, the less poor, and the powerful. But there is a less-recognized, less-researched, less-understood, and less-publicized domain at the other pole: how global crises affect those in developing countries who are poorer, more vulnerable, powerless, and less visible. It is they and their realities who are the focus and concern of *Living through Crises*, showing how these populations were hit and harmed by the food, fuel, and financial crises of 2008–11, and the range of their responses.

To be sure, they have received broad-brush generalized coverage in the media, and journalists may occasionally bring to light individual cases with sound bites of what people say. The extremes of refugee crises and near-famine conditions get prominent and important coverage. But the quieter everyday crises and suffering of ordinary poor people, their struggles and adaptations, and how these evolve, are largely overlooked. Quantitative surveys of income and expenditure pick up some aspects, although such surveys usually take a long time to conduct, process, and report, and so cannot keep up with rapid change. Some cost of living surveys and indices, and some early warning systems, are more timely but leave many significant gaps. Food prices are straightforward for governments to monitor, but labor market impacts are less easy, and migration and remittances harder still. Perhaps most critically, surveys are ill equipped and unlikely to capture and report on the contextual detail of how different groups of poor people are affected and how they cope, and how the effects of crisis and the strategies of coping persist and change. And as this book shows, whole groups of marginalized and excluded people can be missed.

The cases and conclusions presented here go far in showing how these gaps can be filled. They draw on studies of the effects on poor and vulnerable people in 17 countries, and how they responded and struggled to cope through the crises of 2008–11. Eight country studies are presented here: Bangladesh, Cambodia, the Central African Republic, Kazakhstan, Kenya, Mongolia, Senegal, and Thailand. The studies were team undertakings requiring special skills of investigating, listening, learning, analyzing, and presenting. As a form of intermittent monitoring, most of them were repeated, some at three-month intervals, and so picked up changes over time. The approaches and methods varied, but all were qualitative and quick. They were a sort of rapid social anthropology, using sensitive and open-ended methods of inquiry—direct observation and focus group discussions—and listening, being alert for the unexpected, and distilling and presenting insights promptly. The editors and authors do not claim that this kind of research is a substitute for quantitative methods; rather, it is complementary. They make clear that what they find and present is illustrative and indicative, not representative. What they do show many times over is that this approach adds vital new dimensions of understanding. They show just how important it is to be in touch with the changing realities of those who are poorer, more vulnerable, less vocal, and less visible.

Again and again, the diversity of contexts and conditions is striking. Impacts and responses differ by country, livelihood and occupation, age, gender, social and ethnic group, and social relations. There are many differences of locality, economy, politics, institutions, living conditions, family, and person. All of these differences might have been allowed to speak for themselves, as they do powerfully, and left at that. But the authors and editors have practical frameworks and categories to classify and a wealth of detail to analyze so that credible general statements can be made and conclusions drawn. Therefore, the responses to crises are grouped as behavior based, asset based, and assistance based. And the transmission channels of labor market impacts, price shocks, migration, and the decline in remittances from abroad and from urban to rural are identified and analyzed.

Commonalities emerge. Pervasively, those most affected respond actively, many of them with sacrifices and a resilience that command admiration and respect. What they do is diverse. Except when too undernourished, weak, or sick, they struggle and exercise their ingenuity. Adults diversify their activities and, when they can, work for longer hours. Parents protect the food consumption and schooling of their children. Families make many unseen sacrifices and painful choices such as eating less and buying cheaper and less nutritious food; stinting to keep children in school; switching from private to public schools or reluctantly taking children out of school altogether; forgoing medical treatment; mortgaging or selling assets after desperately trying not to, and then becoming irreversibly poorer; or engaging in high-risk activities like sex work, drug selling, or—more commonly—theft and other crime. We see how community and family solidarity can be stretched to the breaking point. And we learn about and can appreciate what is so often missing in the development discourse: the personal and emotional cost, the stress, the exhaustion, the tensions within families, and the agony of the cruel choices that poorer people living at the margins are forced to make.

Living through Crises shows what qualitative research can do, how it reveals significant realities that otherwise would be little recognized or pass unseen. Its value is illustrated by surprises that qualify or contradict common professional views of what happens in crises, who is affected and how much, and how people respond. Perhaps the most widespread and striking finding is how, contrary to expectations, the informal sector was hit harder and for longer than the formal: formal sector employers tried to retain skilled workers, and work for them picked up more rapidly, but the drop in demand for informal sector services and goods was more sustained and recovered more slowly. Then there were other findings that might not have been predicted or adequately recognized. Borrowing from banks dropped. Indebtedness to microfinance organizations became an acute problem. Domestic violence increased not just between men and women, but also between women and children. And some of the very poorest were so deprived already that they noticed little or no difference as a result of the crisis.

Through their professional and sensitive research, the evidence they uncovered, and the detail, analysis, and findings they presented, the editors and authors establish many times over and beyond any doubt the value of similar timely qualitative studies and monitoring. Such research would be valuable not only when there are shocks, but also in "normal" times. Further, studies like these have important contributions to make to policy and practice, not only in low-income or middle-income countries as here, but in rich countries as well. It is not just that in our interconnected global economy all are vulnerable to shocks, but that there are less-visible people in all societies who deserve their realities to be known and to inform policy and practice. The team and qualitative approaches used in this research are then relevant everywhere. All countries would do well to consider mobilizing similar teams and using their findings for bringing to light and keeping up to date with the diversity of conditions and responses of different groups of people affected by crises. By showing the value of timely qualitative insights, this book should lead the way and inspire action by governments and researchers across the globe. If it can do that, its impact for the better will be exponential, in support of those who are marginal, vulnerable, and less visible.

Robert Chambers
Professor, Institute of Development Studies
University of Sussex

Rasmus Heltberg is an economist and senior technical specialist with the World Bank's Social Development Department, where he is the program manager for the Norwegian-Finnish Trust Fund for Environmentally and Socially Sustainable Development (TFESSD). He has published on poverty, vulnerability, and malnutrition; rural development and agriculture; social protection and labor; adaptation to climate change; household energy; and disaster risk management. Before joining the World Bank in 2002, he was associate professor of development economics at the University of Copenhagen, Denmark, where he earned his PhD.

Naomi Hossain is a political sociologist at the Institute of Development Studies at Sussex, specializing in the politics of poverty and pro-poor public service delivery. Her current research interests include unruly politics and women's unpaid care work, both in relation to the economic crises. Past research has included work on elite perceptions of poverty and public service delivery; recently she conducted research on informal accountability, crime and insecurity, and the social impacts of global economic crises. Hossain has been a research fellow in the participation team at the Institute of Development Studies since 2008, before which she worked at BRAC in Bangladesh.

Anna Reva is an operations officer at the World Bank's Poverty Reduction and Equity Department. She has done research on climate change, gender, and social protection. Before joining the Bank in 2008, she worked at the United Nations Development Programme (UNDP) Ukraine on human development issues, including youth empowerment and Internet access. She has a master's degree in international development from Georgetown University in Washington, D.C.

Cheewin Ariyasuntorn graduated with a master's degree in sociology from the Department of Sociology and Anthropology, Faculty of Political Science, Chulalongkorn University.

Warathida Chaiyapa graduated with a master's degree from Southeast Asia Studies Program, Faculty of Arts, Chulalongkorn University.

Supang Chantavanich is professor emeritus at the Department of Sociology and Anthropology, Faculty of Political Science, Chulalongkorn University. She also acts as director of the Asian Research Centre for Migration, Institute of Asian Studies, Chulalongkorn University. She has worked on refugees, migrant workers, human trafficking, and other types of cross-border migration. She served as the first chair of the Asia Pacific Migration Research Network.

Pon Dorina is a fieldwork coordinator at the Cambodia Development Resource Institute, which she joined in 1996. She has experience supervising fieldwork (both quantitative and qualitative), moderating focus groups, and processing data.

Abdou Salam Fall is originally from Senegal. He is the head of the Research Laboratory of Economic and Social Transformation (LARTES) and the head of the doctoral program in Applied Sciences to Social Development at the University Cheikh Anta Diop (UCAD) in Dakar. He is also an Assistant Professor of Sociology at the UCAD Fundamental Institute of Black Africa (IFAN). He holds a dual PhD, one in Urban Sociology at the UCAD and one in Economic Sociology from Amsterdam University. Over the past 25 years, he has coordinated and published many quantitative and qualitative books and studies related to poverty alleviation, vulnerability, local development, and economic, social, and political issues. He is also interested in public policy in other African countries, especially the impact of social and economic changes and their impact on poor people.

Md. Bayazid Hasan is a research associate at BRAC Development Institute (BDI), BRAC University, where he conducts research on local governance and social safety nets. At present, he coordinates BDI's five-slums action research funded by the Rockefeller Foundation. Trained as a political scientist, his academic and research interests also include pro-poor disaster management, food security, and urban poverty.

Sarantuya Jigjiddorj started her research career by joining the Global Reach Center as an executive director. Her research interests include education, gender, microcredit, poverty, and rural development. Sarantuya also works as a consultant for the private sector in business development, strategic management, human resource management, and corporate social responsibility. She is now working as a lecturer at the School of Economic Studies, National University of Mongolia.

Tong Kimsun is a research fellow at the Cambodia Development Resource Institute (CDRI) and is currently the program coordinator for Economic, Trade, and Regional Cooperation. He has worked on poverty dynamics; Chinese investments in Cambodia; the impact of the global financial crisis on households, land tenure, and paddy productivity; the impacts of migration and remittances on poverty and agricultural productivity; and water resource management. His education background is in international finance and microfinance. He was educated at Kobe University, Japan.

Samarn Laodumrongchai is senior researcher at the Asian Research Centre for Migration. He earned a master's degree in sociology at National Taiwan University. His thesis focused on Thai migrant workers in Taiwan, China. His academic interests include international labor migration, particularly in Southeast and East Asia, and internal and overseas Thai migrant workers.

Grace Lubaale is a registered town and regional planner with interdisciplinary training and experience in management, finance, development, and town and regional planning. His main interests and expertise include planning, urban poverty, and policy research, and consultancies in strategic planning and management of local development, evaluation research, and advocacy. He has worked in senior management positions in private and civil society organizations in Uganda, Kenya, and Sudan, and as a consultant in East, Central, Southern, and West Africa.

Veronica Mendizabal is a rural sociologist interested in issues of decentralization and local governance. She has worked as a consultant for the World Bank in the Lao People's Democratic Republic since 2008. Previously, Veronica worked as technical adviser for the Ministry of Finance and the Institute of Public Administration in Papua New Guinea. She holds a master's of science in management of agricultural knowledge systems from Wageningen University in the Netherlands and is currently pursuing a master's of science in public policy and management from the School of Oriental and African Studies, University of London.

Md. Mamunur Rashid is a senior research associate at BDI, BRAC University. Trained as an anthropologist at Jahangirnagar University of Bangladesh, Rashid started his research career at BRAC's Research and Evaluation Division in 2003, where he planned and administered several research projects. He joined BDI in 2008 and continued his work on poverty and local governance. At present, he is a core team member of a large research project on the impact of climate change on urban poverty.

Lea Salmon is a Franco-Ivorian sociologist specializing in poverty and social exclusion in developing countries. She obtained her PhD from Paris X University and is the author of a book and several research papers on poverty reduction, social exclusion, and vulnerable groups. She has been a consultant with the United Nation's Development Programme's Human Development Report, the World Bank's Human Development Network, and the World Bank's Social Development Unit, as well as a staff member with the World Bank Africa Region Conflict and Social Development Unit, supporting excombatant and reintegration projects in Africa.

Sandra Schlossar is a social development specialist (junior professional officer) in the World Bank's Europe and Central Asia region. Sandra specializes in conflict and fragility, good governance, and social inclusion. She edits a regional newsletter on conflict and fragility, works on good governance, and is engaged in projects in the Kyrgyz Republic and Bosnia and Herzegovina. Before joining the Bank, she managed development assistance projects in southeastern and eastern Europe for a nongovernmental organization (NGO) and international education projects at a university in Vienna. She also supported immigrants and refugees at an NGO. She holds undergraduate and postgraduate degrees from the University of New South Wales (Sydney) and the University of Vienna in international social development, educational science, and Slavic studies.

Altantsetseg Sodnomtseren is a social specialist whose studies focus on education, household living standards, and gender. Altantsetseg has provided leadership for a variety of academic and business organizations. She was president of the non-governmental organization Global Reach Center, head of International Affairs of the National University of Mongolia, and executive director of the Asia Research Center. She has served as team leader, researcher, and consultant for projects funded by the Asian Development Bank, European Union, Open Society Institute, Posco TJ Park Foundation, Toyota Foundation, and World Bank. Altantsetseg is now working as a project coordinator for the Bank-funded project "Strengthening the Capacity of the National Statistical System of Mongolia."

Andy Sumner is a research fellow in the Vulnerability and Poverty Reduction Team at the Institute of Development Studies, Sussex, UK, and a visiting fellow at the Centre for Global Development in Washington, D.C. He is a cross-disciplinary economist who has done research relating to human well-being, inequality, and poverty, with particular focus on poverty concepts and indicators, global trends, and Millennium Development Goals (MDG) and post-MDG debates. He is a council member of the Development Studies Association (DSA) and the European Association of Development Institutes (EADI). In 2010, he contributed to the UNDP "MDG International Assessment" for the MDG summit and the Commission for Africa report "Still Our Common Interest." He has published a number of books and articles and is series editor for Palgrave Macmillan's "Rethinking International Development." Most recently his research on the "new bottom billion" (or the 960 million poor people living in middle-income countries) has been covered by the *Economist,* Voice of America, Fox News, and the *Guardian,* and has informed the British Parliament's International Development Committee's inquiry into aid to India.

Pamornrat Tansanguanwong is a social protection and development consultant at the World Bank Office in Bangkok. Her work includes community development in conflict-affected areas, and gender and social safety net issues. She received her master's degree from the University of Wisconsin–Madison in development studies and public policy. She has been collaborating with the Asian Research Centre for Migration since 2009.

Josias Tebero is a Central African socio-anthropologist specializing in decentralization, development, and local government. He studied at the University of Abidjan in Côte d'Ivoire, where he obtained a PhD. He has served as a consultant to international organizations such as the World Bank; United Nations Educational, Scientific, and Cultural Organization (UNESCO); and UNICEF. His current research is concerned with problems of poverty reduction, education, and HIV/AIDS. Since 2000, he has taught at the University of Bangui and directs the Laboratory of Anthropological Studies and Research in the Central African Republic.

Mya Than is a scholar with a specialization in Asia regional economics and a focus on economic corridor and cross-border trade and people movements. He was a visiting fellow at the Institute of Security and International Studies (ISIS) in Chulalongkorn University, Bangkok, Thailand, from 2001 to 2005. He retired from ISIS but continues working as an external lecturer and examiner.

Carolyn Turk is the lead social development specialist and acting sector manager in the World Bank's Europe and Central Asia Social Development Department. She is an expert in poverty policy analysis, including quantitative and qualitative instruments; statistical capacity building; national strategic planning and budgeting processes; and design and implementation of social accountability tools (citizen report cards and governance survey modules). Prior to joining the Bank, she was senior planning officer in the Ministry of Finance in Papua New Guinea, deputy director of Actionaid, and social development adviser at DFID. She has earned undergraduate and postgraduate degrees from Cambridge University in economics and the economics and politics of development.

Theng Vuthy is an agronomist. His research focuses on agricultural development, rural livelihood, and food security in Cambodia. Vuthy joined the Cambodia Development Resource Institute (CDRI) in October 2008 and is a research fellow and program coordinator of the poverty, agriculture, and rural development program. Before joining CDRI, he worked for the Cambodian Agricultural Research and Development Institute (CARDI) as a researcher focused on adaptive farming systems research and agricultural crops improvement. He received his PhD in plant physiology and plant molecular biology from the University of Kagoshima, Japan, in 2007.

Quentin Wodon is an adviser in the Human Development Network at the World Bank. Upon completing business engineering studies, he worked first in Thailand as laureate of the Prize of the Belgian Minister for Foreign Trade, and next in the marketing department of Procter & Gamble Benelux. In 1988, he shifted careers to work on poverty and worked for four and a half years at the International Movement ATD (all together for dignity) Fourth World, a grassroots and advocacy NGO working with the extremely poor. He later completed a PhD in economics at American University, taught at the University of Namur, and joined the World Bank in 1998. At the Bank, he worked first on Latin America and next on Sub-Saharan Africa, where he supervised the Bank's work on poverty. Over the past three years, he has focused on issues related to the delivery of education and health services by nonstate actors. Wodon has published more than a dozen books and 200 papers.

Artit Wong-a-thitikul graduated with a master's degree in public administration from the Department of Public Administration, Faculty of Political Science, Chulalongkorn University. Currently, he is a lecturer at Chieng Rai Rajabhat University, Chieng Rai Province.

Many people have helped shape this book and the crisis monitoring research described herein.

The origins of the book stem from two separate initiatives at crisis monitoring led by the Social Development Department at the World Bank and the Institute for Development Studies (IDS) in the United Kingdom.

When the global crisis first hit in 2008, Carrie Turk from the Bank's Social Development Department set up crisis monitoring activities in select countries as a way to gauge crisis impacts in "real time." The motivation was to inform policy makers formulating crisis responses in settings where quantitative data were not available. Instead, data were gathered by local researchers conducting focus group discussions and other qualitative techniques in affected communities. At IDS, Rosalind Eyben came up with the idea of asking local anthropologists to document the impacts of the crises as they unfolded. Naomi Hossain took on the challenge of producing a rapid report on the impacts of the crisis in time for the G20 meeting in 2009. With the help of (at different times) Robert Chambers, Joy Moncrieffe, Mariz Tadros, Patta Scott-Villiers, and other members of the IDS Participation Team, as well as Andy Sumner, she developed a series of tools and strategies for conducting rapid research in the IDS participatory tradition. Allister McGregor helped steer the IDS group toward a more well-being–oriented approach. Mwila Mulumbi in Zambia and Rizki Fillaili and other colleagues at SMERU (Social Monitoring and Early Response Unit) in Indonesia contributed innovative methodologies and approaches. As the two initiatives—from the IDS and from the World Bank—grew to include more countries and multiple rounds of repeat visits to the same communities, the teams also met to share and coordinate their methodologies. When Carrie Turk moved to the Europe and Central Asia Department of the Bank, Rasmus Heltberg continued crisis monitoring at the Bank's Social Development Department. Andy Sumner was the first to propose a book that would summarize it all, and Anna Reva helped pull all the disparate material together into a coherent whole. Other notable supporters in the Bank include Andy Mason, with the Poverty Reduction Team in East Asia, and Andy Norton, then with the Social Development Department and now with the ODI (Overseas Development Institute).

The country studies would not have been possible without the contributions of teams from local research institutions who did all the fieldwork and wrote the primary research reports. The primary research reports are listed in appendix 1. Chapter authors analyzed and condensed these reports.

We are particularly grateful to the more than 3,000 participants in focus group discussions and individual interviews whose stories shape this book.

Funding for this work was generously provided by the U.K. Department for International Development (DFID) and by the Trust Fund for Environmentally and Socially Sustainable Development housed at the World Bank and funded by the governments of Norway and Finland. Special thanks go to Dennis Pain for the initial support and to Paul Wafer and Tim Conway from DFID for regular feedback and for hosting important seminars and meetings that took stock of the crisis work and led to this book.

We thank the peer reviewers: Allister McGregor from IDS, who commented on the manuscript in its entirety, and Nilufar Ahmad, Nora Dudwick, Elena Glinskaya, Andrew Goodland, Samsen Neak, Frederico Gil Sander, Sandra Schlossar, Carrie Turk, Quentin Wodon, and Xiao Ye, all from the Bank, who commented on individual chapters. All errors and omissions are the responsibility of the authors.

Finally, we are grateful to Denise Bergeron, Pat Katayama, and Dina Towbin from the World Bank's Office of the Publisher.

ADB	Asian Development Bank
ANSD	*Agence Nationale de la Statistique et de la Démographie* (National Agency for Statistics and Demography)
ARCM	Asian Research Centre for Migration
ARV	antiretroviral
BBS	Bangladesh Bureau of Statistics
BDI	BRAC Development Institute
CAR	Central African Republic
CARDI	Cambodian Agricultural Research and Development Institute
CBHI	community-based health insurance
CDRI	Cambodian Development Research Institute
CFAF	Cambodian franc
CIDS	Cambodia Institute of Development Study
CPD	Centre for Policy Dialogue
CR	Cambodian riel
CSES	Cambodia Socio-Economic Survey (2004)
DFID	Department for International Development (United Kingdom)
DSA	Development Studies Association
EADI	European Association of Development Institutes
ECA	Europe and Central Asia
ECASEB	*Enquête Centrafricaine pour le Suivi-Évaluation du Bien-être* (Central African Survey for Welfare Monitoring and Evaluation)
EIG	economic interest groups
ESAM	*Enquête sénégalaise auprès des ménages* (Senegalese Household Survey)
ESPS	*Enquête de suivi de la pauvreté au Sénégal* (Poverty Monitoring Survey in Senegal)

FBO	faith-based organization
FEWSNET	Famine Early Warning Systems Network
FGDs	focus group discussions
GDP	gross domestic product
GoB	Government of Bangladesh
HDF	Human Development Foundation
HEF	Health Equity Fund
ICASEES	*Institut Centrafricain des Statistiques et des Etudes Economiques et Sociales* (National Statistical Office)
IDI	in-depth interview
IDS	Institute of Development Studies
IFAN	*Institut Fondamental d'Afrique Noire* (African Institute of Basic Research)
IMF	International Monetary Fund
ISIS	Institute of Security and International Studies (Thailand)
IT	information technology
KFSSG	Kenya Food Security Steering Group
KNBS	Kenya National Bureau of Statistics
LARTES	*Laboratoire de Recherche sur les Transformations Economiques et Sociales* (Research Laboratory of Economic and Social Transformation)
MDGs	Millennium Development Goals
MFI	microfinance institutions
MOLVT	Ministry of Labour and Vocational Training (Cambodia)
NGO	nongovernmental organization
ODI	Overseas Development Institute
OECD	Organisation for Economic Co-operation and Development
PAD	People's Alliance for Democracy (Thailand)
PPP	People Power Party (Thailand)
PPRC	Power and Participation Research Centre
QUIBB	*Questionnaire Unifié sur les Indicateurs de Base du Bien-être* (Unified Questionnaire on Main Welfare Indicators)
ROSCA	rotating savings and credit association
SESC	Socio-Economic Survey of Cambodia (1993–94)
SMEs	small and medium enterprises

SMERU	Social Monitoring and Early Response Unit
TFESSD	Trust Fund for Environmentally and Socially Sustainable Development
TSA	targeted social assistance
UDD	National United Front of Democracy Against Dictatorship (Thailand)
UNDP	United Nations Development Programme
UNESCO	United Nations Educational, Scientific, and Cultural Organization
UNICEF	United Nations International Children's Emergency Fund
VRF	Village and Urban Revolving Funds
WFP	World Food Programme
WIEGO	Women in Informal Employment, Globalizing and Organizing

Living through Crises: An Overview

Rasmus Heltberg, Naomi Hossain, Anna Reva, and Andy Sumner

The food, fuel, and financial crises that started in 2008 reverberated throughout the global economy, causing job losses; poverty; and economic, financial, and political upheaval in countries all over the world. This book is not about the causes of these crises or the macroeconomic and financial sector issues surrounding their origin, spread, and impact; nor is it about how such crises may be prevented in the future. These are important questions, but they have been dealt with in a large number of books, articles, and even movies.[1] Instead, this book is about the more neglected, mundane, and yet centrally important matter of how people lived through the globalized crises of 2008–11, how these people were affected, and what they did to cope. At the time of writing, in late 2011, global food prices had again spiked, and further waves of fiscal and financial shocks were under way, as world economic growth faltered and the euro area sovereign debt crisis mounted. The timing means this book offers vital insights into how people coped—and how they sometimes did not—at a time when such knowledge is most urgently needed.

The theme of the book is likely to have an enduring significance, as it offers a unique glimpse into the experience of living through a new type of systemic shock wave that is globalized, highly contagious, and multi-faceted. Systemic shocks of the complexity and scale witnessed from 2008 through 2011 are quite unprecedented in world history, but are predicted to be more frequent in the future (Held, Kaldor, and Quah 2010; Goldin and Vogel 2010). The growing integration of developing economies in globalized markets has fundamentally altered the nature of the risks facing the poor: droughts in Australia and housing price collapses in the United States can now create direct threats to the food security of people in Africa

1

and Asia. The capacities of developing countries to manage these new risks have failed to evolve in tandem with the new globalized risk pattern. Nation states have generally lacked the resources and institutional frameworks for formal social protection mechanisms, and they have in many cases struggled to honor precrisis social protection commitments as revenues declined, leaving both the precrisis poor and the newly poor with little or no support (McCord 2010). This situation explains the urgency of understanding how globalized crises affect people and how they cope and has profound implications for design of social protection.

This book came out of two separate initiatives carried out by the Institute of Development Studies (IDS) and the World Bank that aimed to monitor the effects of the crises as they unfolded. The Bank's work was motivated by a need for timely information about the impacts of the crisis, something that the household and labor force surveys available at the time were unable to supply. In East Asia, for example, the most recent poverty data available at the onset of the crisis were two years old, and only one or two countries had labor force data available for 2009 (Turk, Mason, and Petesch 2010). To understand the poverty and social consequences of the crisis more fully, the Bank began a series of rapid qualitative assessments as a supplement to quantitative data. The IDS work was rooted in its tradition of participatory research and drew directly on the pioneering work of Robert Chambers, who contributed to the initial research design. The country studies described in this book were organized in somewhat different ways, but they all relied on qualitative data because statistics and surveys of crisis impacts were not available, had gaps, or would come only after major delays. Under such circumstances, qualitative crisis monitoring held the promise of providing, almost in real time, policy-relevant insights into how people were affected and what they did to cope with shocks.

Local research teams carried out the field work, often visiting the same localities repeatedly as the crisis was unfolding. Their job was to establish "listening posts" that would allow communities to describe what the global food, fuel, and financial crises of 2008–11 meant to them, how they were affected, and what they did to cope with the adverse consequences. To gather the information, field teams used an array of qualitative methods. The research in the various countries was conducted by different people using methods tailored to the country context. No global research protocol was used (although each country used a consistent protocol), and therefore results can be hard to aggregate across countries. In all countries, however, the research focused on essentially the same questions: Who was affected by the crises? How severe were the impacts? What did people do to cope? How were women, men, and children affected differently? What were the sources of support? And what did governments do to help?

Job layoffs, gradual reductions in meals, struggles to keep children in school, the eventual recovery, and the problem of high and volatile food prices were all captured in the accounts produced by our field teams. Over time, common trends started to emerge in the field reports from disparate research sites. These trends relate to the impacts of the crises (often deeper and of longer duration than anticipated); the nature of vulnerabilities (material and emotional, individual and community-wide); and the sources of resilience and available support mechanisms (largely informal). Table 1 organizes some of the trends into a snapshot of common signs of resilience and vulnerability observed across study settings. Chapter 1 and the country case studies provide a further discussion of the evolution of resilience and vulnerability in different contexts as the crises unfolded.

Our purpose in writing this book is to make the bottom-up perspectives on globalized crises available to a larger audience. The research presents a unique and largely untold account of how people lived through the severe economic turmoil of recent years, how they were affected, and what they did to cope, lending a voice to affected communities themselves. The perspectives of people living through crisis are needed to inform and

Table 1. A Mix of Vulnerabilities and Resilience Is Evident in Coping Responses

Evidence of resilience	Evidence of vulnerability
Living off savings	Cutting back basic consumption; fewer and less nutritious meals
Internal migration for opportunities	
Adapting business strategies	Cutting back essential nonfood consumption including soap and shampoo
Cutting back nonessential spending; delaying large purchases	Forgoing health care; switching to traditional healers
Extending working hours	
Working more jobs	Sale of assets needed for livelihood
Striving to keep kids in school	Accumulation of unserviceable debts
Returning to education or training	School dropouts; child labor; switching from private to public schools
Communal meals	High-risk income-generating activities
Mutual support groups; support from family and friends	Depletion or breakdown of community support mechanisms
Savings-credit groups	Theft; crime; drug selling
	Divorce and abandonment
	Increased alcohol and drug use
	Lower resilience to other shocks

Source: Authors.

motivate better policies and interventions against future shocks. We also intend this book to highlight the capacity of participatory approaches to pick up impacts and responses that other research methods may miss, thereby contributing to the methodological knowledge of how to qualitatively assess shocks, vulnerability, and resilience. The book aims to assist development practitioners in understanding how large-scale economic crises affect people's lives and, in so doing, to contribute to what we call an *anatomy of coping*: knowledge of what vulnerability and resilience mean in relation to the new pattern of globalized crises and what the role of public policy may be in protecting against risk.

Research was conducted in 17 countries in the form of interviews and focus group discussions held during 2008–11. Selected sites were visited up to four times and included Bangladesh, Cambodia, the Central African Republic, Ghana, Indonesia, Jamaica, Kazakhstan, Kenya, Mongolia, the Philippines, Senegal, Serbia, Thailand, Ukraine, Vietnam, the Republic of Yemen, and Zambia. To our knowledge, this is by far the most comprehensive qualitative research on crisis impacts and coping ever carried out in developing countries.[2]

The research brings together an analysis of the differences and similarities in coping responses in the 17 countries. In this book, we present eight country case studies to illustrate how people in specific localities were affected by global shocks, which coping strategies they adopted, and which sources of support were available to them. The book contains no quantitative models and uses limited statistics. As such, it is intended to complement other, more quantitative studies of the crises.

Our Approach to Qualitative Crisis Monitoring

Countries were selected based on two criteria: (1) an expectation that they would be vulnerable to crisis, and (2) demand for monitoring data from donors and Bank country teams. Most of the countries did not have relevant quantitative data to assess crisis impacts in a timely manner, sparking interest in rapid qualitative and participatory research. Study sites, respondent samples, and questions were chosen to explore hypotheses about which population groups might be affected in each country. Sampling and site selection was not designed to be nationally representative but rather to cover an illustrative range of social and occupation groups presumed to be vulnerable to crisis.

The guiding principle for the data collection was an understanding of the crisis transmission channels and a broad idea of what impacts and coping mechanisms to look for. In each country, field work design started with an assessment of what transmission channels were likely to be the most important and which groups might be relatively more exposed to the impacts of the crisis (see figure 1). Although they vary by country, the more common transmission channels were labor market impacts, such as layoffs, reduced working time, and increased competition and reduced earnings in the informal sector.[3] Price shocks were another universally important channel—prices of food, fuel, and many of the inputs used in production rose by large magnitudes starting in 2008. Although the labor market situation improved with the economic recovery in some of the countries surveyed, the inability to afford the same basket of food that households consumed before the crisis was a common source of concern for both the vulnerable and the relatively well-off even after the resumption of GDP (gross domestic product) growth. Decline in remittances from family members living abroad or in urban areas away from the household was another common channel by which global shocks hit people.

Figure 1. Transmission Channels

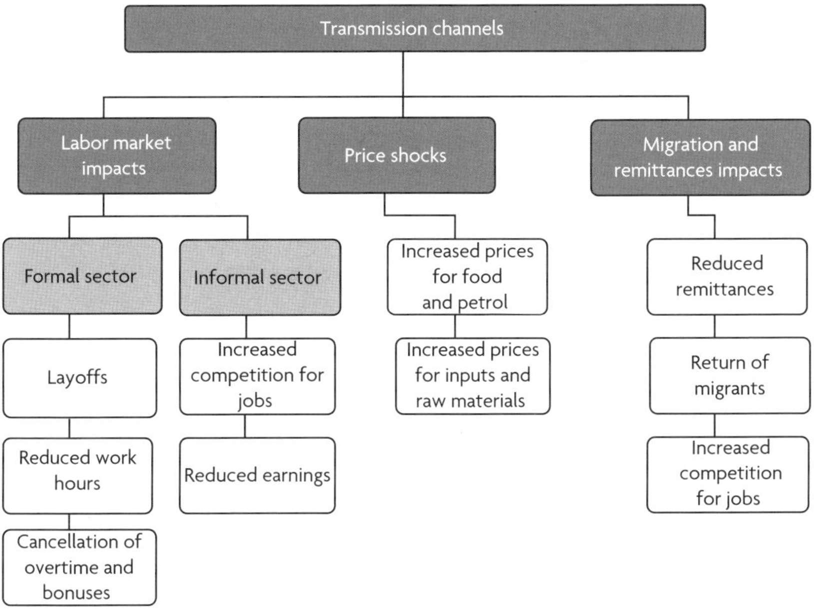

Source: Adapted from Turk, Mason, and Petesch 2010.

Occupation groups selected for research participation varied by country but often included farmers, owners, and workers in the informal sector and employees of export-oriented formal enterprises. Respondents included the relatively well-off (for example, skilled factory workers in East Asia); low-income groups (for example, smallholders, vendors); and the destitute (for example, beggars in Bangladesh). The research also involved a small number of key informant interviews with social workers, NGO (nongovernmental organization) staff, business people, local officials, chiefs, community leaders, and other local elites. These interviews were undertaken to gain an official or institutional perspective on the research findings, as well as to collect relevant local statistical data.

The scope, scale, and emphasis of the field research varied. It typically involved focus group discussions, which encompassed open-ended questions and participatory and visual tools to facilitate discussion and analysis, including prioritization exercises such as matrix ranking and scoring, well-being ranking, examination of daily time use, activities using analyses of food baskets and consumption behavior, occupation and social group impact ranking analyses, and institutional mapping exercises to identify sources of support and resources for coping. In addition, individual semistructured interviews were undertaken to build household case studies, often over repeated research visits. These interviews were with men, women, and, on a few occasions, older children or young adults who were acting as household heads. Around 200 to 300 people were engaged within each country, and study sites were usually visited in several rounds. In all, the research surveyed here draws on interviews involving more than 3,000 participants. Interviewees were of all ages from older people to youth and a small number of children. A strong focus on understanding the gendered dimensions of the impacts and responses in both the World Bank and IDS work meant that women were prominent participants in all the country work.

The interviews covered household livelihoods and coping strategies over the crisis period, discussing changes in work, migration, borrowing, asset sales, social relations, household membership, community and private charitable support received and given, and access to official social protection and other government programs. The research design took into account that the poverty impacts of shocks depend on many factors, including the precrisis structure of poverty and vulnerability; the precrisis social and economic policy package in place (social protection in particular); the nature or type of the shocks; the economic and social policy response to the crisis; the health of the global economy; and household and community responses. As discussed in depth in chapter 1, people who are adversely hit usually respond by attempting to increase income via family members seeking new or additional work; using savings or credit; selling assets; and reducing expenditures, for example, by changing the quantity and quality of diet, health care, and education (see also Lustig and Walton 2009). All of these aspects were covered in the research.

The knowledge obtained through qualitative monitoring can be a useful complement to quantitative data and modeling approaches (Benson et al. 2008; World Bank/IMF 2010). The advantages of qualitative research of the kind presented here in comparison to quantitative studies of crisis impacts include speed, direct observation over estimation, and broader scope of research themes and topics. We therefore find that the qualitative research presented here is a valid and valuable complement to our understanding of the impacts of and responses to crisis and that it sheds light on aspects of those impacts and responses that other methods are less well-equipped to do (see also Hossain 2009a and 2009b).

The study was initiated under the rubric of "real-time crisis monitoring" and aimed to provide early warning to policy makers. Yet in so doing, the research presented in this book also helped document the crisis as it unfolded, and therefore can shed light on some of the processes through which different responses develop, unlike ex-post research, which tends to measure outcomes and be silent on processes. Qualitative research also includes scope for participatory approaches that enable the analysis and findings to reflect the lives and concerns of the people who are the object of the study (Estrella and Gaventa 1998), giving them a voice. Further, qualitative and participatory approaches enable analysis of issues that are not readily quantifiable or captured by conventional survey methodologies. For the purposes of the study of crisis impacts and responses, these include subjective and relational well-being, community cohesion, informal and customary sources of social protection, and issues of women's unpaid and often invisible work within the care economy.

The disadvantage of qualitative work such as the kind presented in this book is primarily the small samples, which, combined with the purposeful selection of the respondents, result in lack of statistical representativeness. This means it is not possible to gauge the scale of the findings or the extent to which they apply more generally. Thus, we cannot say by how much poverty, school enrollment, or community cohesion worsened. Although the inability to measure the change in conditions is certainly a limitation of the data gathered in this collection, we would claim that the advantages of alternative, quantitative approaches are sometimes overstated. One of the striking features of the food, fuel, and financial crisis has been the extent to which the poverty community has had to rely on models and estimations to assess impacts as opposed to observation and measurement (for example, World Bank/IMF 2010). The household surveys commonly used to measure changes in poverty and social indicators are produced rather infrequently and with significant lags. Lacking timely surveys, model-based simulations with their attendant reliance on parameters and assumptions are used to assess likely impacts of crisis in developing countries, even years after the onset of crisis. Better techniques for assessing crisis impacts are needed, and this book explores how qualitative methods can contribute.

Chen and Ravallion (2009) offered an early and often-cited forecast that the crisis would add 64 million people to the population living under $2 a day. This estimate was based on the latest household surveys, a set of growth estimates revised downward in light of the crisis, and an assumption of distribution neutrality. Other quantitative approaches to assessing crisis impacts have used simulation models, either microsimulations or computable general equilibrium models, as in Bourguignon, Bussolo, and Pereira da Silva (2008); Ferreira et al. (2008); and Habib et al. (2010). Although these studies relax the assumption of distribution neutrality, they remain estimates. The current crisis has also seen some progress in using observational data such as labor force surveys, high-frequency administrative records such as unemployment claims, and household surveys where available and sometimes undertaken in response to the crisis (for example, World Bank 2011a). However, many data gaps remain for faster measurement of poverty and social indicators (World Bank 2011a; World Bank/IMF 2011).

Among the various quantitative approaches, crisis monitoring using survey or administrative data has the most in common with the approaches explored in this book because it emphasizes observation over modeling and household impacts over macroeconomic trends. There has been some systematic comparison of qualitative and quantitative findings that suggest broad similarities and some discrepancies in the details. Chapter 4 on the Central African Republic and chapter 8 on Senegal bring together qualitative and quantitative evidence of crisis impacts and find broad concurrence (especially for Senegal) but also paint somewhat different pictures. The quantitative analysis in the Central African Republic suggested that the increase in food and fuel prices may have had only a limited impact on most households because much of the population consumes little of the traded commodities with price increases, but some participants in focus groups reported that the crisis had a strong negative impact.[4] Focus groups consisting of public sector and export-oriented workers, artisans, and traders made such comments, highlighting that even in countries that are poorly integrated in the world economy, certain population groups can nevertheless be strongly affected by global shocks.

Taken as a whole, the qualitative evidence often points to broad and quite adverse social impacts of the crisis, in particular stemming from the food price crisis in low-income countries. Qualitative crisis monitoring shows severe impacts of high and volatile food prices on poverty, food security, and social cohesion in many countries, causing significant hardships and sometimes irreversible damage to human and social capital, even if parents strived to keep children in school. The relative severity of impacts stems, in part, from the fact that the poor often experienced multiple and repeated shocks from various sources (for example, climate, political violence, financial woes), and each shock eroded the capacity to cope with other shocks. The qualitative findings also suggest that second-order impacts, such as declines in remittances or increased competition in the informal sectors that make up a large part of the livelihood of the poor, can be significant; such second-order impacts are ignored in some quantitative simulation approaches. The qualitative work finds very low penetration of formal safety nets in most low-income countries, with people instead relying on informal coping mechanisms often involving family and friends (quantitative evidence confirms this—see, for example, World Bank 2011a). The protracted nature of the crisis in some countries, however, led to gradual erosion of the social cohesion underpinning these informal safety nets—an important finding that would be hard to emulate in modeling approaches.

The qualitative evidence did not always tally well with the macroeconomic indicators. Economic growth resumed in late 2009 and early 2010 in many of the countries where we conducted field work. In East Asia, the recovery of the export sectors was often mirrored in rapid recovery of formal and garment sector workers. But elsewhere, and in the informal sectors, many of the poor households did not benefit from the recovery and were in fact sinking deeper into poverty, while some of the middle-class population was left more sensitive to future shocks. We would therefore caution against naïve attempts to link GDP growth directly to poverty and social outcomes: in practice, impacts differ widely across gender, age, sector, and occupation and depend to a large extent on informal coping responses undertaken in the absence of formal mechanisms of protection.

And even when people appear to be "resilient"—that is, able to adapt, cope, and recover from shocks—there are often economic and social costs to this apparent resilience, as is discussed next.

Key Findings: Resilience and Vulnerability to the Global Economic Shocks

The research covered the impacts of the crises, the nature of vulnerabilities, and the sources of resilience including available support mechanisms. Table 1 provides a snapshot of signs of resilience and vulnerability across the different study settings. This section attempts to discern key findings and lessons from country case studies. In doing so, it also illustrates the advantages of qualitative methods in analyzing certain impacts of the crises.

The crises have had a severe impact on poor people in all communities surveyed. Putting food on the table and keeping children clothed and in school during a severe food crisis and recession extracted a heavy toll on poorer people and communities. Researchers commonly observed serious personal stress and anxiety over the daily struggles to make ends meet, family and community solidarity at the breaking point, and breadwinners working unusually long hours or getting involved in precarious activities to afford a basic food basket.

Resilience has economic and social costs that are paid today and in the future. The economic costs include sales of vital assets, compromised health from eating inferior foods and forgoing health care, taking children out of school, depletion of common property natural resources, and reduced investment in business growth. The social costs of resilience include family breakdown; weakened community cohesion; transgressions of social, legal, and personal norms made in order to cope; and increase in crime and violence. Some of these costs were temporary and disappeared once the recovery got under way. But some hardships are likely to have long-lasting and possibly irreversible consequences in the form of stunted development of children, loss of health and of social and economic assets, and occasional loss of life when someone could not afford timely health care or became destitute.

Because of second-order impacts, exposure to economic shock was often a poor predictor of vulnerability. Although this fact is well-recognized in the vulnerability literature, many analysts had expected that formal sector workers in export-oriented enterprises would be the most affected by the economic shocks, as these sectors appeared to be the most directly exposed. Yet in all countries surveyed, we found that export-sector workers may have taken the first hit, but they often benefited from some degree of labor protection (even if it was often weakening) or were retained by employers eager to keep skilled workers for the expected economic recovery. In contrast, many poorer people employed in the informal sectors experienced deeper and more protracted hardships stemming from reduced demand for their goods and services, higher input prices, and fierce competition from workers laid off from other sectors. In all surveyed sites, marginalized and poor people with weak social capital experienced the most severe and most irreversible hardships. Again, many modeling approaches, unless very careful, would struggle to pick up such nuance.

The research uncovered high levels of stress and deterioration of relational well-being in nearly all surveyed locations. The noneconomic and subjective dimensions of well-being are sometimes neglected or underplayed because they are difficult to measure quantitatively. They are, however, an important aspect of people's lives and are relevant for policy due to, first, the direct contribution of stress and reduced social cohesion to measurable development outcomes such as income poverty and the MDGs (Millennium Development Goals) via impacts on maternal health, child care, labor productivity, collective risk sharing mechanisms, and domestic and community violence (see Harper et al. 2011; Mendoza 2009; McGregor and Sumner 2010; Hossain and McGregor 2011); and, second, the contribution of worsening relationships to social and political unrest, intergroup tensions, and conflict (see Brinkman and Hendrix 2011). This area is one where the qualitative methodologies demonstrated their value. Research participants commonly reported that worries about how to feed families, rising debt, job layoffs, or failing businesses led to personal anxiety, marital strain, family breakup, or emergency migration that divided family members temporarily or indefinitely. Economic downturn also contributed to social or ethnic tensions over access to employment opportunities or support resources in several research sites. Partly because stress and conflict are endemic to poverty, the research participants had a range of strategies for alleviating these pressures on their individual and collective well-being. In many instances, people were resorting to their families and friends, turning to religion, or consuming alcohol and drugs.

Women played an important role in shock absorption, possibly more than during the previous crises (Horn 2009). The research collected for this book highlights the central significance of women in enabling the "resilience" with which societies managed the crises and suggests two reasons for the particularly direct impact on women and their work. First, the increase in women's participation in the labor force worldwide has often involved a concentration in the highly flexible export sectors, which were most exposed to the financial crisis. Therefore, compared to previous crises (not compared to men during the present crisis) women's formal sector employment is likely to have been hit harder than in the past. Not only have women lost more jobs faster than in the past, but also their employment in export sectors has been under even greater pressure for flexibility or casualization in the wake of the recession (see also Hurst, Buttles, and Sandars 2010; Miller-Dawkins, Irwansyah, and Abimanyu 2010; Gaerlan et al. 2010; Hossain, Fillaili, and Lubaale 2010; Hossain et al. 2010). The second reason to view women's roles as shock absorbers as particularly important is their responsibilities for food sourcing and cooking as well as for child care. Reports from a number of countries showed women spending considerably longer hours and making more effort to gather wild foods and fuel, to travel around to shop more frequently in more affordable small quantities, and to bear the brunt of the stress involved in comforting, coaxing, and disciplining hungry or unhappy children. It is important to note that neither the impact on women's care work nor the shift into the informal sector will be picked up by conventional crisis monitoring exercises or poverty surveys, as neither sector is fully recognized and measured in standard economics practice (Folbre 2006; Hoskyns and Rai 2007; Razavi 2011).

The research uncovered many encouraging signs of resilience, usually driven more by the initiative of poor people and the strength of community solidarity than by any government policy (more on this in chapter 1 and the country studies). People affected by income loss were quick to seek out new livelihood options. They usually tried to avoid selling their house and the assets vital to their continued livelihoods, such as land or cattle. And one of the most encouraging signs of resilience was that in nearly all study sites, parents sought to shield children from the worst impacts of the crisis, forgoing meals so children could eat and keeping them in school if at all possible. Although it is true that economic shocks can disrupt children's schooling, the research reported in this book finds that parents strive to avoid that outcome. Free schooling and provision of school meals and uniforms where available were important in helping parents in their struggle to protect children's education.

Customary and localized sources of support were considerably more widespread and typically more substantial determinants of resilience against economic shocks than formal social protection systems. The reason is partly that coverage continues to be inadequate to protect all vulnerable groups against covariate shocks, such as food price spikes, and partly that official social protection and emergency coping measures are sometimes triggered after a shock, rather than acting as automatic stabilizers. A related finding was that where formal social protection was covering the population, serious design flaws limited its effectiveness (see Davies 2011). Informal sources of support included help with jobs and migration networks, meals, or small loans from friends and neighbors; private charitable support through faith-based or community institutions; and traditional assistance to beggars and other vulnerable groups. The research also confirmed certain known limitations of informal social protection systems. Some of the very poorest people were left unprotected by the informal safety nets, even where the safety nets were reasonably comprehensive, because the people were outsiders. They could be migrants, members of socially excluded groups, or in other respects not considered members of the moral community protected by the safety net, such as members of another faith. In addition, the covariate nature of the globalized crises meant that better-off groups within the communities were themselves facing economic stress and were less able to provide the customary level of charitable assistance to poor people in hardship.

Attribution in an Era of Complex Shocks

In an era of complex globalized crises, direct attribution between individual global shock waves and local hardships is difficult. We cannot assert with confidence which shock caused which hardships because the nature of the research was never designed for attributing causality. It is also because of the way different local and global shock waves interact (see also McGregor, Hossain, and Butters 2010).

First, many hardships were often indirectly linked to global crises and in ways dimly perceived by respondents. Poor people's lives often consist of continuous episodes of shocks and coping, which may include rebuilding their livelihoods after natural disasters and dealing with food price inflation, political upheavals, and severe illness or death of family members. Kenya has been suffering from the effects of the political violence of

2008 and a seven-year drought. In Bangladesh, severe floods and cyclones have turned thousands of people into environmental refugees and completely changed their livelihoods. In Kampong Tnaot village, Cambodia, the most negative change in the community during 2008–09 was depletion of fish stocks from illegal fishing vessels. Rural Mongolia was battered by the *dzud*, a severe snowfall that leaves livestock unable to find grazing. Some of these more "local" shocks may have had a stronger impact on surveyed communities (although attribution is generally impossible, some of the local climatic shocks may be caused by climate change and are hence another example of global shock). Finally, many idiosyncratic shocks emerged from the research—the death of an infant or breadwinner, a migration or divorce, the loss of a harvest or the failure of a small business. All of these crises—at global, regional, national, subnational, local, community, household, and individual levels—could be reasonably established as causes of hardship and stress.

Second, from the epistemological perspective taken in this research—the viewpoint of the people whose lives we aim to study—a focus on attribution makes little sense. Some interviewees were not aware of the ongoing global food, fuel, and financial crises; others attributed worsening livelihoods and subsequent recovery in the later rounds of research to activities by local or national governments. In some chronic poor communities (for example, in the Central African Republic and Zambia), many respondents had not noticed any change in their lives, which were already so difficult prior to the crises that they could hardly get any worse.

Third, different sources of shocks and crisis interact and make attribution more complex. In the short term, much of the qualitative evidence suggested that the food and fuel crises were experienced more directly and more widely than the effects of the global financial crisis, albeit with some exceptions among export sector workers. The impacts of food price spikes were direct and urgent for many of the groups studied, particularly the urban populations who grow little of their own food and who benefit little from rising rural wages. The available qualitative evidence does not easily support comparison of the severity of different sources of shocks. Quantitative estimates, however, suggest that the food price crisis pushed many millions of people into hunger and poverty, and did so very rapidly (see World Bank/IMF 2010; World Bank 2010, 2011b; Ivanic, Martin, and Zaman 2011). In contrast, the general verdict on the 2008–09 financial crisis seems to be that its poverty impacts were both more muted and better handled in developing countries than had been anticipated. But there were other, less easily observed factors, which included localized wage and price effects from the financial crisis and the impact of the global financial turmoil on global commodity prices. By 2011, there were also early signs of fiscal austerity measures that could affect poverty over the longer term. Thus, the crises have interacted throughout, and although some crises are felt more directly by people, other crises may still exert influence. In such a context, how confident can one be about attribution and causality? The series of overlapping and interlocking shocks since 2008 suggest that causality may be intrinsically difficult to determine. From the point of view of research, precise attribution of impacts to shocks may ultimately matter less than establishing what works to protect poor and vulnerable people from shocks, whatever their source.

Outline of the Book

After this introduction, Chapter 1 analyzes coping responses and the sources of support that people relied upon during crises across all the countries for which we have data (a somewhat larger data set than the number of country case studies that we could include in the book). Chapter 1 also discusses implications of the research findings for policy making. Chapters 2–9 present the country case studies, documenting crisis impacts and coping responses in Bangladesh, Cambodia, the Central African Republic, Kazakhstan, Kenya, Mongolia, Senegal, and Thailand.

Many similarities were apparent in the transmission channels of the global economic shocks and people's adaptation responses, but the research also uncovered some differences. For example, the impacts of the financial crisis in Bangladesh (chapter 2) were muted with continuous GDP growth of 5 percent to 6 percent throughout the studied period. The major transmission channel of the global economic shocks over 2008–11 was the price volatility of food and fuel, which eroded people's incomes and pushed many into debt. The impact on the garment industry was delayed and short lived as the recession initially increased demand for cheap goods in the West. The chronic poor and the informal sector workers were most affected as in other countries discussed in this volume.

In Cambodia and Thailand (chapters 3 and 9), the initial impacts of the crisis were felt most strongly by workers in the export-oriented industries (garments, tourism, electrical appliances) who lost their jobs or were forced to work part time. The recovery of these industries was, however, relatively fast, while informal sector workers and landless farmers suffered more lasting damage. Many sold their productive assets or houses to finance basic consumption or pay off high interest debts from informal moneylenders. Thailand's population had access to a number of social assistance programs (although the most vulnerable were often excluded from them), but the poor in Cambodia had to rely primarily on their social networks and own resources to cope with the worsening hardships.

Chapter 4 on the Central African Republic and chapter 8 on Senegal combine qualitative crisis monitoring with the simulations based on household surveys. In the Central African Republic, chronic poverty and malnutrition was so pervasive that many of the vulnerable groups did not notice any changes in their already-constrained livelihoods resulting from the global economic crises—a finding confirmed by the quantitative analysis. Yet, even in this relatively isolated country, export-oriented workers, those engaged in trade, and public sector employees were affected through reduction of job opportunities, sales, and incomes. There were no official social assistance programs in the Central African Republic, and people relied on faith-based organizations and social networks for support. The impact of the global economic downturn was much more pronounced in Senegal, where it was felt through labor market shocks and increased food and fuel prices. Focus group participants did not benefit from any government-sponsored social assistance programs and reported that rampant corruption was hindering their coping responses.

Chapter 5 on Kazakhstan focuses primarily on the analysis of the government's Road Map program established specifically to address the short-term impacts of the global economic crisis. The chapter shows that although the program largely achieved its goal of providing a temporary relief, it did not address the long-term needs of the poor. These findings suggest that temporary crisis response measures could be usefully followed up with further interventions to reduce chronic poverty.

Chapter 6 finds that the key transmission channel of the global economic shocks in Kenya was the increase in the food and fuel prices, which was further compounded by a five-year drought and the consequences of the political violence of 2008. The interviewees in visited communities reported drastic reduction in food consumption, depletion of natural resources, and increases in crime and prostitution, family breakup, and social fragmentation. The assistance programs of government and the donor community did not have sufficient outreach and generosity to address the vast needs of the impoverished communities.

Chapter 7 describes crisis impacts on Mongolia, where they were felt through the drop of prices for export commodities and labor market shocks. In rural areas, poor herders engaged in distress sale of meat to compensate for the reduced prices of cashmere. They were left with smaller herds (their major asset) and were disproportionately affected by the dzud. In urban areas, the crisis was felt primarily through the reduction of job opportunities, sales, and incomes. Migrants from rural areas and the low skilled were the most affected. Government assistance, albeit small, was an important source of support to poor households throughout the 2008–11 period.

Notes

1. See, for example, Raghuram Rajan's account of the inequality roots of the subprime crisis (*Fault Lines*, 2010); Gillian Tett's insider ethnography of financial sector risk taking (*Fool's Gold*, 2009); Niall Ferguson's historical account of the roots of the crisis (*The Ascent of Money*, 2008); and Slavoj Žižek's Marxist analysis of the "crisis as shock therapy" (*First as Tragedy, Then as Farce*, 2009) to name a few.

2. The studies *Voices of the Poor* (Narayan 2000) and *Moving Out of Poverty* (Narayan, Pritchett, and Kapoor 2009) had larger samples but were not specifically focused on crisis impacts and coping. The *Moving Out of Poverty* study, however, found large downward movements triggered by shocks (both idiosyncratic, such as health shocks, and covariate, such as crop loss due to drought) and lack of effective social protection. As such, there are many similarities in approach and findings between this book and the *Moving Out of Poverty* study.

3. The transmission mechanisms identified in the country chapters are similar to those discussed in recent literature (Baldacci, de Mello, and Inchauste 2002; Lustig and Walton 2009; Pernia and Knowles 1998; Prennushi, Ferreira, and Ravallion 1998). Financial crises impact poverty through several transmission mechanisms. Baldacci, de Mello, and Inchauste argue that 60 to 70 percent of the poverty impacts of a crisis are due to four factors: unemployment, inflation, reduced public expenditure, and GDP contraction. Prennushi, Ferreira, and Ravallion (Vol. 1) identified five main types of transmission mechanisms between shocks and welfare: (1) changes in relative prices that lead to changes in relative wages, consumption baskets, and employment patterns;

(2) changes in aggregate labor demand that can reduce employment levels and wage rates; (3) changes in the rates of return on assets; (4) changes in levels of public transfers, in cash and kind; and (5) changes in community environment, in terms of public health or safety. Lustig and Walton (2009) identify a similar set.

4. Research in Indonesia also found broad agreement between quantitative and qualitative indicators of crisis impacts (McCulloch and Grover 2010), as well as some dissimilarities: the labor force survey showed that real wages in the formal sector increased during the crisis period, but this was not picked up in the qualitative research, which had focused on areas hard hit by the crisis. The qualitative study also uncovered weaknesses in the way the labor force survey treated migrant workers.

References

Baldacci, E., L. de Mello, and G. Inchauste. 2002. "Financial Crisis, Poverty and Income Distribution." Working Paper 02/04, International Monetary Fund, Washington, DC.

Benson, T., N. Minot, J. Pender, M. Robles, J. von Braun. 2008. "Global Food Crises: Monitoring and Assessing Impact to Inform Policy Responses." Food Policy Report, International Food Policy Research Institute, Washington, DC.

Bourguignon, F., M. Bussolo, and L. Pereira da Silva. 2008. "Introduction: Evaluating the Impact of Macroeconomic Policies on Poverty and Income Distribution." In *The Impact of Macroeconomic Policies on Poverty and Income Distribution*, ed. F. Bourguignon, M. Bussolo, and L. Pereira da Silva, 1–23. Washington, DC: World Bank.

Brinkman, H. J., and C. S. Hendrix. 2011. "Food Insecurity and Violent Conflict: Causes, Consequences, and Addressing the Challenges." Occasional Paper 24, World Food Programme, Rome.

Chen, S., and M. Ravallion. 2009. "The Impact of the Global Financial Crisis on the World's Poorest." Development Research Group, World Bank, Washington, DC. http://www.voxeu.org/index.php?q=node/3520.

Davies, M. 2011. "Designing Social Protection as an Effective and Sustainable Investment." IDS In Focus Policy Briefing Issue 17, Institute of Development Studies, Brighton, U.K.

Estrella, M., and J. Gaventa. 1998. "Who Counts Reality: Participatory Monitoring and Evaluation: A Literature Review." IDS Working Paper 70, Institute of Development Studies, Brighton, U.K.

Ferguson, N. 2008. *The Ascent of Money.* New York: Penguin Press.

Ferreira, F., P. Leite, L. Pereira da Silva, and P. Picchetti. 2008. "Can the Distributional Impacts of Macroeconomic Shocks Be Predicted? A Comparison of Top-Down Macro-Micro Models with Historical Data for Brazil." In *The Impact of Macroeconomic Policies on Poverty and Income Distribution*, ed. F. Bourguignon, M. Bussolo, and L. Pereira da Silva, 119–75. Washington, DC: World Bank.

Folbre, N. 2006. "Measuring Care: Gender, Empowerment, and the Care Economy." *Journal of Human Development and Capabilities* 7 (2): 183–99.

Gaerlan, K., M. Cabrera, P. Samia, and L. E. Santoalla. 2010. "Feminised Recession: Impact of the Global Financial Crisis on Women Garment Workers in the Philippines." *Gender and Development* 18 (2):229–40.

Goldin, I. and T. Vogel. 2010. "Global Governance and Systemic Risk in the 21st Century: Lessons from the Financial Crisis." *Global Policy* 1 (1): 4–15.

Habib, B., A. Narayan, S. Olivieri, and C. Sanchez. 2010. "The Impact of the Financial Crisis on Poverty and Income Distribution: Insights from Simulations in Selected Countries." Economic Premise 7, Poverty Reduction and Economic Management (PREM) Network, World Bank, Washington, DC.

Harper, C., N. Jones, P. Pereznieto, and A. McKay. 2011. "Promoting Children's Well-Being: Policy Lessons from Past and Present Economic Crises." *Development Policy Review* 29 (5): 622–41.

Held, D., M. Kaldor, and D. Quah. 2010. "The Hydra-Headed Crisis." LSE Global Governance. London School of Economics, London.

Horn, Z. E. 2009. "No Cushion to Fall Back On: The Global Economic Crisis and Informal Workers." Women in Informal Employment: Globalizing and Organizing (WIEGO)/Inclusive Cities Project report.

Hoskyns, C. and S. M. Rai. 2007. "Recasting the Global Political Economy: Counting Women's Unpaid Work." *New Political Economy* 12 (3): 297–317.

Hossain, N. 2009a. "Crisis Impact Monitoring Methodology: Lessons from a Pilot Study in 2009." Institute of Development Studies, Brighton, U.K.

———. 2009b. "Accounts of Crisis: Poor People's Experiences of the Food, Fuel and Financial Crises in Five Countries," Report on a Pilot Study, January–March 2009. Institute of Development Studies, Brighton, U.K.

Hossain, N., R. Fillaili, and G. Lubaale. 2010. "Invisible Impacts and Lost Opportunities: Evidence of the Global Recession in Developing Countries." *Journal of Poverty and Social Justice* 18 (3): 269–79.

Hossain, N., R. Fillaili, G. Lubaale, M. Mulumbi, M. Rashid, and M. Tadros. 2010. *The Social Impacts of Crisis. Findings from Community-level Research in Five Developing Countries*. Brighton, U.K.: Institute of Development Studies.

Hossain, N., and J. A. McGregor. 2011. "A 'Lost Generation'? Impacts of Complex Compound Crises on Children and Young People." *Development Policy Review* 29 (5): 565–84.

Hurst, R., M. Buttle, and J. Sandars. 2010. "The Impact of the Global Economic Slowdown on Value Chain Labor Markets in Asia." In *Poverty and Sustainable*

Development in Asia: Impacts and Responses to the Global Economic Crisis. Manila: Asian Development Bank.

Ivanic, M., W. Martin, and H. Zaman. 2011. "Estimating the Short-Run Poverty Impacts of the 2010–11 Surge in Food Prices." Policy Research Working Paper 5633, World Bank, Washington, DC.

Lustig, N., and M. Walton. 2009. *Crises and the Poor: A Template for Action.* Washington, DC: World Bank.

McCord, A. 2010. "The Impact of the Global Financial Crisis on Social Protection in Developing Countries." *International Social Security Review* 63: 31–45.

McCulloch, N., and A. Grover. 2010. "Estimating the National Impact of the Financial Crisis in Indonesia by Combining a Rapid Qualitative Study with Nationally Representative Surveys." IDS Working Paper 346, Institute of Development Studies, Brighton, U.K.

McGregor, A., N. Hossain, and S. Butters. 2010. "Crisis Effects: Impacts, Attribution and Resilience: A Crisis Watch Background Report for DFID."

McGregor, J. A., and A. Sumner. 2010. "Beyond Business as Usual: What Might 3-D Well-Being Contribute to MDG Momentum?" *IDS Bulletin* 41 (1): 104–12.

Mendoza, R.U. 2009. "Aggregate Shocks, Poor Households and Children: Transmission Channels and Policy Responses." *Global Social Policy* 9: 55–77.

Miller-Dawkins, M., Irwansyah, and R. Abimanyu. 2010. "The Real Story Behind the Numbers: The Impacts of the Global Economic Crisis 2008–2009 on Indonesia's Women Workers." Oxfam GB Research Report.

Narayan, D. 2000. *Voices of the Poor. Can Anyone Hear Us?:* Vol. 1. New York: Oxford University Press for the World Bank.

Narayan, D., L. Pritchett, and S. Kapoor. 2009. *Moving Out of Poverty.* Vol. 2 of *Success from the Bottom Up.* Basingstoke, U.K.; Washington, DC: Palgrave Macmillan and World Bank.

Pernia, E., and J. Knowles. 1998. *Assessing the Social Impact of the Financial Crisis in Asia.* Economics and Development Resource Center Briefing Notes Number 6. Asian Development Bank, Manila. http://aric.adb.org/pdf/edrcbn/edrcbn06.pdf.

Prennushi, G., F. Ferreira, and M. Ravallion. 1998. "Macroeconomic Crises and Poverty: Transmission Mechanisms and Policy Responses." Working Paper, World Bank, Washington, DC.

Rajan, R.G. 2010. *Fault Lines: How Hidden Fractures Still Threaten the World Economy.* Princeton, NJ: Princeton University Press.

Razavi, S. 2011. "Rethinking Care in a Development Context: An Introduction." *Development and Change* 42 (4): 873–903.

Tett, G. 2009. *Fool's Gold: How Unrestrained Greed Corrupted a Dream, Shattered Global Markets and Unleashed a Catastrophe.* London: Abacus.

Turk, C., A. Mason, and P. Petesch. 2010. *Impacts of the Economic Crisis on Vulnerable Population Groups: Midcourse Findings from a Qualitative Monitoring Project in 12 Developing Countries.* Washington, DC: World Bank.

World Bank. 2010. *Food Price Increases in South Asia: National Responses and Regional Dimensions*. Washington, DC: World Bank, South Asia Region.

———. 2011a. *The Jobs Crisis: Household and Government Responses to the Great Recession in Eastern Europe and Central Asia*. Directions in Development. Washington, DC: World Bank.

———. 2011b. "Food Price Watch August 2011." Poverty Reduction and Economic Management Group Report, World Bank, Washington, DC.

World Bank/IMF. 2010. "Global Monitoring Report 2010: The MDGs after the Crisis." World Bank/International Monetary Fund, Washington, DC.

———. 2011. "Global Monitoring Report 2011: Improving the Odds of Achieving the MDGs." World Bank/International Monetary Fund, Washington, DC.

Žižek, S. 2009. *First as Tragedy, Then as Farce*. London: Verso.

CHAPTER 1

Anatomy of Coping: Evidence from People Living through the Crises of 2008–11

Rasmus Heltberg, Naomi Hossain, Anna Reva, and Carolyn Turk

The purpose of this chapter is to survey qualitative research on the coping responses used by poor and vulnerable people in 17 countries to deal with the local effects of the global food, fuel, and financial crises that started in 2008 and are still affecting many parts of the world at the time of writing in early 2011. The data come from focus group discussions (FGDs) and interviews with respondents selected to represent groups exposed to economic shocks and food and fuel price volatility (for example, workers in export-oriented sectors, informal sector workers, and farmers). As such, the data offer insights into the perceptions and behaviors of people as they live through economic volatility and crisis. As described in the introductory chapter, the 17 country case studies were designed for the local context and carried out by local researchers in collaboration with the Institute of Development Studies (IDS) or the World Bank, leading to differences in study design across countries (Hossain 2009; Turk, Mason, and Petesch 2010). Nevertheless, broadly similar qualitative research designs were employed with the common objective of monitoring crises impacts and responses as they unfolded and of complementing quantitative and model-based approaches to crisis monitoring with qualitative approaches. The data therefore permit broad, qualitative comparisons of impacts and coping responses across sites in different countries.

The overriding themes of this chapter are the extent to which people were able to remain resilient against the shocks of recent years and how they did it. The themes are important for understanding the design of crisis response programs and the efforts aimed at building resilience more broadly. We address them through the following questions:

- What were the most common coping responses used by the poor and vulnerable and how effective were they at averting major impacts?
- How were the costs of coping distributed among women, men, children, and youth?
- How did the crises affect gender roles and community cohesion?
- Which sources of support were the most useful and what role did social protection, other government programs, and community organizations play?

At our disposal to address the questions are thousands of pages of country reports and focus group discussion transcripts from up to four rounds of qualitative research at select sites in Bangladesh, Cambodia, the Central African Republic, Ghana, Indonesia, Jamaica, Kazakhstan, Kenya, Mongolia, the Philippines, Senegal, Serbia, Thailand, Ukraine, Vietnam, the Republic of Yemen, and Zambia. By including all 17 countries, we are able to generate a large body of qualitative data on crisis impact and coping.

The chapter is structured as follows. The next section presents the conceptual framework and summarizes the major coping responses across all the study sites and countries. The section on qualitative research discusses the hardships faced by people during the crises. The next section surveys the sources of support people could rely upon, and the final section offers concluding reflections and implications for policy.

Major Coping Responses

Conceptual Framework

The analysis of coping did not adhere to any single academic concept; rather, it was guided by a broad-based framework of coping mechanisms (see figure 1.1). The analytical framework is based on observations in the field and inspired by a range of studies on poverty and vulnerability, both quantitative and qualitative, including *Voices of the Poor* (Narayan 2000); *Moving out of Poverty* (Narayan, Pritchett, and Kapoor 2009); and the work by Anirudh Krishna (Krishna 2004, 2007; Krishna and Shariff 2011), Robert Chambers, and Stefan Dercon (for example, Dercon 2004). By coping responses (or mechanisms), we refer to actions that households take to deal with shocks and avoid the worst impacts: eat cheaper foods and

Figure 1.1. Coping Mechanisms Determine the Ultimate Impact of Shocks

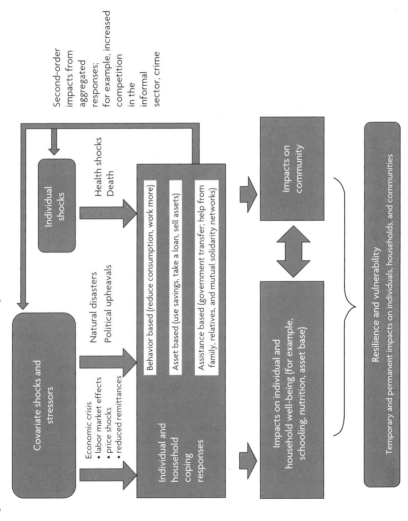

Second-order impacts from aggregated responses; for example, increased competition in the informal sector, crime

Individual shocks
Health shocks
Death

Covariate shocks and stressors
Natural disasters
Political upheavals

Economic crisis
• labor market effects
• price shocks
• reduced remittances

Individual and household coping responses

Behavior based (reduce consumption, work more)

Asset based (use savings, take a loan, sell assets)

Assistance based (government transfer; help from family, relatives, and mutual solidarity networks)

Impacts on community

Impacts on individual and household well-being (for example, schooling, nutrition, asset base)

Resilience and vulnerability
Temporary and permanent impacts on individuals, households, and communities

Source: Authors.

25

fewer meals, work harder, look for new income opportunities, seek support from relatives and community support networks, and so forth. Following Heltberg and Lund (2009), we distinguish among three broad categories of coping responses: (1) behavior-based responses related to consumption and labor supply; (2) asset-based responses that use savings, assets, and common property resources for coping; and (3) assistance-based responses involving accessing support from various sources.

In all study sites, people experience both covariate (common across many people) and idiosyncratic (household-specific) shocks. The most common covariate shocks included the sharp economic contraction starting in 2008; food, fuel, and input price volatility; reduced remittances; droughts and other natural disasters; and political shocks. Health shocks and deaths were common idiosyncratic shocks. As mentioned in the introductory chapter, sharp distinctions between crises and other shocks is difficult, and we therefore need to be cautious with attributions. Our framework, however, distinguishes between the direct impacts of the crises—wage and employment shocks, food and fuel price hikes, and reduced remittances—and the second-order impacts that result from the consequences of coping responses (see figure 1.1). The studies show that that coping responses led to further, or second-order impacts: the women who work long hours to feed their families become exhausted and may have to leave infants in the care of minors; people unable to afford meat, dairy, and vegetables for long periods become malnourished and more susceptible to illness and disease; the sudden influx of workers into the informal economy lowers everyone's earnings; and criminal activities erode trust and cohesion within the community. Thus, second-order impacts from crisis responses led to both individual and covariate shocks, the latter stemming from the accumulated impacts of many peoples' individual responses.

We also distinguish among impacts on men, women, youth, and children; on families; and on communities. Our observations in the field tell us that not all family members experience the same hardship and, moreover, that local communities can be important to coping. Although community is often a source of support, it can also be affected by people's coping responses, such as when norms are violated through theft, sex work, or the drug trade.

Some coping responses are relatively benign, but others can have adverse and possibly long-lasting consequences that could impede people's ability to recover. Adverse coping responses include sales of assets needed for livelihoods, compromised health from eating inferior foods and forgoing health care, children dropping out of school or attending erratically, depletion of common property natural resources, and reduced investment in business growth. Some community impacts can also be long lasting—family breakdown; weakened community cohesion; transgressions of social, legal, and personal norms made to cope; and an uptick in crime and violence.

Overview of Coping Mechanisms

The people interviewed relied on a wide range of coping mechanisms, often simultaneously, to help adjust to worsening circumstances and to avert the worst outcomes such as hunger or loss of house and major assets. Here, we give a brief overview of coping mechanisms; the remainder of the chapter elaborates on them. Table 1.1 summarizes the coping responses that were commonly observed and cited as important in study sites in each of the 13 countries for which we had enough data to make comparisons.

Reducing the quality of food and the number of meals was the most common behavior-based coping response—and often the first one to be used—observed in study sites in all countries. Reducing nonfood consumption, working more hours, and diversifying sources of income (for example, by entering a new informal occupation) were common nearly everywhere. Migration was also fairly common, sometimes including reverse migration to the home area. Increase in crime, petty theft in particular, was another common occurrence. Pulling children out of school happened quite a bit in many countries, but was not necessarily perceived as an important coping response.

Among asset- and loan-based coping responses, sales of assets was fairly common in many surveyed sites, and collection of food and fuel from common property natural resources (a use of communal natural assets) was important only among some of the low-income countries. Loans were important for coping in study sites in many countries, but the lender varied. Family, friends, and moneylenders were the most frequent sources. Banks and microfinance institutions were a common source of loans for coping in sites in only two countries; such loans were more common before the crises forced financial institutions to cut back lending. As the economic conditions worsened, many vulnerable groups were struggling with repayment of existing loans and were no longer eligible to borrow from banks or microfinance institutions. In fact, interviewees often had to borrow from family, friends, and informal moneylenders or sell essential assets to repay

Table 1.1. Coping Responses Cited as Common or Very Common

Common coping responses	Philippines	Thailand	Vietnam	Mongolia	Cambodia	Kenya	Ghana	CAR	Zambia	Bangladesh	Kazakhstan	Ukraine	Serbia	Total
Behavior-based responses														
Reduce the quality and quantity of food	•	•	•	•	•	•	•	•	•	•	•	•	•	13
Reduce nonfood expenditures	•	•	•	•	•	•	•	•	•	•	•	•	•	13
Stop primary or secondary education	•	•	•		•	•	•	•		•				6
Stop higher education	•			•										2
Work more	•	•	•	•	•	•	•	•	•	•	•	•		12
Take up illicit occupations:														
Sex work							•		•					2
Drug dealing		•				•								2
Crime/theft	•	•	•	•		•	•	•	•	•		•		10
Income diversification	•	•	•	•	•			•		•			•	9
Migration		•	•	•	•					•		•		6

Asset-based responses

Response	Count
Sell assets	6
Loan from formal lender	2
Microfinance loan	2
Loan from family/friends	7
Loan from moneylender	4
Use common property natural resources for fuel and food	5

Assistance-based responses. Source of assistance:

Source	Count
Government	4
NGO	4
Religious organization	5
Mutual solidarity group	7
Relatives	13
Friends and neighbors	11

Source: Authors' coding based on qualitative research at sites in the mentioned countries.

Note: Data from Indonesia, Jamaica, Senegal, and the Republic of Yemen are discussed in the text but not included in this table because the data were not in a format that readily permitted comparison.

Mutual solidarity: There was a lot of help exchanged within occupational groups, for example, with finding work or housing. It is included here even though it may not involve assistance in cash.

their bank loans as no refinance schemes were available (see the section on sources of support).

Assistance most often came from relatives, friends, and neighbors. Informal groups organized around mutual solidarity, often along occupational lines, were common in sites in around half the countries; moral and financial help from religious organizations was commonly reported in five; and nongovernmental organizations (NGOs) provided assistance in four. NGOs had a presence in additional study sites, but did not always provide assistance in a form that the respondents perceived as important or helpful for coping. Government assistance was important for coping only in sites in the former socialist countries of Eastern Europe, Central Asia, and Mongolia—countries that had fairly large national social protection programs in place prior to the crisis.

How effective were the coping responses in averting the adverse impacts of the crises? This question is addressed in the next section.

Qualitative Research on Impacts on Individuals, Families, and Communities

Coping came at significant costs to poor individuals, families, and communities, and, as mentioned, some of these costs may continue to be felt well after the crises subside. Indeed, the impacts of reduced food consumption in the context of chronic malnutrition, the sale of productive assets, the forgone education and health care, the high levels of stress incurred by individuals struggling to cope, and the uptick in antisocial behaviors such as theft are likely to reverberate for a long time. In the following, we discuss the major forms of hardship felt by individuals and families, how these hardships were distributed within households, and how community cohesion was affected.

Hardships for Individuals and Families

—*"How can you afford a smile if you slept hungry?"*

Impacts differed in their timing, duration, and severity. Groups tied to the formal economy were affected first and most directly through layoffs, reduced working hours, and cancellation of bonuses as the global economy contracted. Yet formal sector workers turned out to be relatively resilient. They could often count on severance payments and live off savings without drastic reduction of food consumption or sale of essential assets. Workers in the informal and agricultural sectors reported many indirect impacts through reduced domestic demand for their products and services, increased competition as the laid-off factory workers sought informal sector jobs, and reduced remittances from urban workers to rural areas. Many of the informal sector workers were struggling to make ends meet even before the crises and saw the most damage to their livelihoods due to coping responses that often included accumulation of unserviceable debt, sale of productive assets, or forgoing medical care. In many countries, the impact of the global economic downturn on this group appeared likely to be long lasting, and they were not able to recover as the national economies started to grow (documented in the later rounds of research).

Food insecurity emerged as the most severe impact of the crisis. It was most pronounced in the Central African Republic and Kenya where the impacts of global financial and food price crises were compounded by domestic shocks such as breakdown of the hydropower plant in the Central African Republic and prolonged drought in Kenya. In both countries, food shortages were widespread among children and adults, and respondents described major stress over securing the daily meal. In the Central African Republic, even employees of state-owned enterprises reported barely ever eating meat. Some reported that low food intake resulted in deaths:

> *"I lost my two children a year ago. Since their birth they never knew a happy life, they were always sick. The last time I sent them to the health center, the diagnostic was the lack of blood cells and malnourishment. The nurse told me to feed them with more milk and beans. Because I didn't have enough money to buy these products, they died."*
> Fifty-one-year-old woman, mother of six children, Central African Republic, August 2010

> *"These days it has become very difficult. Even though we are alive, our health is deteriorating. I used to have three meals each day, but now I am hardly managing a meal each day. When I am unable to get food, I just sleep, with hope that tomorrow will be better."*
> Rural woman in Lango Baya, Kenya, March 2009

Severe food insecurity was also common in Bangladesh and Zambia, where respondents often complained of weakness, dizziness, and lack of energy due to poor diets. Although no instances of starvation were reported in East Asia, many poor households were reducing the quantity and quality of food. Adults were sometimes forgoing meals so their children could eat. Less drastic reductions in the food expenditure were also reported in Eastern Europe and Central Asia (ECA). Reduced calorie intake combined with the need to work longer hours can have long-term health consequences, particularly for individuals engaged in hard physical work.

High levels of stress, anxiety, and even trauma resulting from inability to provide adequate food for the family, maintain the previous level of remittances to parents and siblings in rural communities, pay off debts, and cope with other negative conditions of the crises were reported in nearly all communities. Both men and women were often working extremely long hours and reported physical and emotional exhaustion.

> *"We have so little money we can almost not survive. How can we be happy? Now there are only headaches and tears."*
> Participant, Baboang Village, Cambodia, July 2009

In Eastern Europe, interviewees reported increased use of counseling and psychological assistance provided by social workers either in person or by phone through dedicated "trust numbers." In Serbia, women expressed appreciation of the counseling provided by Centers for Social Work.

> *"I can only praise the Center for Social Work because they call me often just to talk. They ask me how I'm doing, how is it for my children, if they should see a psychologist. I am happy when they call me."*
> Single mother from Belgrade, October 2009

> *"We get more people coming to us for help. People go for help to psychologists, social workers. People started to ask more for their consultations, and the number of such people increased three-fold during last year. We even resumed the operation of the telephone line for psychological counseling, which had been closed long time ago. . . . But now, once again, we had to open such line on a voluntary basis, because people simply need it."*
> Participant, Slavutych, Kiev region, Ukraine, August 2010

In site after site in most study countries, poor people were forgoing medical services because they could no longer cover health care costs. Interviewees were increasingly self-medicating, relying on traditional healers, and buying medicines from street vendors instead of pharmacies. Some interviewees in the Central African Republic reported the deaths of family members unable to afford health services. In Kenya, people living with HIV/AIDS reported worsening conditions as they often had to take their antiretroviral drugs on an empty stomach. Some respondents in Bangladesh reported postponing serious medical treatment.

> *"Because of lack of money, I had to drive my wife who was sick to a pygmy healer, but she died three days later."*
>
> Wood factory worker and father of six children, Central African Republic, August 2010

Increased indebtedness and sale of assets was reported in sites in most countries. The situation was particularly dire in Cambodia, the Philippines, and Thailand where many households had lost or were living in fear of losing their land and houses from their inability to service debts. Pawning of assets (jewelry, televisions, and other appliances) and sale of motorbikes, boats, and other productive equipment was also very common in these countries. In Bangladesh, people reported selling electronic equipment and mobile phones. In Kazakhstan, respondents sold houses, cattle, and cars to pay off debts incurred before the crisis. In the African sites, sale of assets was observed in Ghana, where poor shea nut gatherers reported layers of coping: they would first sell off shea nuts, which represent a major form of savings, and then sell livestock in a particular order, poultry first, then ruminants, and cattle as last resort. In the Central African Republic and Kenya, sale of assets was not common, possibly because poor households had already exhausted their resources and had little left to sell.

Distress asset sales disadvantage the poor. Mongolian herders were severely affected by declining world cashmere prices, which prompted a massive sale of meat and a reduction of prices. The poor had to sell a large number of animals to finance basic consumption, and it will take years to rebuild the herds. The wealthier herders, however, could wait for cashmere prices to recover by drawing on savings and alternative sources of income. These herders also had a better sense of price movements and could afford transportation costs to sell their produce at higher prices in urban markets.

Coping with economic crisis has eroded the savings and asset base of households in most study sites, leaving many people with few resources to cope with other shocks such as adverse weather conditions, natural disasters, and health and education expenditures. Prolonged and repeated shocks clearly exhaust the coping capacity of families and communities.

Continued high and volatile global food prices are therefore a source of concern.

Economic Shocks Are Not Gender Blind

—*"When they know that a woman has a small child, they don't want to employ her, they just say 'I need a worker who will work every day.'"*

Men and women both were affected by rising unemployment and reduced incomes and reported high levels of psychological stress, the need to work longer hours just to make ends meet, increased competition in the labor market, and worsening treatment or even abuse by employers. In most countries, these effects had a larger impact on women who were more likely to work in low-paying occupations even before the crises and had the major share of child care and household responsibilities. In East Asia, women also suffered disproportionately from industrial downsizing. In this region, women were overrepresented among low-skilled workers employed in manufacturing, and they were the first to get fired as companies engaged in a strategy to retain skilled employees, who were primarily men.

There were some reports of rising gender discrimination. In Mongolia, women reported discrimination in hiring decisions based on their physical appearance. In Thailand, some interviewees said that women received less in severance payments when companies incorrectly reported laid-off female employees as having resigned voluntarily while reporting laid-off male employees correctly, resulting in higher severance payouts. In export factories in Indonesia, workers reported that as the sector recovered, there was a stronger demand for female employees who would agree to work long hours without secure contracts and accept more pressure for productivity. In Serbia and Ukraine, it became much more difficult for women with small children to find work as job market competition increased, and these women were also more likely to be laid off if the company was downsizing. In addition, interviewed single mothers in Serbia said that employers were trying to take advantage of their vulnerability by asking them to work long hours and weekends for low pay; they also reported instances of sexual harassment.

"Most likely to get into a list of people whose jobs can be cut in the first place are mothers with children. Especially when their children tend to get sick frequently. . . . It may happen that in one month one child gets ill, but in the other month another child may also get sick and so on."
Woman from Donetsk, Ukraine, August 2010

"When they know that a woman has a small child they don't want to employ her, they just say 'I need a worker who will work every day.'"
Woman in rural Zrenjanin, Serbia, October 2009

"I found a job and my employer soon told me that we had to become close. I rejected his offer and lost the job."
Woman in rural Zrenjanin, Serbia, October 2009

Surveyed sites in many countries found that economic hardship often made women shift from a concentration on nonpaid domestic labor to income-generating activities. The increased labor force participation of women usually entailed informal sector work and low pay and led to the stress of working long hours away from home with small children left in the care of older siblings. It appeared that contractions in labor market earnings sometimes led to more hours worked, not less, as people had to supplement with less remunerative occupations. Starting to work outside the home had an impact on gender roles. In Mongolia, it resulted in improved self-esteem and an increased role for women in household decision making and social life at large, while in the Republic of Yemen, women's paid work outside the home was perceived by some men as a threat to social norms as well as to their own employment.

The emotional pressure of facing hungry children often forced women to be more entrepreneurial in their search for income-generating opportunities. In many sites, interviewees perceived women to be somewhat more likely to diversify into new activities, while men were more likely to continue doing the same jobs but for longer hours wherever possible. In the export industries in Bangladesh and Indonesia, men and women both reported loss of overtime and shorter working hours. The noticeable diversification by women across the wide range of contexts may result from the more direct pressures women face in terms of feeding children and other household members, which pushed them to continuously look for new opportunities. When faced with economic hardship, they were also more prepared to accept low status and physically demanding jobs, like cleaning, laundry, and sex work. In Cambodia, for example, garment workers who lost their jobs went to work in karaoke bars and massage salons—jobs that entail a high possibility of sexual harassment.

Women with children were sometimes constrained in their coping options. For example, in ECA, many interviewed women complained about lack of kindergartens, which limited their employment opportunities. In East Asian study sites, women often had to take poorly paid subcontracting jobs that would allow them to work from home and fulfill caretaking responsibilities. Married men were generally more likely to accept jobs that were far away from home or to move to a different locality for work.

Women were also better able to manage household budgets, save up, and remit money to relatives in difficult times. Women were usually responsible for stretching household budgets by buying food at cheaper places or in bulk at wholesale prices; walking long distances to collect firewood to save on fuel (mostly in the African countries); sewing new clothes from old ones; and collecting wild fruit, leaves, or mushrooms to supplement food consumption. Respondents in Vietnam also noted that women were better at remitting money to rural relatives:

> "Now youngsters travel to the city to seek employment by themselves. They get information from their friends through mobiles so it is clearer. Fewer people are cheated. Normally, more women migrate than men, and the former also send more money home, as their savings capacity is better."
> Official from Thúy Hòa village, Trà Vinh, Vietnam,
> July–August 2009

Women continued to bear the burden of household responsibilities despite experiencing longer hours in paid work and income activities. In many communities, interviewees noted that when the time women spent in income-generating activities was added to the time they spent cooking, cleaning, caring for children, and other household needs, women worked much longer hours than men. This was particularly apparent in the Central African Republic, where an interviewee noted, "*It is the sleep which drags her away from her daily housework,*" and in Kenya, where rural women reported 18-hour working days.

In some sites, reduced incomes and rising unemployment contributed to an increase in domestic violence, both by men against women and by women against children. Economic hardships increased tensions and arguments in family relationships, which sometimes resulted in violence. Focus group participants in a Cambodian village reported an increase in domestic violence, which they linked to reduced incomes as a result of the crisis:

> "Many families seem to have very frequent arguments and most of the cases relate to income. . . . Some wives cannot stay in their house because they are afraid of their husbands."
> Participant, Donn Vong Village, Cambodia, July 2009

In Mongolia, unemployment among men and alcohol abuse were seen as the reason for the rise in domestic violence, which was more common in urban areas. Focus group participants explained that the rural areas still had herding jobs, which kept men busy throughout the year:

"Presence of domestic violence is often observed among our khoroo *[subdistrict] citizens. Sometimes we find women having black eyes. I observe that unemployed men usually spend their time drinking alcohol and playing game. When they are at home, drunk men often get into conflict with family members and start fighting. It is very depressing for women, children and older family members. Households, who suffer from a drinking family member, do not call police. They feel that after a few cases they would be sentenced by court. In this case, the family members will be responsible for paying an attorney fee, therefore they don't call police and attend women's centre."*
Social worker of 25th khoroo, Songino Khairkhan district,
Ulaanbaatar, Mongolia,
November 2010–January 2011

The crisis sometimes contributed to the increase in female-headed households as men left for urban areas or abroad (but not necessarily sending remittances), were sentenced to jail (crime rates went up in nearly all countries surveyed), or simply abandoned their families. Single mothers and their children were particularly vulnerable to food insecurity, and children of woman-headed households were more likely to leave school to contribute to family incomes. The more common situation, however, was men migrating for work and sending remittances while women managed household responsibilities.

Men who lost their jobs were, in some communities, reported as those who were most affected by the crisis. Men are traditionally seen as having a major responsibility of providing for the family, and being unable to fill that role sometimes resulted in a deep emotional stress. Men were also very likely to engage in hard physical labor for many hours while denying themselves proper nutrition, to risk their personal safety by saving on accommodation (for example, migrant construction workers and cyclo drivers in urban Cambodia lived and slept on the street), and to migrate away from home. Overall physical and emotional exhaustion was quite common among men:

"With the beginning of the crisis, I started to work more, and practically speaking I don't live at home. Because I come home practically to take a shower, have dinner and sleep. Therefore, personally for me, our relations in the family have deteriorated. From material point of view everything is OK, because I started to work more. But in my family they tell me 'we

do not need your money, you better stay at home more time. Why do we need all these money, give it up, all of it,' but I cannot stop such work, because after that they will tell me 'it is enough for you to sit at home, high time to go and earn money.' . . . I cannot get into situation, when I come home and they will tell me 'give us something' and I wouldn't be able to give it. . . . No, it's not my way."

Man in Donetsk, Ukraine, August 2010

Children's Hardships

—*"We did not want our children to drop out of school. But they said that they could not study because we faced such problems and they had to help the family."*

In site after site in all covered countries, parents sought to protect their children's food consumption and schooling. Adult household members often reported skimping on the quantity and quality of food they consumed to ensure that children had proper diets. At the onset of the crisis, parents were reducing school allowances and in some instances transferring children from private to public schools (or to less expensive schools run by churches, madrassas, or NGOs), yet doing everything possible to ensure that children continue their studies. Impacts on schooling overall were more muted than expected on the basics of knowledge of responses to previous crises. The strong emphasis on keeping children in school may reflect the widespread investments in improving access to education across the developing world since the 1990s, particularly through reducing the direct costs (through school fee abolition) and the indirect costs of school (through cash or food transfers). Factors that influenced whether students remained in school during the hardships included the value that parents attached to education, free education policies or subsidies for fees, distance to schools, and the availability of school feeding.

There were nevertheless many instances of erratic attendance and school withdrawal either because of the need for children to contribute to household income or because education costs had become prohibitive. In the Republic of Yemen, people reported that costs of schooling, such as the customary payment toward teachers' lunches, had risen. In Jamaica, some people felt that despite policies of free education, the actual costs of schooling remained a burden. An NGO-run school in a Bangkok slum registered a 20 percent drop-out rate, with many of the dropouts becoming street vendors. There were concerns for the safety of these children, and, according to staff of a port hospital, 2009 had the highest rate of pregnant girls under 14. In the Cambodia sites, many children in rural areas left school. Young teenagers (aged 13 to 15) tried to engage in paid economic activities. Girls often found employment in Phnom Penh as domestic workers, and boys worked as laborers in agriculture, fishing, and construction. Younger children helped their parents by looking after animals and collecting wild foods such as mushrooms, crabs, and snails from the commons:

> "My children dropped out of school a few months ago. I did not want them to stop but they stopped themselves. Now they go to collect wild mushrooms and morning glory to sell to help the family."

> "Now we are faced with this tough time, lack of income and outstanding debts, our children go to seek jobs—carrying rice bags in our village or going out of the village, such as to uproot cassava in Kampong Cham or to work in construction in urban areas."

> "My children, aged between 13 and 15, dropped out of school and now have gone to work as domestic workers in the city for 100,000 Riel a month. This helps mitigate the burden of feeding them and they help us with their remittances."
>
> Participant, Baboang Village, Cambodia, July 2009

In 2008–09, drop-out rates increased in Bangladesh where the head teacher in an NGO-run school in Dhaka reported:

> "On average if we had 30 students in every class, then we lost five students in every normal year. But this year, 10 to 15 students have dropped out from every class of our school. Many are not able to pay the fees while others do not have uniforms or books."

Teachers, however, felt that the situation had returned to what they considered normal in 2010 and 2011. Dropouts were particularly acute in many of the African sites due to long distance to schools, unaffordability of fees, and lack of school feeding programs. In a number of contexts, it was clear that even when children had not dropped out, hunger and casual work opportunities meant their attendance became more erratic during this period. Erratic attendance often has long-term consequences for school performance and the transition to higher levels of education.

The situation was markedly better in the ECA and Mongolia sites, countries that have long traditions of universal education. Although these countries reported almost no dropping out or a rise in absenteeism, parents often had to reduce expenditures on extracurricular activities, clothes, supplies, transportation, and children's allowances for school lunches and leisure activities.

Although generally quite rare, violence against children was reported in Jamaica and the Republic of Yemen. In Jamaica, some people noted that stressed women took their frustrations out on children, and in contexts where children's views were elicited, it was clear that financial stress created tense domestic situations:

> *"Women beat their children more than men do. When women have nothing to eat, they beat their children and verbally abuse them. Women are more stressed."*
>
> Participant, in Kingston, Jamaica, 2009

> *"When I don't have anything in the house and I am upset, I beat up the children."*
>
> Woman in the Republic of Yemen, 2010

Children were often left alone or in the care of older siblings as all adult family members had to work long hours away from home. In Serbia, single mothers complained that their children had behavioral problems and low academic performance as mothers had no time to support them: *"My child is not doing well at school. I was working all day long and I couldn't follow what she was doing,"* said a single mother from Belgrade. Lack of public kindergartens often forced mothers to leave small children unattended or in the care of older siblings. In the Central African Republic, this practice reportedly resulted in increased disease prevalence among small children as their brothers and sisters did not know how to feed them properly or take care of them when they were ill.

Children were suffering most in the Kenya sites where the effects of the global financial crisis were greatly compounded by a seven-year-long drought. Most families could afford only one meal per day, porridge or *ugali*, a maize dish with vegetables. Teachers reported a drastic decline in student attendance and a growing number of children engaged in waste collection, crime, and prostitution to be able to provide food for themselves and their siblings. According to interviewees, some parents encouraged their daughters to engage in prostitution and sold their sons to wealthy Asian traders so that households could eat. Teachers reported an increase in pregnancies among schoolgirls, attributed to the shortage of food. There were also stories of children robbing each other of food in primary schools. School feeding programs, where functional, were extremely useful in improving school attendance and academic performance, but school lunch programs were terminated in many schools when the economic conditions worsened. In the rural community of Lango Baya, there were concerns about the growing number of abandoned children, whose parents went to urban areas in search of jobs but never returned.

Youth during Crises

—"They have to steal because they have no food."

In many of the countries surveyed, young people were seen as among the most vulnerable to the crisis. Youth found it difficult or impossible to find jobs, struggled with paying college or university tuition, and were tempted to engage in illegal activities from lack of other opportunities.

The crisis appeared to have a mixed impact on secondary and higher education. In Mongolia, students who completed their course of studies and who come from wealthy families decided to continue their education until the job market improved, but poor students had to terminate their university education or take a temporary leave of absence as their parents could no longer afford tuition fees. Similarly, in Kazakhstan, many university graduates unable to find jobs reported continuing their education to obtain an additional specialization and be more competitive in the market; students from the poorest families switched to part-time studies to be able to earn an income, which resulted in a negative impact on their academic achievement. In Ghana, university and secondary school students reported missing lectures or deferring their courses as they could no longer afford tuition, while in Jamaica, promising students were shelving their university plans. In Vietnam, however, the increased competition for jobs due to the crisis made workers pay greater attention to education. The number of workers enrolled in vocational schools increased substantially during the crisis. Many of these workers were taking advantage of the flexible class schedules and combining work with studies.

Increased alcohol and drug use and engagement in criminal activities by youth was cited as a negative impact of the crisis in sites in several countries. The situation was worst in Kenya and Zambia, which experienced a rise in drug and alcohol abuse and prostitution by youth. In Lusaka, youth reported a rising number of girls and young women entering sex work as one of the most significant problems facing their community, caused by poverty, unemployment, and pressure from families to help pay for food or siblings' education. In both countries, there were concerns about an increased incidence of sexually transmitted diseases including HIV/AIDS. In Kenya, a number of interviewees also mentioned increased theft, particularly food theft by youth.

> *"Children, especially the youth, have to stay home. The ones who have completed school just stay at home, without jobs even when they have completed primary school. Most of these were not able to proceed to secondary school. A lot of these youth have ended up organizing themselves into groups. They end up on the centres and in town (Malindi) engaging in crime to survive. They have to steal, even violently; because they have no food and they must have at least a meal each day."*
>
> Participant in Lango Baya, Kenya, March 2009

An increased number of drug users and sellers among the youth was also observed in Thailand. The interviewees reported that drug dealers were using children as young as 10 to sell drugs for them. The types of drugs used are amphetamines and glue, which are cheaper and easier to use and sell than other drugs. An increase in young people engaged in sex work to earn money was also reported.

Community Cohesion

> —*"Theft is increasing because of hardship in the area . . . but we are not afraid of it anymore because we are living in empty houses . . . we have nothing for them to steal."*

Economic hardship also had high social costs in many of the communities surveyed, with increases in crime, drug and alcohol abuse, erosion of social norms, and the breaking or weakening of solidarity mechanisms. Alcohol abuse, mostly among men, increased in nearly all countries, and unemployment and stress were cited as major reasons. Drug abuse and prostitution also became widespread in several countries, as already mentioned. Kenyan interviewees noted increased consumption of a lethal local brew known as "kill-me-quick" to "kill the stress." In the Republic of Yemen, some men reported consumption of *qat* (a stimulant) had declined, but women felt it had generally increased. Some women said they encouraged use of qat, as it was an appetite suppressant. One Sana'a mother of a baby reported that her breast milk had dried up, a fact she attributed to her qat use and poor diet.

"In the black market when the working day ends, people all get drunk. They sell something and drink the money. Homeless people come to collect leftover food and steal things."

Candy and fruit trader from Narantuul market, Ulaanbaatar, Mongolia, August–September 2009

Crime, particularly theft, was reported to have increased and was a major source of concern in rural and urban sites in nearly all countries. Some interviewees were afraid not only for the security of their possessions but also for their personal safety. In the Philippines, women were more affected by the rise in crime, including kidnapping and rape. In many rural communities, people were concerned about the increased incidence of crop and livestock theft. In Kenya, interviewees commonly complained about food theft. It seemed that there was no outright condemnation of it as the thieves were stealing just to eat and not for further commercial resale. Young people have noted that it is better to steal and be nabbed than to be malnourished and eventually die of hunger. In rural Kenya, a farmer explained that food crops were being stolen from the fields, creating disincentives to increase cultivation. In Mongolia, the poor were more likely to have their animals stolen as they lacked hired help and were more likely to leave animals unattended.

"I had very nice cows. Last year the cows were stolen. My wife was herding the animals and she came in to have some tea. We saw the animals near our ger. It became dark and one car passed through our ger. That evening we could not find our cows."

Herder from Bayandelger soum, Tuv province, Mongolia, August–September 2009

"I have no idea what to do for a living . . . maybe I am going to be a thief myself!"

Participant, Donn Vong village, Cambodia, July 2009

"Security here is now a matter of concern. This is because previously we never had theft, especially theft of food. But today, because of this, food and economic crisis and hunger, everyone is vigilant. Theft of food is increasing; one cannot simply die of hunger when there is food."

Participant in Lango Baya, Kenya, March 2009

Despite reports of weakening community cohesion and solidarity, there was no evidence of violent conflict in the study sites. Competition for scarce work and resources available sometimes divided people and communities.

In Thailand, port workers expressed hostility toward illegal migrants from other countries who agreed to work for lower pay. In Serbia, the Roma reported increased discrimination by employers. In Kenya, interviewees noted that mosques were providing generous assistance to Muslims but not to people of other faiths, which created animosity among non-Muslims. Women market traders in rural Kenya said that some of them used witchcraft to win customers over fellow traders. Women beggars in Bangladesh felt that the norm of assisting the extreme poor had been destroyed during this period, with better-off people abusing and rudely advising them to seek help from the government or NGOs.

Sources of Support

An important part of coping everywhere was to reach out for help. Assistance came, with varying frequency and effectiveness, from formal, micro, and informal finance; social protection; NGOs and religious groups; and informal sources such as community-based groups and remittances from relatives. Informal safety nets played the most important role for coping (even if the amount of assistance was inadequate relative to the large and growing need) and were often the only sources of support available. Formal sources of support were largely absent, except in the ECA and Mongolia sites.

The Role of Formal, Micro, and Informal Finance

—"We fear the credit agent like we fear the tiger."

Formal financial institutions were usually inaccessible to low-income groups both before and during the crisis, as these groups lacked collateral. In addition, banks rarely locate in rural areas, where many focus group participants live. The main sources of credit were family, friends, neighbors, coworkers, and informal moneylenders. In all the countries surveyed, the availability of credit from both formal and informal sources went down. Banks and moneylenders were lending smaller amounts at higher interest rates, and family and community-based credit sources were often exhausting themselves.

Kazakhstan, Mongolia, Serbia, and Ukraine were the four countries where bank credit was widely available to most employed people, but with mixed evidence on the usefulness of formal credit for coping. Bank credit was instrumental in helping herders and wage employees in Mongolia survive the crisis and cover school expenses and university tuition for their children. Furthermore, in Mongolia, microfinance institutions were viewed positively and praised for support in development of nonpastoral economic activities. In Ukraine, some interviewees reported that credit from banks had helped them cover basic consumption needs during the crisis. Unsustainable debts to banks became an issue of concern in Kazakhstan, where interviewees resorted to sale of assets, including cars and housing, to repay the loans taken before the onset of the crisis. They also started hiding from bank agents or even changing the place of residence to escape their credit obligations. High levels of indebtedness to banks were also reported among the Roma in Serbia.

> *"People took out so many loans. Nobody thought about interest rates. Now they are unable to repay a loan. Sometimes people escape, hide from the bank officers, sell their houses in order to repay a loan, and in other times they are even left outdoors. Nobody helps them. When they took out their loans, they had jobs, but the crisis took away their jobs. I took out a loan with my husband. Then my husband was selected for a redundancy during the job cuts at his workplace, while I was on maternity leave. We failed to repay our loan in due time, then bank officers came and threatened us that they will take away our apartment. Now, in order to repay a loan, our family budget had to be reduced."*
>
> Participant in urban area, Kizilorda oblast, Kazakhstan,
> June–July 2010

Access to formal finance was constrained in other areas. In Africa, very few FGD participants reported having any access to bank loans or microcredit, while in East Asia, credit from banks was available mainly to formal sector employees. Informal sector workers and farmers were relying primarily on loans from family members and friends and on high interest loans from moneylenders. In Indonesia and the Philippines, customary community-based savings groups were accessed. Yet in Indonesia, interviewees reported that the *arisan*—traditional savings groups that bring together between tens and hundreds of community members—have been weakening. In some communities, they were terminated altogether; in others, they were meeting every two or four months as opposed to every week before the crisis.

Indebtedness to microfinance institutions and informal moneylenders and the inability to service those debts were major sources of distress for households in Bangladesh, Cambodia, the Philippines, and Thailand. In Cambodia, interviewees from rural areas took loans from microfinance institutions before the crisis to invest in agricultural inputs or houses, or to cover other essential needs. With the onset of the crisis, many people had to borrow from moneylenders at very high interest rates to pay back their microfinance debts. As their incomes kept falling, they could not service these debts, prompting many to sell motorbikes, boats, livestock, land, or even their homes to pay their debts. Others were living in constant fear of creditors taking possession of their property.

> "People took the money from the microfinance institutions. They thought they could return it . . . but they could not because of the crisis. Now the institution has taken their land and house . . . many more households here will become homeless soon."

> "We sell whatever we have to get the money to cope with the loan, but it is still not enough . . . we are afraid of the credit agent like we are afraid of a tiger. Any time they come we leave our home and go somewhere else."

> Participant, in rural Cambodia, July 2009

Similar accounts of high levels of indebtedness and stress over the potential loss of land or houses were observed in Thailand and the Philippines, where vulnerable population groups could not borrow from banks and most of their loans were from loan sharks at very high interest rates. People were afraid of debt collectors who often publicly humiliated and embarrassed the borrowers to collect the debts. For example, an interviewee from Klong Toey, Thailand, took a loan to start a new business and borrowed 5,000 Thai baht as an initial investment for it. Six months later she had a debt of B 60,000. She could not explain how it happened and did not see a way out of her situation: "If we stay where we are, we know how much debt we have, if we tried to earn more and struggle to work, we might end up having more debt than before." In Bangladesh, interviewees complained that families had to go without food for days to continue making weekly repayments to microfinance institutions.

These examples call for public action to improve financial literacy, regulate and facilitate the development of formal lending institutions (including those that provide microcredit), and perhaps create mechanisms for debt refinancing in times of crisis. Of the countries surveyed, only in Thailand did the government pursue a debt refinancing scheme, but because it did not have much success in refinancing moneylender loans, it did not help the most vulnerable population groups.

The Role of Social Protection

—"Who can feed their family on $3 per month?"

Across sites and countries, vulnerable population groups rarely benefited from formal social protection programs, with the exception of the ECA and Mongolia sites. Many countries lacked effective preexisting social assistance programs, and governments were rarely able to design and launch new programs promptly as the crisis unfolded. The reported problems with social protection included poor design and targeting, low generosity, and downscaling during crisis. This being said, free or subsidized education and school feeding programs were instrumental in keeping children in school, and greatly valued by families and communities. Likewise, in countries whose governments subsidized health services, such assistance was widely appreciated by recipients.

Kazakhstan, Mongolia, Serbia, and Ukraine were the exceptions in that many FGD participants in these countries benefited from government transfers such as universal old age pensions, subsidies for utilities, child allowances, and unemployment benefits. Some also benefited from the support of employment centers in finding jobs. But even these countries were not completely spared from the problems observed elsewhere: corruption in program implementation, failure to reach some vulnerable groups (informal gold miners in Mongolia, the Roma in Serbia), and inadequate level of benefits. The magnitude of these problems was less severe than in other countries covered in this research. In general, government transfers, albeit small, were perceived to have helped low-income households weather the crisis. Despite that, FGD participants in Eastern Europe and Central Asia were often critical of their social protection systems, largely because they had memories of the much more generous assistance packages of the socialist regime and high expectations of the quality of public services.

In other countries, some government programs were in place, but they were ineffective in helping people cope with growing food insecurity, loss of jobs, lack of income-generating opportunities, and mounting debt. In many cases, the programs did not address the particular vulnerabilities that mattered to respondents, such as the widespread indebtedness in Cambodia and the Philippines or the pervasive food insecurity in the Central African Republic, Senegal, and Zambia. People in rural Kenya complained that those few who were fortunate enough to access the food-for-work program found it to be a mixed blessing, as the amounts of food earned were not adequate compensation for the excessively hard work

they performed. In addition, after the long period of chronic food insecurity resulting from the drought and election violence, most people who
sought such work were physically weak and generally malnourished, and
they found it difficult to perform the work required.

In other instances, the programs were not well targeted. For example,
the government of Thailand launched a loan refinancing program and a
utility subsidy program for electricity and water. Although both initiatives
seem to have been generally useful, they excluded some of the most vulnerable groups. Urban slum dwellers without access to basic infrastructure could not benefit from utility subsidies. Poor people who borrowed
from loan sharks could not apply for the refinancing program because the
informal lenders did not allow their borrowers to disclose their names, a
prerequisite to access the program.

In some countries, political considerations and corruption were alleged
to play a role for targeting. In Mongolia, where the winter dzud compounded the effects of the crisis, the government's fodder and hay
distribution never reached some of the *soums* (subdivisions) headed by
opposition party governors. In Cambodia, food aid in rural areas was
provided based on the loyalty to local authorities rather than on the
objective poverty criteria. In Ukraine, interviewees indicated that jobs
could sometimes be found by paying a bribe to employees of the state
employment centers. And, in Kazakhstan, nepotism and corruption were
alleged to be widespread in the implementation of the Road Map program, which aimed at helping the vulnerable groups obtain employment
or receive vocational training.

Benefits, when received, were often too small to have any significant
impact. The government of Mongolia has been distributing Tog 10,000
a month (around $8) to every citizen of the country since August 2010.
FGD participants found the amount too small to have any real impact.
In rural Bangladesh, recipients of the old-age and widows' allowances
complained that the transfers (between 200 and 300 taka) were grossly
inadequate because of food price hikes: "*Can anyone feed themselves
on only Tk 200 ($2.89) per month?*" complained one of the intervie-
wees. In Zambia, to increase the outreach of the Farmers Input Support Program, the government halved the amount of fertilizer and seed
distributed to eligible beneficiaries. Interviewees complained that the
amount of inputs received was negligible and could not have any impact
on production; even so, a number of eligible households never received
any fertilizer.

Assistance provided in-kind was sometimes of inferior quality. In Quezon, the Philippines, the fertilizer distributed by the government was thought to have had a negative impact on crops. In Kenya, the Ministry of Agriculture provided farmers with "improved" male goats that were expected to mate with the local goat varieties and produce kids better adjusted to local climate conditions. Most of the male goats died because they could not survive in the local climate. In Bangladesh, women complained that the cheap rice subsidized by the government had a bad smell and would spoil if not eaten immediately after it was cooked.

There were also instances of downscaling and termination of precrisis initiatives due to fiscal constraints. With the onset of the crisis, some governments were no longer able to continue their social assistance programs at the previous level. In Kenya, some school feeding programs were threatened with funding withdrawals, which negatively affected student attendance and academic performance. In Mongolia, the Child Benefit Program, which provided regular monthly and quarterly transfers to all families with children, was terminated in late 2009 due to fiscal constraints. The program had been widely appreciated by recipients because the payments were predictable, and its termination during a time of hardship was viewed very negatively. Instead of this program, the government provided a one-time payment of Tog 70,000 to all citizens of Mongolia as the "mineral resource sharing money." This money was quickly spent for Tsagaan Sar (New Year) celebration, and the recipients were left with no predictable source of cash income.

> *"Child support money was a major income source for poor and very poor households. Moreover, the child support money documents were used as a collateral in the shop to get some daily food. Unfortunately, the support stopped; livelihood will worsen more."*
>
> Participants, Dundgobi aimag, Mongolia,
> January–February 2010

In Thailand, the government launched several new social programs in response to the economic and political crisis, but their implementation started only as the economy had already begun its recovery. Field work based on focus group discussions was used to assess the early implementation experience of these programs (World Bank, Thailand 2010).

Government programs of all kinds tended to exclude informal sector workers and enterprises even though the informal sector arguably did the lion's share of crisis adjustment by absorbing the laid-off workers and new entrants to the labor market. In Vietnam, large formal enterprises were eligible for subsidized loans, but no such assistance was available for small and cash-strapped informal businesses. In Thailand, tax cuts and credit at low fixed interest rates were available for formal businesses in key industries if they retained workers, but efforts to help small and medium enterprises (SMEs) by increasing the capital of the SME bank did not have much success, and no support was offered to entrepreneurs in the informal sector. Similarly, in both of these countries, workers laid off from formal enterprises were receiving severance payments, while those losing jobs in the informal sector were left with no assistance. In addition to the lack of access to finance, informal sector employees also suffered from the lack of access to markets, poor knowledge of consumer demand, lack of skills, and increasing incidences of crime and racketeering as a result of the crisis.

NGOs and Religious Organizations

—"*The church is also waging a war against the increasing levels of poverty but it does not have enough resources so you can't expect much.*"

NGOs and religious organizations played a positive but limited role in mitigating the effects of the crisis. Although both types of organizations ran well-regarded assistance projects in the surveyed communities of several countries, the amount and type of aid they provided was often too small to make significant impacts. Furthermore, the number of people receiving assistance seemed to be negligible relevant to the number of the needy. There was no evidence in the surveyed countries that NGOs or religious organizations had changed or scaled up their operation strategies to better serve the needs of the poor during the crisis.

NGOs often implemented good projects but had a limited number of beneficiaries. In addition, many of their projects were aimed at long-term needs and did not provide the kind of support that poor people needed at the height of the crisis: cash or food transfers, income-generation opportunities, and access to affordable loans or credit refinancing. In rural Mongolia, NGOs promoted nonpastoral livelihoods. The Human Development Foundation (HDF) mercy center in Klong Toey slum, Thailand, ran a school to support children of informal sector workers and provided basic health services, including support to people living with HIV/AIDS. Action Aid Kenya implemented an irrigation project in Lango Baya, distributed improved seeds, organized training in modern farming methods, renovated classrooms, and provided some school assistance. In Zambia, however, some respondents were highly critical of NGO activities, including one that distributed dolls to hungry children.

Religious organizations were widely appreciated as a source of moral and material support in numerous communities, but the amount of support fell as contributions declined and the need grew during the crisis period. Respondents in many sites held support from religious groups in high esteem, particularly in Bangladesh, Cambodia, the Central African Republic, Kenya, Senegal, Thailand, and Zambia, even though the assistance was often small relative to the needs (that is, the assistance was appreciated even when it was not particularly effective). In Kenya, both the school feeding program and other assistance provided by the Catholic Church were open to people of all confessions, according to FGD participants. The assistance given by mosques was limited only to practicing Muslims, which created hostility toward the Islamic community:

> *"Although we are suffering as youth in Mukuru, and our parents and friends are struggling, the Muslims always have food. Every Friday, the Mosque opposite provides food and even clothing. This support is only for Muslims. We have been to the Mosque a few times dressed in* buibui *[black shawl] like the other Muslim women and managed to get food. It seems the people at the Mosque found [out]. We are told they cannot give food to* kafirs *[non-Muslims]. A few weeks back our friends, young men, were caught dressed in buibui like women; it was embarrassing, but we must survive."*
>
> Participant, Mukuru, Kenya, March 2009

In Thailand, a Buddhist temple provided food to some families in need. A team of motorcycle taxi drivers in Romklaow slum were taking turns asking for food from the nearby temple. *"It helps us a great deal. The food is not only for the team to eat every morning, sometimes we could also take leftovers back to our families,"* a motorcycle taxi driver said. In Bangladesh, a Sufi shrine was providing meals to some 500 people per day at the height of the 2008 food price crisis. In Cambodia, pagodas have traditionally provided support to the poor in rural areas, but since the onset of the crisis, the number of beneficiaries and the amount of aid declined because of reduced contributions and was then limited to the extreme poor and the sick. The moral support provided by churches was also deeply valued by respondents in Zambia. Churches in Zambia were providing some material assistance as well but it declined in comparison to the previous years.

"The spiritual support we receive from the church is important for our general well-being. In the face of any crisis, having a connection with God gives one a sense of peace."
Participant in Kabwata, Zambia, 2010

"The church is also waging a war against the increasing levels of poverty, but it does not have enough resources, so you can't expect much"
Participant in Kabwata, Zambia, February 2009

"The pagodas in our village barely assist the people since they are also poor [as] it is the people who usually donate to the monks and contribute towards building the pagodas."
Participant in Trapieng Prey village, Cambodia, July 2009

In the Central African Republic, religious organizations along with the mutual solidarity networks were a key source of support to poor households, more so than in many other countries. People appreciated the moral support from other faith members as well as the psychological relief from prayers. Religious organizations also provided assistance during important life events such as birth, marriage, death, or illnesses. The assistance was usually limited to members only. With the onset of the crisis, reliance on religious organizations and adherence to faith increased.

"There are no mutual aid organizations in this locality. We find such an organization in religious faiths. They are currently active. Only members benefit from their help in case of difficulty."
Bagandou farming groups, Central African Republic, August 2010

Informal Support
—*"We will not allow any people to die from hunger in our village."*

In all countries surveyed, informal safety nets played a major role in softening the impacts of the crisis and were often the only support mechanism available for the poor. Informal support was usually exchanged among family, friends, neighbors, and within solidarity networks made up of workers belonging to the same occupational groups or coming from the same locality. As the crisis unfolded, many interviewees were complaining of weakening solidarity mechanisms, with the exception of support provided by close relatives. What such statements actually meant was that the amount of aid given to poor households was diminishing or was given only to the neediest. There was no evidence that the solidarity mechanisms were destroyed; rather, they were merely underfunded, reducing the capacity of traditional resilience mechanisms (Global Pulse 2010).

> *"How can we help and take care of each other like we used to in our village? Every family is facing its own difficulties. We struggle to survive ourselves, so how can we help other people when we can barely help ourselves?"*

> *"We help only elderly people who have nobody (no children or no relatives) to look after them—giving them food or anything they need to survive. If elderly people have children or relatives we do not help them, because we are also poor and have to take care of ourselves as well. But we will not allow any people to die from hunger in our village."*
> Participants in rural Cambodia, July 2009

It seems that a sense of belonging to the group (community or occupational) made people stronger and helped them to weather different shocks:

> *"In emergencies we organize fundraising to help the person in need. . . . The group constitutes a family or one body, so if a part of the body is suffering than the whole body is suffering."*
> Artisans group, Central African Republic, August 2010

> *"People like each other. We never have any violence in the group or towards other cyclo drivers, but instead we try to help each other during hardships like sickness or other difficult circumstances. . . . We all come from rural areas. . . . Nobody can understand us and assist us beside ourselves and our friends."*
> Cyclo drivers, Cambodia, August 2009

The research found no decline in nonfinancial support such as moral support, help with finding jobs, or sharing of productive equipment. In Kenya, farmers who belonged to the irrigation association shared water pumps; in Senegal, small traders shared market spaces; in Hanoi, Vietnam, day laborers (many of whom came in groups from the same localities) shared the available work with each other so that nobody should have no income at all. In Cambodia, construction and garment workers were pooling money or rice sent from the villages and cooking and eating together in large groups. The eating groups kept on growing as the crisis was unfolding. Homeless cyclo drivers and unskilled construction workers were living together as a group to reduce safety-related risks, as they were often attacked by gangs. In Cambodia, Kazakhstan, and

Mongolia, people relied on their friends and relatives to find jobs in urban areas.

Informal savings and credit groups such as the *tontines* in West Africa run by women or professional groups were often the main source of financial assistance. In many FGDs, participants said that although membership in tontines was helpful, the resources received were not enough to start a new business. In Senegal, many poor people could no longer make contributions to tontines and ended their membership.

Small businesses were another source of credit. In sites in Cambodia, Kazakhstan, Mongolia, the Philippines, and Serbia, stores were often selling food and other basic items on credit. In some instances, these practices resulted in big losses for small business owners and even in closures of the stores:

> "*People borrow goods and food. Some people borrow money to go home or if somebody passes away. They pay back when they earn money. Their payment period is getting longer. Some people disappear without paying for what they borrowed.*"
>
> Shop owner at the gold mining site, Bayanteel soum,
> Uvurkhangai aimag, Mongolia, May–June 2009

Support from direct family members was extensive and included domestic and international remittances, sharing of food and other in-kind assistance (for example, lending livestock), providing interest-free loans, and paying tuition fees for close relatives. Family ties were also used widely to search for jobs by migrants, the laid off, and new job market entrants.

Remittances from urban or international migrants were important for coping: "*Migration is the most important solution for employment and incomes. If all migrants returned home, we would come back to eating porridge only,*" said an official from a village's Women's Union, Trà Vinh, Vietnam. Yet as the crisis unfolded, many families and communities reported sharp reductions in the amount and regularity of remittance transfers, causing significant hardships. The return of some urban migrants increased competition for jobs and reduced the already low wage rates, while households with returning international migrants struggled to repay large debts that they had incurred to send family members abroad.

Agricultural land was important for coping in East Asia and sometimes fed reverse remittances. Rural landowners in Cambodia, Thailand, and Vietnam were more resilient to the negative impacts of the crises than the landless. They could intensify production to compensate for the loss of remittances, get access to loans using their land for collateral, and even provide support to family members living in urban areas. In East Asia, remittances were flowing not only from urban workers to families in rural areas but also in the reverse direction. As urban workers faced reduced working hours and unemployment, their rural families were often sending them food and sometimes money.

Thus, informal safety nets provided by relatives, friends, and community and religious organizations were important for coping everywhere. Even though the amount of support through informal safety nets was inadequate relative to the large and growing need, it was often the only source of support available.

Lessons Learned from Qualitative Crisis Monitoring and Implications for Policy

The research conducted for this book has shown that qualitative analysis of how people lived through the crises can be a valuable addition to the quantitative studies on the subject. First, the research permitted a closer look at the impacts on the informal sector that employs the majority of population in developing countries, yet is rarely covered in sectoral assessments or industrial growth strategies prepared by government ministries. Second, the research helped draw attention to the plight of the people who are usually excluded from household surveys, such as the Roma in Serbia, beggars in Bangladesh, informal gold miners in Mongolia, or the illegal cross-border migrants in Thailand. Third, it was useful for an in-depth analysis of crisis impacts by age and gender, highlighting in particular the role of women's unpaid work in household resilience. Fourth, qualitative monitoring helped assess a wider range of impacts beyond the material, pointing to the enormous psychological stress inflicted by the crisis and its effects on family and community relationships and demonstrating the importance of communal solidarity in cushioning against shocks. Qualitative monitoring also assessed the damaging impact of prolonged economic stress to traditional support mechanisms.

This study has shown that the analysis of macroeconomic indicators alone can conceal important aspects of the process of economic recovery. In particular, the resumption of GDP growth in late 2009 or 2010 in many developing countries gave optimism to governments and the donor community that the impacts of the crises were relatively short lived and that the livelihoods of the poor were not strongly affected. The findings of this study do not support this argument. Despite the narrow employment base of export production in developing countries, formal sector workers fuel the rural economies through remittances and provide a customer base for a large number of informal sector workers. Therefore, even temporary labor shocks to the formal economy have long-lasting impacts on the urban and rural poor. The reason is that often the first wave of coping responses adopted by poor people (incurring debt, forgoing health care, diversification) led to the second wave of impacts (selling assets or increased competition in the informal sector). In many surveyed countries, poor people were living through this second round of negative impacts at the same time the national economies were showing strong signs of economic recovery.

Three years of compound crises depleted the resources of vulnerable people (Mongolian herders with less than 100 animals, households across East Asia that lost their land or houses to creditors, impoverished smallholders in rural Kenya). Many people may not be able to take advantage of new economic opportunities without targeted assistance. Furthermore, food and fuel prices remained high or increased further with economic recovery while incomes stagnated or rose insignificantly. Even formal sector workers in countries like Bangladesh, Cambodia, and Thailand, where wages rose with the revival of the export sector, felt that income increases did not fully compensate for food price inflation. These are some of the reasons that resumed growth rates had not yet translated into noticeable improvements in the livelihoods of poor people in surveyed sites.

Although the types of coping mechanisms used by the poor to cope with the global food, fuel, and financial crises are often similar to those used when coping with more localized shocks, there is a sharp difference in their effectiveness. The large and protracted crisis rendered the traditional informal safety nets of the poor ineffective. The informal sector was hit by the crisis and exposed to suddenly increased competition and reduced remittances, and religious and mutual solidarity dried up as needs grew and fewer could afford to contribute. Interviewees were trying to avoid sale of major livelihood assets, particularly houses and land. They would rather send children to work and eat less than sell their property. Many families, however, were on very poor diets but kept children in school. People often tried to identify new livelihood options and move to other sectors, localities, and occupations. These attempts were often unsuccessful, in part because they were simultaneously pursued by many other competitors, yet there were also examples of adaptation of business strategies and creative diversification that helped people cope through the bad times.

What kind of policies and programs should governments consider to help reduce vulnerability to future shocks? The analysis of the case studies demonstrates the need for more effective and more generous social protection systems; support packages for informal enterprises and smallholder farmers, including access to credit and debt refinancing schemes; as well as measures to strengthen community cohesion.

Improve Social Protection and Access to Public Services

The analysis of the country case studies confirmed the importance of pre-existing social protection schemes in responding to shocks of massive scale. In countries where such programs have been in place (in our sample, the formerly socialist states), poor people were better protected in comparison to countries that did not have such schemes. In all countries surveyed, the crisis also exposed the weaknesses of existing social assistance programs—low generosity, poor targeting, low quality of in-kind assistance, and in some cases, inability to sustain the precrisis initiatives due to fiscal pressures. This research also showed that the vision of comprehensive shock response programs should be wider than in most current social protection programs in developing countries, which tend to focus on modest cash transfers to the chronic poor. In particular, the country case studies demonstrated the value of free or subsidized health and education programs in protecting human capital during the worst of the crises. Free schooling and provision of school meals and uniforms were critical to keeping children in school. Many findings also pointed to a pressing lack of short and flexible skill-building programs to address the needs of the informal sector and to improve employment outcomes for laid-off workers from formal enterprises.

Support SMEs and Smallholders

The qualitative crisis monitoring showed the importance of the informal sector for the livelihoods of the poor and its role in absorbing shocks to formal enterprises during times of crisis. It also demonstrated that local and national government regulations often preclude rather than facilitate the operation of small-scale entrepreneurs. For example, transport workers in Kenya and Senegal complained of harassment by traffic police; rickshaw pullers in Dhaka were banned from major streets; the rates for market rent space were prohibitively expensive for workers in imitation gold ornaments in Thailand and informal vendors in Senegal; and porters and women doing laundry work in Kenya complained of harassment by the security personnel of the city council. Secondary roads in poor condition and high transport costs were an issue in most countries surveyed, limiting access to markets for smallholders. In an extreme example, rural women in the Central African Republic had to spend 3.5 hours to bring their produce on foot to a local market.

Rising food costs necessitate public investments in new seed varieties, extension services, irrigation infrastructure to increase productivity, and the development of supply chains to lower the cost of food for consumers while increasing producer price share of agricultural products. Poor shea nut gatherers in Ghana, coconut farmers in the Philippines, and herders in Mongolia complained that they were unable to get a fair price for their products: when prices were low, it was hardly worth selling; in good times, traders took advantage of the remoteness of rural communities and demanded a large margin. Organizing smallholders into groups to purchase inputs, negotiate with buyers, and sell produce in bulk can help overcome these constraints.

In addition, development of affordable microfinance schemes for individuals and small businesses can help weather a crisis and increase production in good times. Microfinance ought to include credit, savings, insurance options, and protection against abusive collection practices. It is equally important for governments and microfinance institutions to develop loan refinancing schemes in case of another global shock or a local disaster.

Strengthen Community Organizations

Community-based organizations were often the first and the only institutions to provide support to the poor during times of hardship (Turk, Mason, and Petesch 2010). In places where local government and community institutions are strong, governments can partner with local institutions to support community development priorities. Initiatives could include improvement of local infrastructure, creation of vocational programs for youth, establishment of counseling centers to address the problems of domestic violence and drug and alcohol abuse, and the development of community watch programs to address safety concerns. In cases where communities are divided over ethnic or religious lines or where local institutions are underdeveloped, a number of approaches can be applied to strengthen transparency and accountability of local governments and facilitate dialogue among various civic groups. In both contexts, support for community initiatives can create vital social networks and increase household and community resilience to shocks.

Note

We are grateful to Veronica M. Joffre for helpful comments and to the local researchers who carried out the country studies surveyed here. The list of country studies is provided in appendix 1.

References

Dercon, S., ed. 2004. *Insurance against Poverty.* Oxford, U.K., and New York: Oxford University Press, in collaboration with United Nations University World Institute for Development Economics Research.

Global Pulse. 2010. *Voices of the Vulnerable: Recovery from the Ground Up.* New York: United Nations.

Heltberg, R., and N. Lund. 2009. "Shocks, Coping, and Outcomes for Pakistan's Poor: Health Risks Predominate." *Journal of Development Studies* 45 (6): 889–910.

Hossain, N. 2009. *Accounts of Crisis: Poor People's Experiences of the Food, Fuel and Financial Crises in Five Countries. Report on a Pilot Study in Bangladesh, Indonesia, Jamaica, Kenya and Zambia, January–March 2009.* Brighton, U.K.: Institute of Development Studies.

Krishna, A. 2004. "Escaping Poverty and Becoming Poor: Who Gains, Who Loses, and Why?" *World Development* 32 (January): 121–36.

———. 2007. "For Reducing Poverty Faster: Target Reasons before People." *World Development* 35 (November): 1947–60.

Krishna, A., and A. Shariff. 2011. "The Irrelevance of National Strategies? Rural Poverty Dynamics in States and Regions of India, 1993–2005." *World Development* 39 (April): 533–49.

Narayan, D. 2000. *Voices of the Poor: Can Anyone Hear Us?* Vol. 1. New York: Oxford University Press for the World Bank.

Narayan, D., L. Pritchett, and S. Kapoor. 2009. *Moving Out of Poverty.* Vol. 2 of *Success from the Bottom Up.* Basingstoke, U.K., and Washington, DC: Palgrave Macmillan and World Bank.

Turk, C., A. Mason, and P. Petesch. 2010. "Impacts of the Economic Crisis on Vulnerable Population Groups: Midcourse Findings from a Qualitative Monitoring Project in 12 Developing Countries." World Bank, Washington, DC.

World Bank, Thailand. 2010. *Thailand Economic Monitor* (November). Bangkok.

CHAPTER 2

Bangladesh: Pathways and Impacts of the Global Economic Shocks

Mamunur Rashid, Bayazid Hasan, and Naomi Hossain

The Complicated Impacts of the Global Economic Crisis on Bangladesh

In 2008, when the global financial crisis struck, observers predicted that Bangladesh would be hit directly and hard because of its dependence on migrant remittances and garments exports. Garments and knitwear together constituted some 79 percent of export earnings, and migrant workers' remittances comprised 9.4 percent of gross domestic product (GDP) in 2008–09 (GoB 2009). Both sectors were expected to be vulnerable to the global downturn. The social consequences for Bangladesh—where despite steady economic growth and good poverty reduction performance since the 1990s, one-third of the people still lived below the poverty line in 2010 (BBS 2011)—looked set to be serious. At the peak of the crisis in 2009, however, the impacts of the global financial crisis felt less serious than expected. The explanation is partly a matter of contrast: immediately before the financial crisis struck, Bangladesh, like most other countries, had been reeling from the effects of the food and fuel crisis of 2008. This crisis had hit Bangladesh hard, particularly because rice alone made up 24 percent of average household spending at that time (World Bank 2008).

The political context meant the handling of the 2008 food price spike was itself complicated. Bangladesh was ruled by a (military-backed) unelected caretaker government in 2007 and 2008. Popular opinion was that the nature of the regime explained the high prices: democratic pressures, it was widely felt, would have forced an elected government to act to reduce food prices more promptly. Ironically, however, it was the democratically elected government that came to power in January 2009 that ultimately benefited from the many initiatives undertaken by the caretaker regime to stabilize food prices. The rice price began to decline just as the popularly elected Awami League government took power in early 2009, creating the belief that it was the actions of the elected government rather than the drop in global food prices or the open market sales programs of the previous caretaker regime that had brought food prices down.

When the financial crisis struck, Bangladesh had just weathered a complicated transition back to multiparty rule and was recovering from the 2008 price spike. In early 2009, the government then put in place a series of stimulus measures that enabled it to take credit for the fact that, compared to other Asian countries (most of which had also proven to be resilient to the shock), Bangladesh's growth rate barely dipped below 6 percent (see figure 2.1). At the height of the financial crisis in 2009, Bangladesh looked to be relatively immune from the shocks. One indicator of this immunity was that at first the growth in migrant remittances slowed down only slightly. A second indicator was that Bangladeshi garment exports were initially boosted by the so-called "Wal-Mart effect," as global demand for cheap clothing grew in 2009. Garments dominate Bangladeshi exports, but

Figure 2.1. The Impacts of the World Financial Crisis on Economic Growth Rates in Selected Asian Countries, 2006–12

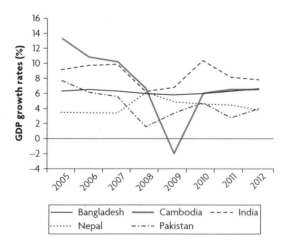

Source: IMF 2011.

Note: Figures for 2011 and 2012 are projections.

the good fortune was not spread evenly, and other sectors (frozen food, electronics, leather) were hit hard by the downturn. Yet the spectre of thousands of returning migrants and unemployed garment workers on the streets of Dhaka did not materialize. The mere possibility of masses in the streets was an important concern because Bangladeshi garment workers had for several years been protesting against the inadequacy of their wages at a time of rising food costs. These protests had become increasingly violent and had led to significant disruption to factory production and city life. The protests trailed off after the minimum wage was almost doubled in early 2011, although workers' groups continued to campaign for further wage increases.

The general consensus among informed observers, the business community, economists, and other policy researchers about the impact of the economic crisis was that Bangladesh got off lightly in 2009. At one end of the social and economic scale, a Dhaka rickshaw-puller said that they had heard about the global economic crisis but that it *"didn't come here."* At the other end, the head of the main business association in the country asked rhetorically: *"Why is it that when the U.S. has a crisis it's a global financial crisis, whereas when Asia has a crisis it's only an Asian financial crisis?"* As a garments manufacturer and exporter, he was alert to the effects of global markets on Bangladesh and felt it had fared well.

By 2011, however, it seemed that the global financial crisis had affected Bangladesh, but that the effects were less direct and more lagged than initially predicted. Understanding the impact of the global financial crisis in Bangladesh has been complicated because, as noted, rather than feeling the immediate effects of the financial crisis, Bangladesh was hit harder by the crisis' other face—the rise of food and fuel prices. The effects of food and fuel price rises in 2008 and again in 2010–11 were to affect household consumption directly and to affect the macroeconomic situation indirectly, through fiscal pressures as fuel subsidies widened the budget deficit.

By 2010, when the global economy was officially in recovery, Bangladesh began to experience the lagged effects of these shocks. Official statements on the state of the economy were still buoyantly optimistic, but independent analysis became more ambivalent. By 2011, it was clear that there were reasons to be concerned after all: one report noted that remittances from migrant workers to the Middle East had begun to decline and that the numbers of workers going abroad had halved compared to 2006–07 (CPD

2011). In 2011, the turbulence of the Arab Spring began to heighten concerns about the impacts on Bangladeshi migrant remittances, as workers returned from Libya and elsewhere in the region. The decline in remittances was somewhat counterbalanced by strong export performance in 2011 (CPD 2011).

But in 2011, attention was once again fastened on global food and fuel price volatility. Civil society observers and the International Monetary Fund (IMF) noted pressures on the national economy, including those arising from food and fuel price inflation. Macroeconomic management was under stress because of the budgetary pressures arising from inflation (particularly fuel subsidies), but there were also serious concerns about the direct negative effects of inflation on poverty and food security.[1] General inflation reached 8.1 percent by October 2010 compared to 5.1 percent a year earlier, and food inflation was at 9.8 percent in October 2010, nearly double the 5.3 percent 12 months before. Food inflation was higher in rural than in urban areas (9.1 compared to 6.8 percent in October 2010), suggesting particularly strong pressures on the masses of the rural landless poor.[2]

The overall picture that emerged was that although Bangladesh initially fared better than predicted in the global financial crisis, there were lagged and indirect impacts, particularly on remittances and on nongarment exports. By 2011, the more serious concern was the recurring problem of global commodity price rises and inflation. Because of Bangladesh's history of political instability and regime overthrow following episodes of acute food insecurity, the authorities tend to regard rapid food price rises as a politically urgent matter, and they put in place or ramped up a number of safety net measures to mitigate the effects.

The Community Case Study Research

How have these varied and unpredictable effects of global economic shocks since 2008 played out in people's lives in Bangladesh? In particular, what have they meant for those who were already living in conditions of poverty and vulnerability? The aggregate impacts of these shocks on poverty are only beginning to emerge, and it is too soon to take a firm position on what these shocks will ultimately mean for poverty or well-being in the medium term.

A small-scale qualitative monitoring exercise involving rounds of research throughout the peak crisis period, in early 2009, 2010, and 2011, however, affords some insights into how these shocks affected the everyday lives of poor Bangladeshis. The final outcomes and impacts on poverty are not yet known, but this unique micro-level perspective on the unfolding shocks makes it possible to understand something about the coping responses. This chapter draws on qualitative research in two community "listening posts," one in Dhaka and one in rural northwest Bangladesh, to draw some preliminary conclusions about the nature of the pathways on which these shocks are likely to have set people who were already living on low incomes or in poverty. This effort involved repeat rounds of research, including three visits to the rural site in the northwest and four to the urban site in Dhaka. To take seasonality into account, three of the visits in each site took place at the same time of year in 2009, 2010, and 2011.

The research took the form of community case studies and drew participants from across the range of occupation and social groups in each location. The main component of the research was focus group discussions (FGDs) around the cost of living, the state of jobs and businesses within the local economy, the social protection and government responses to the hardships being faced, and coping and adaptive responses to the situation. Focus groups were conducted with informal sector workers; factory workers; working children; small farmers and landless laborers and migrants; and men, women, and children. A small number of household case study interviews were conducted in each place to gain a sense of the process and dynamics of change and coping within individual households. Key informant interviews were also undertaken with local officials and community leaders and NGO (nongovernmental organization) and government service providers. In 2010, a research dissemination workshop was conducted to enable the participants to comment and give feedback on the research findings and analysis. Over the three years, the research involved around 300 participants.

Research Sites

The listening posts for the research included Notun Bazaar, a slum settlement in Dhaka, and a village in the poor northwest district of Naogaon on the border with India. These two locations were selected principally because they offered the scope for exploring the impacts on different occupational groups, including through presumed exposure to the direct effects of the global financial crisis. The Naogaon village was selected in part because it falls within the larger belt of extreme poverty and deprivation that is characteristic of that region. Its location means its occupation profile is characteristic of other border areas, including a tendency to rely on smuggling as a livelihood option, but less so of other rural regions of the northwest. The population of Notun Bazaar comprises many climate change refugees as is characteristic of Dhaka slums more generally. The researchers had already had some contact with both communities. Aside from the importance of smuggling in Naogaon, neither location is particularly unrepresentative of urban or rural communities in Bangladesh. From the perspective of the process of economic crises being played out, there are no good reasons to believe the experiences of the people of Naogaon or Notun Bazaar would differ greatly from those of people from comparable occupation groups and areas. The research, however, makes no claims to represent the national experience of the global economic crisis, as this would be impossible for any qualitative research of credible scale to undertake.

Notun Bazaar is a teeming slum settlement with a highly mobile, economically active population, most of whom are "people of the broken river"—people who lost their lands in the south to river erosion. They face the constant threat of eviction from the government land on which many have lived for more than 20 years. The latest effort to evict them was in 2002, but the possibility remains the greatest single risk in their collective life. The main occupations are various activities related to waste recycling, garment factory employment, rickshaw-pulling/owning and other transport services, domestic services, and petty trade. Because it is an informal settlement with no official health or education services and ramshackle infrastructure, Notun Bazaar's levels of social deprivation are high, child labor and school dropouts are visible and common, and the monsoon often means flooding and a sharp rise in water-borne illnesses. Reflecting its status as an informal settlement, there are no official or other statistics available to aid a social or economic profile of the area.

The village in Dhamuirhat, Naogaon, is an agricultural community with a high concentration of extremely poor people. The Dhamuirhat village is far from any big—or even small—city, but is on the border with India. There are some medium-sized landowners, but the population is mainly smallholders and landless households. Agriculture is officially the main occupation, but cross-border smuggling has periodically provided a lucrative livelihood for those willing and able to run the risk. Fertilizer smuggling was reportedly common prior to 2009, but an official crackdown has forced the smugglers into other occupations. Since 2010, brickfield employment has grown in importance, giving rise to concerns about environmental and agricultural impacts. Seasonal and other forms of short-term migration are reasonably common, including to the garment factories in Dhaka.

The Impacts of the Financial Crisis on Occupations and Businesses

Notun Bazaar was initially selected as a community particularly vulnerable to the global financial crisis because it is in the Mirpur area of Dhaka where garment factories (and hence, garment factory workers) are clustered. The researchers soon discovered that the main sector most directly exposed to volatilities in global trade was the waste recycling industry. Relatively little attention has been paid to the impacts of the global financial crisis on this industry at a global level.[3] But repeat research visits to Notun Bazaar indicated that livelihoods connected to waste recycling were highly vulnerable to the downturn in global trade and to associated commodity price volatility. When commodity prices rose in 2008, merchants of recycled waste were earning unprecedented high incomes, and the work drew more local people, including poor women and children, into waste-picking and waste-sorting activities. The global financial crisis meant a sharp downturn in the global waste price in 2009, however, and in mid-2009 and early 2010, waste recycling merchants were facing hard times, and children reported that they had stopped collecting waste for sale because the prices were too low. One waste recycling business owner reported having had a good year in 2008, but hard times in 2009:

> "Last year, every day I profited with big margins. Price of everything increased every day, even overnight. Even a kg of PVC pipe would fetch me [a good price]. Even if the prices were high last year I faced no trouble. This year the picture is different, the price of everything is normal now, but so are the prices of waste materials. Lots of shops have closed down. My business is on the brink of closing. Now I cannot collect anything from homes. When I tell them the price, the housewives chase me with brooms or start swearing. They cannot accept that I will pay 10 taka for the same thing I bought for Tk 30 a month ago."

Waste recycling merchant, Notun Bazaar,
Dhaka, February 2009

The fortunes of the waste trade appear to mirror the cost of living, as the waste recycling merchants were doing better once again when food and fuel prices rose in 2011. One implication of the direct effects of the global crisis on workers and traders in the waste sector is that a focus on formal sector employment impacts was likely to miss many of those more directly affected by the shocks, including many of the poorest and those in the most vulnerable livelihoods.

By contrast, as noted, garment workers were assumed to be highly vulnerable to the downturn, as the ready-made garment export sector is inherently flexible and responsive to global market forces. The transmission channels through which garment workers were affected, however, meant they experienced the impacts indirectly, and at least initially, in reverse of what was expected. In early 2009, as the crisis effects unfolded through the world economy, workers in Notun Bazaar noted that jobs were still available in the sector and no factories had closed; some small new sweatshops were thought to have set up operations during this period. Yet the quality of the jobs available was low: factories that were hiring were reportedly mainly those where wages were paid irregularly, abuse was common, and instant layoffs likely.

Garment work in Bangladesh is a semiformal occupation into which people move in and out relatively rapidly, which means that hard data on employment levels in the sector are not available, and it is difficult to assess the extent to which the local perception that employment stayed steady was reflected across the sector more widely. Yet these local findings were consistent with macroeconomic data showing that by January 2009 the sector had yet to be adversely hit by the crisis. Possibly because of the higher demand for cheaper products during the recession, January 2009 garment exports were up 20 percent from their January 2008 levels. This rise was, however, reported by factory owners to have come with increased market volatility and uncertainty and a sharp squeeze on profits (Rahman et al. 2009). By August 2009, the sector had taken a hit, and workers were facing job losses, factory closures, and no overtime. Later in 2009, growth in the sector started to decline, but this had already slowed by the end of the year.

By early 2010, it was clear that as far as the Notun Bazaar garment workers were concerned, the sector had recovered. Jobs were more freely available, and, although pressures on productivity remained high, working conditions were also said to have improved, partly because smaller sweatshop-type units had been forced out of business during the slowdown. Workers said that larger companies were buying up failed units and were better employers—wages and overtime were paid regularly, benefits and bonuses provided. Some factories employing local people were selling subsidized rice to factory workers. In addition, the manufacturers' association was believed to have become stricter about labor regulations, and workers reported cases where workers who were fired unjustifiably and without being paid owed salary successfully sought compensation. For the garment workers, this change was evidence that the long period of often violent worker militancy since 2006 was paying off. Their belief was confirmed when the minimum wage for garment workers was increased from a pitiful Tk 1,600 per month to a basic level of Tk 3,000 in late 2010. The workers' movement argues that even with this rise, garment workers' pay remains too low to live on, given the pace of inflation.

The sector has some wider significance for Notun Bazaar, because the garment industry is an important source of regular cash incomes, particularly for younger people. The knock-on effects are also felt very directly through spending on rent, food, travel and entertainment, and in rural homes of origin, as many workers remit to support extended families.

The Effects of Food and Fuel Price Rises on Farmers and Consumers

The effects of food and fuel price inflation were arguably both more direct and more widespread than the impacts on jobs and livelihoods transmitted through the global financial crisis. Food and fuel price volatility over the 2008–11 period had a number of direct and indirect effects on livelihoods and jobs and on people as consumers. As consumers, people mainly felt the effects of the crisis at the beginning and the end of the period; the months between the second quarter of 2009 and the middle of 2010 were, by contrast, a relatively comfortable time when the all-important price of rice came down (see figure 2.2).

For farmers in the semiarid Naogaon area, the aftermath of the 2008 food price spike was an unpredictable period, contributing to what was widely reported as "a sense of uncertainty" around agriculture. The supply response to high food prices was complicated in part by the high fertilizer prices during that period. Farmers in Naogaon reported trying to cultivate with less fertilizer, reverting to compost or organic fertilizers, and mixing more costly fertilizers with cheaper varieties to make them stretch further. The steep drop in the rice price in 2009 and early 2010 meant many smaller farmers were unable to get the prices anticipated on the basis of high prices in 2008.

Figure 2.2. Prices of Staple Foods, 2008–11

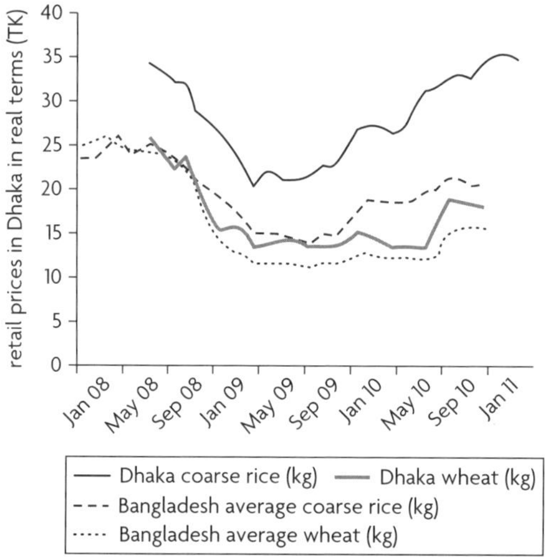

Legend
—— Dhaka coarse rice (kg) —— Dhaka wheat (kg)
- - - Bangladesh average coarse rice (kg)
····· Bangladesh average wheat (kg)

Source: Department of Agriculture Marketing, Bangladesh, http://www.fao.org/giews/pricetool/.

Among the other commodity spike factors that affected farmers was the cost of irrigation: although the diesel price dropped as the 2009 financial crisis struck, the 2009 costs of diesel (which powers irrigation in Bangladesh) remained around 30 percent higher than it had been in 2007. Fertilizer smuggling relieved some price pressures, but farmers who bought cheap Indian fertilizer soon found it to be of poor quality. And farmers who invested in expensive fertilizer and seeds at the height of the rice price spike were suffering because rice prices had dropped substantially. The price drop also negatively affected poor people engaged in paddy and rice trading. A further recent change, not associated with economic crisis, was a reported change in production relations, with output-based contract production increasingly replacing the use of daily labor on larger farms.

Another livelihood that was affected by the price spike was smuggling. The high demand and high price for fertilizer encouraged a rise in fertilizer smuggling from across the Indian border in 2009. This lucrative, if risky, livelihood was later clamped down on through official measures. But even though fertilizer smuggling remained highly risky, so many local people were drawn into it that local businessmen and landlords reported it had became difficult to find agricultural labor.

The 2010 economic recovery in Naogaon took the form of increased agricultural production, mainly because agricultural input costs had come down compared to the year before. With farmers cultivating larger areas of land, there was more work for agricultural wage laborers and transport workers. In an exercise to rank livelihood change that year, men noted that most of the main occupation groups—farmers, agricultural laborers, van drivers—had improved their livelihoods over the previous 12 months, and the only group that had not done well was the vegetable traders. Even rice traders—traditionally a group believed to do well out of episodes of food insecurity—were believed to be better off under the more stable food prices of 2010, as extreme volatility reduced returns on their investments in 2009. By 2011, farmers reported that fertilizer prices were stable and were being protected by government intervention. Despite stable input costs and high prices, however, smaller farmers noted that they were not greatly better off, primarily because farmgate prices remained low as a result of a rising number of agricultural intermediaries.[4] The volatility in food prices and returns from agriculture are likely to have contributed to the shift noted among agricultural wage laborers and smaller farmers into brickfield employment toward the end of this period.

The food price spike encouraged livelihood diversification, particularly among women. Rural Muslim women were reported to be working publicly in restaurant kitchens and on the new 100 Days Employment Guarantee scheme—forms of employment they would not customarily have taken on. New forms of food retail also emerged, often involving women, in a sector that is traditionally male. One new niche livelihood involved the gathering and sale of rejected vegetables in 2008. This trade began when people recognized the possibilities for gathering broken or partly spoiled vegetables, previously discarded as unsalable, from the local wholesale vegetable market. After the floods of 2007, new migrants from flood-hit areas started to collect these vegetables; they were soon followed by local children and adults, and finally even by unmarried girls (who would not be expected to engage in public activities of this kind). One elderly woman explained that she had lost her job as a cook-housekeeper at the height of the food crisis when her middle-class employers could no longer afford her services. She began to notice her neighbors going to the bazaar [market] to pick up rejected vegetables: *"From that day my hunger won over my dignity."* Soon, she realized there was a market for cheap vegetables in small quantities:

> *"One day, I got a large amount of chili at a cheap price. I was sitting with that wondering what to do with that quantity of chili . . . suddenly a woman came to me and asked, 'Will you sell a little portion of these*

to me?' My greed took over and now I have saved Tk 7,000 by selling these vegetables."

Market trader, February 2009

This new livelihood developed in part because the food price crisis created a new group of lower-middle-class customers who, although not ready to bear the shame of collecting rejected vegetables, were prepared to buy them as cheap alternatives to standard vegetables. This kind of low-return adaptation to the economic situation appeared to be fairly typical of the gendered dimensions of crisis coping. Women and girls—whose time and labor is priced low even during boom times—were likely to display great creativity and dexterity in their efforts to carve out small sources of income in competitive markets. Their resourcefulness demonstrates the great resilience characteristic of poor Bangladeshi women. They can cope with multiple disadvantages, but it is also clear that doing so draws down their resources and has negative implications for their personal status and well-being. Young, unmarried girls were said to be moving into managing market stalls—an activity generally considered for men only—in a society in which the importance of unmarried girls' sexual purity ensures they are kept out of rough public spaces like markets. The older woman who had developed her market niche in selling spoiled vegetables noted how she had "won over her dignity," having to swallow her pride to enter into sales of what in previous times had, in effect, been rubbish.

The combination of the global financial crisis and the commodity price volatility has had fairly varied effects on different occupation groups at different times, but all groups have been struggling to cope with the sharp rise in the cost of living, particularly the urban community (see figure 2.2).

By early 2011, it was clear that the recurrence of the food price spike in late 2010 meant that the wage and income rises that some groups had managed to secure were, in effect, being negated by inflation. Table 2.1 summarizes findings about how different occupation groups were faring during the 2011 spike. Note that the occupation groups doing worst are at the top of the table; farther down are groups that reported to be doing about the same as the previous year, and at the bottom are those who were said to be better off than last year. The pattern of change suggests a considerable amount of diversity in terms of the impacts of the economic crisis at different times even within these communities.

Table 2.1. Livelihood Changes in Bangladesh, 2010–11

Place	Occupation groups	Current reported wages or earnings	National wage comparisons	What people said about why real earnings have changed
Dhamuirhat, Bangladesh	Agricultural day laborers	Tk 100–120 per day ($1.37–1.65) (low season)	National average agricultural wage per day: Tk 233[a] ($3.18)	The daily wage rate has increased, as many laborers now work in the brickfields creating a shortage. But this raise has not been enough to cope with the price hike.
	Van drivers	Tk 100–150 per day ($1.37–2.06)	Garment workers' minimum wage as of 2010: Tk 3,000 per month (based on 5-day week; roughly Tk 125 or $1.70 per day)	Earnings have declined because people are increasingly using "easy-power" auto-rickshaw transport instead of pedal-driven vans.
	Small rice traders	Tk 700–800 per week ($10.00–11.00)		Price of paddy is too high. When this high cost is added to storage costs, it becomes difficult to make a profit.
	Vegetable sellers	Tk 100–150 per day ($1.37–2.06)		People do not have much money to spend, so vegetable sellers' incomes are down.
Notun Bazaar, Dhaka, Bangladesh	Rickshaw-pullers	Tk 200 daily ($2.75)	Garment workers' minimum wage as of 2010: Tk 3,000 per month (based on 5-day week; roughly Tk 125 or $1.70 per day)	Fares have increased but are almost matched by the rising cost of living. Restrictions on the roads that rickshaws can use have meant longer, more circuitous journeys. Police harassment and seizures of vehicle parts are more common. Because it is strenuous work, rickshaw-pullers need to eat snacks and food all through the day, which have become less affordable. Some rickshaw-pullers have shifted to the garment factories, where pay is better and more regular.
	Hawkers (snack vendors)	Tk 150 daily ($2.00)		Costs of food items have increased, so street vendors are not doing much better than before.

(continued next page)

Table 2.1. Livelihood Changes in Bangladesh, 2010–11 (continued)

Place	Occupation groups	Current reported wages or earnings	National wage comparisons	What people said about why real earnings have changed
Notun Bazaar, Dhaka, Bangladesh	Bhangari (recycled waste) merchants	Tk 20,000 month ($275.00)	Garment workers' minimum wage as of 2010: Tk 3,000 per month (based on 5-day week; roughly Tk 125 or $1.70 per day)	The price of recycled waste has increased. But those who collect the waste for the bhangari businessmen have not done well, because people sell their waste directly as the price is good.
	Housemaids	Various; increasingly paid per task		Demand for domestic servants has been outstripped by opportunities in garment work. Pay has increased, as maids are now paid per task rather than per hour and can earn more this way. They may receive food and clothing benefits from employer households. Improvements in domestic servants' incomes directly reflect employment and wages growth in the garments sector.
	Garment workers	Minimum: Tk 3,000 per month ($41.00)		The new minimum wage for garment workers came into effect in November 2010, almost doubling basic pay from Tk 1,600 to Tk 3,000 per month. This came after a 5-year campaign in which garment workers waged pitched battles against factories and police, arguing that pay failed to keep pace with inflation. Other groups (both men and women) have entered the factories over the past year.
Dhamuirhat, Naogaon, Bangladesh	Farmers with their own land/landowners	Not known	National average agricultural wage per day: Tk 233[b] ($3.18)	Those who have their own land (do not lease or share-crop farmland) are getting a good price for their goods and, with fertilizer prices low, their profits are higher.
	Brickfield workers	Tk150–200 ($2.06–2.75) per day		Wages have increased significantly since last year; there are more opportunities in this sector and for a longer period of the year than agricultural labor (from which most workers come).

Source: Focus group discussions in Dhamuirhat, Naogaon, and Notun Bazaar, Dhaka, February 2010 and February 2011.

a. According to the World Food Program, "Bangladesh Food Security Monitoring Bulletin, 2011;" Dhaka: World Food Program. http://home.wfp.org/stellent/groups/public/documents/ena/wfp231366.pdf.

b. Ibid.

Coping with Economic Crises

Adjustments to Food

Bangladeshis came up with numerous ways to adapt livelihoods to their new circumstances, but the most common category of coping response was to find ways to curb spending on food. The importance of this coping strategy is not surprising given the prominence of food in the budgets of poor households in these communities.

The first way of coping, however, was to cut down on expenses such as transport, communications, clothes, and social activity, while spending a larger share of income on food. In 2009, this practice was common across the communities. But in 2011, the impacts were more differentiated, and some groups who had seen their wages go up were better able to bear the rising costs of food than others, who had not had comparable income increases (see table 2.1). Those who were forced to sacrifice other spending to continue to feed their families noted the embarrassment and shame going without could entail:

> "I used to have 5 to 6 pairs of underwear, and now I wear one [pair] for a whole week. In the past, I did not wear a lungi [men's garment, like a sarong] for more than one month, and now I wear a lungi for more than three months. When it gets torn, I get it sewed. Listen, with my income, I don't have any money after buying food items, so how can I have the luxury of buying more underwear or lungis? . . .people can see my ass. And the thing is, as I wear the same underwear for the whole week, people get a bad smell from me. What can I do?"
>
> Rickshaw puller in Notun Bazaar, February 2011

A common response was also to change food shopping habits: buying smaller quantities more often, shopping around more for bargains, and buying from cheaper sources. It often meant buying nonbrand items, which was a source of some anxiety in a context in which food adulteration is a major concern of the average citizen.[5] It also involved more time and effort on the part of those doing the shopping, which in Bangladesh is traditionally men.

Equally common was reducing the quality and diversity of food. Poorer people in Notun Bazaar changed to the coarsest variety of rice, which was being sold in rationed military-run outlets. Other changes were buying unpackaged flour from street vendors, broken eggs, old fish, overripe fruit, and parts of chickens or cows that they would not previously have eaten. Even these items became more costly in 2009 during the latter period of the first food spike as the middle and lower-middle classes also started to resort to some of these foods. Women in Notun Bazaar said they did not expect to eat meat other than during one of the two main Eid festivals. In both rural and urban Bangladesh, however, poor people complained that they got poorer cuts and smaller quantities of meat after Eid-ul-Azha, suggesting a source of charity that was in decline:[6]

> *"After I prepared the meat this year, my employer stored it all in the freezer, and gave me just bones and fats. They are still eating it after nearly one year."*

Housemaid in Notun Bazaar, February 2009

There was also some rationing or prioritizing of who eats first and best. As in past crises and as is usual in poor households in general, it was sometimes reported that women were eating only after all other household members had been fed:

> *"While cooking, I try to use less rice. Because if I can save some, I will be able to use it for another day. I always try to make sure that the male members have enough to eat. They are working hard and they need food to perform their laborious jobs. Then I try to feed the children. We [the female members of the family] eat the remaining food. Well, this is not enough. But what can I do? How can I give less food to my children? They need fish, meat, milk, and eggs, and we cannot provide them. The only thing that I can feed them is rice and if I cannot give them enough of that, how will they live?"*

Woman in Naogaon, February 2011

That women should always and automatically eat last was not heard from all households or all women, as had been expected. One response that had not been anticipated was that parents jointly prioritized their children's food and ate only after the children had been adequately fed. Although the evidence from these two community case studies is limited in what it can suggest about the wider population, the prioritization of children's food over that of parents seemed to be more common in circumstances where men were not in unusually physically demanding manual occupations (such as agricultural wage labor or rickshaw-pulling). Another reason may be that feeding children was more of a priority in households in which children's education was seen as an investment, such as households employed in the garments sector, which requires more education than other unskilled manual trades. Whether this relatively more gender-equitable outcome, and the emphasis it suggests on investments in children, applies more widely in people's coping responses during this crisis in Bangladesh and elsewhere clearly merits closer investigation.

Gathering wild foods appeared to be mainly a strategy of the poorest communities or the poorest within communities. Women in Naogaon reported rising conflict over common property resources as middle-class people were also gleaning as well as protecting wild foods and fuel found on their property. Women had to work considerably harder than in the past—traveling farther and spending triple the time they previously had spent to gather enough twigs and items to use as cooking fuel when fuel costs increased.

Some people were eating less and going hungry, which often resulted in lack of energy and sometimes difficulty in performing the usual tasks, particularly for those engaged in jobs requiring physical labor. The poorest people were struggling to cover their basic food needs. Garment workers in Dhaka in 2009 reported having to make do with only potatoes; by 2011, however, they had successfully fought for an increase in the minimum wage, which, with the recovery in the global garment trade, the availability of overtime, and access to subsidized rice meant they were better off in food terms. Even relatively affluent households were said to have cut down on meals at the height of the crisis in 2008. For parents, and particularly mothers, the burden of caring for hungry children could be heavy:

> "Where children are not able to eat properly even if you tell them to, they don't want to go to school . . . you have to feed the children a bit more because they don't understand and when they get hungry they start crying."

> Women beggars in Naogaon, February 2009

Health and Education

Most parents emphasized their efforts to retain children in school throughout this period, but some additional dropout from school was reported in response to the shock, mainly in 2008 and early 2009. The reason for children leaving school was very likely the rise in food prices in 2008, which caused more household hardship than the financial crisis. In 2010 and 2011, teachers in both areas felt that the situation had returned to what they considered to be normal levels. Changes in child labor were mixed, illustrating that its supply is driven not only by the push of poverty but also by the pull of lucrative work available for children. Waste picking, a common activity for slum children, became less lucrative after the commodity price spike ended, and fewer children were said to be actively involved in this trade after 2009 than before. In the rural community, a small number of children continued to be drawn into the brickfields, despite wages being low as brick prices and demand dropped with a downturn in the construction trade. The manager of the local brickfield and local people explained that children had started working in the brickfields two years previously, at the height of the food price crisis. Yet children were reportedly working there mainly after school and on weekends. The garment industry in urban areas also continued to draw whole families into migration. Some older children were known to have dropped out of school to migrate to work in the garment factories in the past year. From what teachers and parents said in the rural community, incentives for children to attend school (such as the cash stipend for selected poor children who meet certain performance standards) made a positive difference.

With respect to health and health-seeking behavior, reports fluctuated with the cost of living. Following the drop in the rice price in 2009, there was less evidence of high stress levels, domestic conflict, and health-related shocks in the 2010 research. People were reportedly able to access allopathic health systems again, having relied more on traditional healers at the height of the 2008 crisis. Yet a year later, mirroring the rise in the rice price, reports of high stress and ill health were also on the rise, and people were again said to be rationing medical care and only seeking help for acute conditions:

> "Now we have to devise a number of strategies to sell medicines. People demand less medicine. For example, if I tell someone that you have to buy medicines worth 80 taka and have to take these for some time, he will think about the price and then will tell me to wait, and he will come back to me later. The thing is, he will never come back. Due to price hike, people are making a choice between buying medicine and buying foods."

Village doctor and pharmacy owner in Naogaon, February 2011

In 2011, an elderly man in Naogaon who depended in part on begging for his livelihood explained the calculations and sacrifices he had to make to afford the medicines he needed:

> "I am feeling really weak. I came to the doctor and he told me that I should buy medicine worth Tk 80. I was thinking whether I should buy

these medicines. The thing is if I become too weak, I will not be able to work. So, finally I decided to buy the medicines and paid Tk 50 for that. I could not get up from bed for a couple of days. Today, I somehow managed to come to the market. I had a small chicken. I sold it for Tk 50 and bought medicines. Now I am thinking how I shall buy food. I do not have any money left. I could not even pay fully for the medicine. Even last year was better for me. Now, price of everything is so high people are not willing to help me [provide free food]. . . . I have taken very little food in the morning. It is afternoon now and I have not taken anything. I have spent all the money by buying medicine and thus will not be able to buy anything. I will try to beg now and if I can get anything, only then I will be able to eat today."

Migration

Internal migration and a considerable degree of labor mobility were found in response to the economic crisis. People in general prefer not to split up their families or to leave rural homes to seek better livelihoods, but the combination of a difficult economic context and idiosyncratic shocks such as ill-health or the loss of household land through erosion tended to create conditions in which migration was likely.

Although labor mobility is a source of considerable economic resilience in Bangladesh, it also comes at some costs. In one case in Naogaon, a woman had interspersed periods of work in the garment factories in Dhaka with periods in the village home, where she had been caring for her partially paralyzed husband (an occasional smuggler, sometimes given latitude by the border police because of his condition) and his ailing mother. The flexibility of her employment meant she was confident of being able to reenter the sector whenever she returned to Dhaka, but the short stints weakened her rights: she recently lost two months' wages because the factory refused to pay when she left in a hurry to attend to an emergency in Naogaon. During one period of work in Dhaka, she withdrew her adolescent daughter from school and left her in the village to care for her disabled father, while she took her son with her to Dhaka. Within a year, the daughter, aged around 14 or 15, was married off by her parents.

Different forms of migration featured in several household's accounts of how they had coped with economic turmoil. One family in which both parents worked mainly in garment factories had sent their children to the village to stay with the father's parents while living costs were at their height. The pair had struggled through the slight downturn in the garment industry in 2009–10, partly because the man was also recovering from tuberculosis. But by 2011, with wages up, they were able to bring their daughter back to live with them in Dhaka and keep a close eye on her schooling.

Not all labor mobility strategies are so successful. Those who struggle the most are also likely to be those most continually on the move, and therefore also those whom research of this kind fails to reach. The research team met one recent migrant from the poor northwest in Notun Bazaar in 2009. She was a heavily pregnant woman and had a daughter aged around five and no obvious source of livelihood. She was deeply distressed—it is no exaggeration to describe her as desperate—as she had recently been abandoned by her husband and had no relatives or other kin nearby. On our return visit in 2010, we asked after her. Local residents related that her daughter had died and that she had "sold" her newborn son to a middle-class woman from the next neighborhood and then left in search of work. From these community case studies, it was clear that in the worst cases, there could be significant negative impacts on children. Given the nature of the research, however, it is difficult to comment on how likely such impacts are to have been across the wider population.

Credit, Debt, and Asset Sales

People were relying on a number of strategies to cover increased costs of living. Asset sales, such as livestock in rural areas, production equipment (for example, agricultural tools or a mosaic machine), and mobile phones and electronic devices were quite common. In some cases, consumer items were replaced when income flows returned to their previous levels. Unlike in some other countries surveyed in this book, land sales were not very common.

However, households were increasingly going into debt to cope with the crisis. One form of debt widespread among poor people is dowry debt. The Naogaon woman who married off her teenage daughter had incurred a Tk 45,000 dowry debt in so doing; this was a major incentive for her to return to work in Dhaka.

Bangladesh is known as a pioneer in the field of microfinance, but it is clear that for many poor people in the Naogaon community, such credit had become a burden and not a benefit during the economic crisis:

"Almost everyone [here] has taken [microcredit] loans from the NGOs. People spend most of their money paying these installments and are left

with very little money to buy food. The NGOs are very 'professional' about collecting installments—they will come to your house regularly and will wait for you. It does not matter whether you can eat or not, you have to pay the installments."

Village veterinarian in Naogaon, February 2011

Indebtedness became a growing concern. The branch of a microfinance NGO in Notun Bazaar closed down in the middle of the research period and relocated outside of the slum, near the more settled and middle-class *mohalla* area. The NGO stopped providing credit to waste merchants, rickshaw-pullers, and others from the slum because of the high risks of default. Yet microfinance continued to thrive in the rural community in Naogaon. Microcredit-lending NGOs were seen as competitive lenders but tough creditors, whom only death could shake off:

"The situation is so severe that even the death of a family member does not make people sad—instead they are often relieved. I know someone whose wife died two day ago. But he showed no tension or sadness. I tried to understand the reason and found out that his wife had a loan of Tk 6,000 ($82). Besides, the price hike was making his life really difficult. Now, as his wife is dead, he will not have to worry about the loan or installments and at the same time, he no longer has to buy food for his wife. So overall, he is quite relieved."

Village veterinarian in Naogaon, February 2011

As these accounts are from only one of Bangladesh's 80,000 villages, around 90 percent of which have microfinance lenders, they should be treated with caution and merely as illustrative of how some people are experiencing their debt burdens. The manager of an NGO branch office in the area, one of a handful of large microcredit lenders in the country, noted that there had been pressure on repayment rates with recent volatility. His organization responded by being more flexible and adapting repayment schedules to help people cope and by adopting more rigorous screening of borrowers, particularly because loan sizes were increasing alongside inflation. Despite the positive spin, it seemed clear that the office (one of more than 3,000 branches nationally) had been feeling the effects of people's inability to repay: during the interview, a staff member rushed in to inform the boss that another borrower had just run away without repaying the loan. It emerged that 25 borrowers ran away without repaying in 2009, but only 12 in 2010. Yet in just the first two months of 2011, seven borrowers had already run away.

Increased Reliance on Informal Safety Nets

Support from family members, private charity, and assistance from religious organizations was vital for coping strategies of vulnerable people in surveyed sites. Most interviewees, however, noted that the amount of charitable donations by private individuals was reduced, as the relatively affluent had also been hit hard by the crises, while the number of people asking for assistance was growing. Beggars in the two surveyed communities reported that they were visiting many more houses, but were receiving much less rice and cash than before the crisis. They also had to endure a lot of verbal abuse.

Other than microfinance institutions, NGOs were not frequently mentioned as a source of support, but religious organizations were an important source of food security in some communities. For example, a shrine of a Sufi saint near Dhaka was feeding up to 500 people at the height of the crisis. Contributions, mainly from local people, increased as a result of new regulations (brought in after the change in government, these regulations were unrelated to the crisis), which allowed musicians to perform in the shrine attracting larger number of visitors and therefore more donations.

Policy Responses and Implications

The Bangladesh case raises interesting and important questions for thinking about the politics of the policy response to economic shocks. Throughout the 2009–11 period, the Bangladeshi state made a range of efforts to address the crisis, establishing stimulus programs to support businesses, scaling up food and cash transfer schemes, fixing fertilizer prices, conducting open market sales to moderate food prices, and continuing with fuel subsidies, despite their controversial status with the multilateral agencies (see CPD 2010, 2011; Rahman et al. 2009, 2010). The significant rise in the minimum wage for garment workers took place during this period. The central bank also took steps to address concerns about monopolies in rice distribution (CPD 2011). State systems were in place to monitor food prices, and NGOs, donor agencies, and the mass media all paid close attention to the effects on people of global shocks.

The rural community in Naogaon felt the positive effects of the increased spending on agriculture in the stimulus package and 2009–10 budget through fertilizer subsidies. Rural people also noted increased coverage of the targeted Primary School Stipends scheme, and the new provision of "tiffin" or the school feeding program for rural children, to be valuable support. Allocations to safety nets increased by 26 percent, mainly through expanded programs, particularly the Open Market Sales of subsidized rice (Rahman et al. 2010). One study found that subsidized rice and later other sales of food items in 2007–08 were considered most valuable during the peak of the food crisis (PPRC 2009), and it seems that this remains an important visible element of the official response. Subsidized food sales were valued more by the Notun Bazaar residents than by their rural counterparts, for whom the costs and time involved in traveling to the distribution center and queuing would outweigh the small amounts one was allowed to buy. In addition, as women in both communities noted, the *controler chal* (as the subsidized rice is called), smelled bad once cooked. Notun Bazaar women complained that the cheap rice was a mixed blessing, as it would spoil unless eaten immediately, creating additional work for women because meals had to be cooked fresh rather than once daily and requiring more fuel, which women were responsible for collecting. Nevertheless, as rice prices rose, the subsidy could mean a considerable saving—although at greater costs to women's time and labor.

Despite what is generally understood to have been a timely and wide range of responses, it is clear that the overall goals of social protection were not met. The amount of assistance was too small relative to people's needs: households were limited in the amount of subsidized rice they were permitted to buy, and recipients of old age and widow's allowances complained that monthly payments of Tk 200–300 (about $3) were insufficient to cover their food expenditures. Another important concern was that coverage of social protection schemes was inadequate to protect all of those seriously affected. Social protection coverage has increased (25 percent of the population had received some kind of safety net benefit, according to the 2010 household income and expenditure survey), but a high proportion of poor people continue to be excluded from such benefits in some of the poorest regions of the country (BBS 2011).

Furthermore, action to regulate food prices plainly failed to keep them within bounds that poor people considered to be affordable. To some extent, this problem reflects the size of the poor and extremely poor population in Bangladesh. With 13.5 percent of the population of 160 million living below the poverty line, it is safe to assume that more than 50 million people will have been struggling to maintain basic standards of living when the basic costs of living—in particular, the price of rice and other staple foods—have increased by more than half since 2005.[7] Although considerable progress has been made on agricultural production, concerns have arisen that greater production has not translated into a cushion against global food price rises. Domestic food production increases in recent years meant that by 2011, domestic production was projected to meet domestic demand (CPD 2011). That food prices continued to rise during this period may reflect inaccuracies in the data (on population size, per capita food intake, or domestic food grain production estimates). Another possibility may be changes coming in Bangladesh's food grain market, such as an increased role of intermediaries in these markets, which has led to the delinking of domestic food grain production from domestic food prices (CPD 2011, 46, 49).

It was clear from what people said in these two communities that they expected their government to act to protect them against sharp food price rises. This idea that the state should and will intervene during times of acute food insecurity is firmly grounded in the Bangladeshi political culture. The long history of political unrest and regime overthrow associated with episodes of famine and economic crisis has created a powerful aversion among the ruling elites to food-related shocks and has encouraged the establishment of a well-developed institutional framework to respond to natural disasters and food-related shocks (see Hossain 2005, 2007).[8] The government elected with a large popular mandate in early 2009 was credited by people in the two communities with having successfully taken action to control prices, as prices came down sharply after the new government took office. The facts all seemed to support this view: prices came down; they did so immediately after an unelected government (which people deemed unresponsive to their needs) had been replaced by one elected with a large majority; the party of the new government had a better reputation for caring about poor people than its competitors; and, above all, it took immediate and highly visible steps to ensure wider access to at least some affordable food (despite considerable problems with the open market sales program it established). The theory that a popularly elected government would do more to protect people against economic shocks appeared, at first, to be borne out by the realities. In 2010, people in both communities were broadly satisfied with the performance of their government in managing the crisis on their behalf.

The improvements in well-being, however, may have had less to do with the visible and popular actions of the new regime and more to do with less overt efforts on the part of the preceding caretaker regime, as well as fiscal prudence in the preceding years (see PPRC 2009), and the drop in commodity prices globally. By 2011, when food prices had returned to (in some places) their 2008 peak, there was considerable anger and dissatisfaction with the government. The idea that markets could not be successfully regulated because of corruption and collusion among politicians, officials, and big and small businessmen was widely held. Some of the views expressed by transport workers in Notun Bazaar captured this sense of frustration and disappointment and the firmness of the view that the government was responsible for taking direct action against unfair business practices:

> *"The government should send officials of different agencies to the market on a regular basis. If they go to the market on a daily basis, the shopkeepers will get afraid, and they will sell food items at the right price. However, the key issue again is whether the government is sending 'honest' and 'competent' officials to the market. If not, they will not look after the interest of the people; rather, they will serve the interest of the businessmen. Nowadays, most of the committee members of the government investigation committees are dishonest, they are not afraid of Allah and are not concerned about life after death."*

> *"Whenever the prices start to rise, the government should send its police forces to the godown [warehouse] of the big businessmen. The police will seize all the goods, will bring them to the stadium and will announce that these food items will be distributed among the poor people free of cost. And then the free distribution will take place. If the government can do this only once, that will send the right message."*

> *"If price continues to rise, in reality people cannot do anything. If 25–30 people show their dissatisfaction and engage in protest, police will simply beat them up and will send them to home. Despite this, people should protest. Without this, the Food or the Commerce Minister will not realize the situation and will not take necessary steps."*

In light of the last quotation, it is worth noting that hundreds of rickshaw-pullers rioted in Dhaka less than two weeks after this research was completed. Their main point of contention was that they had been banned from using main city streets—an issue that was also raised during the focus groups. For people who are struggling to make ends meet to be faced with official regulations that prevent them from doing their work is likely to be seen as unjust and to elicit unruly political responses. In 2011, as the consequences of the Arab Spring continued to unfold, it became clear that popular discontent arising from economic crises and the lack of adequate response by governments is a growing concern in many countries. In this context, it remains to be seen whether even the relatively responsive government of Bangladesh has the capacity and the fiscal space to mount a response that will address popular concerns and needs.

Concluding Thoughts

The impacts of the complex (and apparently ongoing) economic crisis that first struck in 2008 have been variously unpredictable, lagging, and contradictory in Bangladesh. Disentangling and attributing shocks from effects and transmission channels is a daunting challenge given the complexity of the crisis, in particular the interaction of commodity price volatility with (largely separate) financial crises. In Bangladesh, as elsewhere, understanding the effects of such external shocks requires understanding the near-crisis situation in which many poor people routinely live their lives, in addition to the effects of climatic episodes such as cyclones and floods.

Despite these challenges, the research approach tested here indicates that it is possible to gain an understanding of what global economic crises mean in people's lives. In this chapter, we have reviewed some findings from three years of research visits to two communities, in which teams of anthropologists looked closely at how people's lives had been shaped by the events of the three years from 2008 to 2011. We believe the research offers some insights into the process of global economic shocks as they unfold in local communities. They are admittedly limited and partial insights, based on small-scale community work. But the findings sketch a picture of winners as well as losers in occupational terms, of livelihoods at turning points, of adaptive and resourceful individuals, and of workers taking control of their working conditions. Bangladeshis are accustomed to economic ups and downs; even in formal sector employment, such as in garment factories, conditions of work can be tenuous and insecure. From the perspective of real lives, the financial crisis ultimately meant some more churning in the job market, but there was little net sense of hardship. By contrast, food and fuel price spikes were felt directly and were experienced as significant sources of hardship. The politics of the official response to these different crises merits more attention than it has been possible to give it in this chapter, but it is clear a quality of responsiveness to poor people exists within the Bangladeshi state that has helped to shape a reasonably effective social protection response.

A concluding point is to strike a note of caution about the celebration of resilience in relation to coping with economic crisis. Poor Bangladeshis, and particularly poor Bangladeshi women, are often lauded for their extraordinary capacities to cope, adapt, and recover. Yet the accounts given by the people in Notun Bazaar and Naogaon are of significant declines in well-being, in some instances likely to lead to irreversible—yet not necessarily measurable—changes in trust, social relations, and quality of care. They cope, it is true, but would be far better off if the were protected against the need to do so. The resilience of poor people—particularly of poor women—is not without its costs. Given the likelihood that complex crises of the kind experienced between 2008–11 will recur in the near future, we need to find ways and tools of documenting and measuring the costs of this so-called resilience before it is completely depleted.

Notes

1. "Economy Under Stress: IMF," *Daily Star,* March 22, 2011, http://www.thedailystar.net/news-details.php?nif=178631.
2. Twelve-month average inflation rates, from Centre for Policy Dialogue, 2011.
3. Although there is some evidence of the impacts on waste recycling sector workers, particularly Horn (2009) and WIEGO (2011).
4. On a national scale, analysis of retail and farmgate prices during 2010 by the Centre for Policy Dialogue provides support for this point (CPD 2011).
5. An unpublished survey by the World Bank of experiences of crime in Bangladesh found that food adulteration was ranked among the top three greatest concerns.
6. Eid-ul-Azha is the festival when wealthy Muslims traditionally sacrifice animals, and a portion of the meat is supposed to be shared with the poor. Domestic staff will customarily expect to receive a proportion of the meat sacrificed in the households for which they work, and for many this will be the only time of year when they have meat.
7. Estimates of the poverty impact of the 2008 food price rises in Bangladesh noted that the price of rice had increased by 50 percent in the first nine months of 2008, and the peak price during the second spike of June 2011 was slightly above the previous high in 2008. At Tk 32 per kg, average retail prices in 2008 were double their 2005 level of Tk 16 per kg. Based on the rising price of rice alone, one estimate was that the poverty headcount ratio would have increased by 6 percent. Taking into account how people adjust to food prices,

the overall poverty impact was likely to have been closer to 3 percent (World Bank 2010).

8. This point was brought to our attention by Hossain Zillur Rahman of PPRC in Bangladesh, a political sociologist and researcher who had himself been the adviser/minister in charge of the crisis response during the interim nonparty caretaker government period (2006–08).

References

BBS (Bangladesh Bureau of Statistics). 2011. "Preliminary Report on Household Income and Expenditure Survey 2010." Bangladesh Bureau of Statistics, Ministry of Planning, Dhaka.

CPD (Centre for Policy Dialogue). 2010. "State of the Bangladesh Economy in FY2009–10." Independent Review of Bangladesh's Development, Centre for Policy Dialogue, Dhaka.

———. 2011. "State of the Bangladesh Economy in FY2010–11 (First Reading)." Paper prepared under the Independent Review of Bangladesh's Development (IRBD), implemented by the Centre for Policy Dialogue, 46, 49. Dhaka.

GoB (Government of Bangladesh). 2009. "Bangladesh Economic Review 2009 (English)." Ministry of Finance, Dhaka.

Horn, Z. E. 2009. *No Cushion to Fall Back On: The Global Economic Crisis and Informal Workers*. Women in Informal Employment: Globalizing and Organizing (WIEGO)/Inclusive Cities Project report, http://www.inclusivecities.org/pdfs/GEC_Study.pdf.

Hossain, N. 2005. *Elite Perceptions of Poverty in Bangladesh*. Dhaka: University Press Limited.

———. 2007 "The Politics of What Works: The Case of the Vulnerable Group Development Programme in Bangladesh." Chronic Poverty Research Centre Working Paper 92, Chronic Poverty Research Centre, Manchester, U.K.

IMF (International Monetary Fund). 2011. *World Economic Outlook April 2011: Tensions from the Two-Speed Recovery: Unemployment, Commodities, and Capital Flows*. Washington, DC: International Monetary Fund.

PPRC (Power and Participation Research Centre). 2009. "Food Price Inflation: Impact and Response: Lessons from Recent Experiences." PPRC Policy Paper 22. Power and Participation Research Centre/Concern Worldwide, Dhaka.

Rahman, M., D. Bhattacharya, M. A. Iqbal, T. I. Khan, and T. K. Paul. 2009. "Global Financial Crisis Discussion Paper 1: Bangladesh." Overseas Development Institute, London.

Rahman, M., M. A. Iqbal, T. I. Khan, and S. Dasgupta. 2010. "Bangladesh Phase 2." Global Financial Crisis Discussion Series Paper 12, Overseas Development Institute and Centre for Policy Dialogue, London.

WIEGO (Women in Informal Employment: Globalizing and Organizing). 2011. *Coping with Crises: Lingering Recession, Rising Inflation, and the Informal Workforce.* WIEGO/Inclusive Cities Project report.

World Bank. 2008. *Poverty Assessment for Bangladesh: Creating Opportunities and Bridging the East-West Divide.* Washington, DC: World Bank.

———. 2010. *Food Price Increases in South Asia: National Responses and Regional Dimensions.* Washington, DC: World Bank South Asia Region.

CHAPTER 3

Crisis Monitoring among Low-Income Workers in Cambodia: Monitoring Vulnerabilities and Discovering Resilience

Veronica Mendizabal, Theng Vuthy, Tong Kimsun, and Pon Dorina

Introduction

Between 1998 and 2008, Cambodia grew at a remarkable and steady pace. The country's annual growth averaged 9.1 percent, and the income per capita more than doubled from $287 in 1997 to $593 in 2007 (World Bank 2009a). This achievement has been impressive, but the benefits of growth have been spread unevenly leading to widening disparities. Poverty has been reduced from 47.0 percent in 1993 to 30.1 percent in 2007, which means that a third of Cambodians still live below the national poverty line, calculated at CR 2,473 or $0.61 per day (World Bank 2009b). The exchange rate used throughout the chapter is 4,080 Cambodian riel (CR) to $1, as of September 22, 2009. Inequality has increased not only between rural and urban areas, but also within rural areas (World Bank 2007). Approximately 1.5 million people in the countryside and more than 150,000 people in the cities remain food insecure (CDRI 2008). Progress has been made toward reaching the national Millennium Development Goals (MDGs) targets on child mortality and combating HIV/AIDS and malaria, but Cambodia is off-track in its targets for poverty and hunger eradication, maternal mortality, primary education, and environmental sustainability.[1]

Vulnerability in Cambodia is pervasive, with a large proportion of the population highly susceptible to shocks that can push them into poverty, particularly in rural areas where 80.5 percent of the population and 93.0 percent of Cambodia's poor reside (MoP 2010). The sources of vulnerability include chronic food insecurity, lack of land and productive resources, heavy reliance on single crop subsistence agriculture, and dependency on irregular weather patterns that can determine the fate of a whole harvest. Unemployment and underemployment are endemic risks (Braithwaite et al. 2009). Moreover, most of the workforce is engaged in the informal sector. By 2004, only 20 percent of Cambodians were paid employees (World Bank 2006).

The pace of growth slowed from the last quarter of 2008 and during most of 2009 as the global economic crisis reached Cambodia, severely affecting its three main engines of growth: construction, tourism, and garment exports, which account for 88 percent of total exports (World Bank 2009a). Garment exports to the United States fell by 20.9 percent,[2] and 93 garment factories closed between January and November 2009.[3] Although tourist arrivals rose by 1.7 percent in 2009, arrivals of higher-spending tourists declined (ADB 2010). Construction slowed mainly as a result of the 35 percent decrease in inflow of foreign direct investment. The Cambodian economy contracted by 2 percent in real gross domestic product (GDP) in 2009 (World Bank 2010b). As a consequence, the labor market suffered a shock, with thousands of people losing their jobs; the garment sector alone recorded 43,000 job losses between 2008 and 2009 (World Bank 2010b). Many of the workers who remained employed went on involuntary part-time arrangements or reduced working hours.

How were the lives of workers affected by rising unemployment, labor insecurity, and falling incomes? In particular, how did vulnerable workers manage to cope with these sudden negative changes? What sources of support—formal or informal—were available to them during the crisis? This chapter presents the evolving conditions of a sample of low-income urban workers and rural householders who, between 2009 and 2010, participated in a year-long qualitative multiround monitoring study, carried out by the Cambodian Development Research Institute (CDRI) and financed by the World Bank.

The Cambodian economy started recovering by the end of 2009 with growth expected to reach 6 percent in 2010 and 2011 (World Bank 2011). The storm has passed, but the strength with which it hit Cambodia has exposed important weaknesses in the current growth model. First, it has become clear that the economy is too narrowly specialized and diversification has not taken place, a weakness the government is serious about addressing as reflected in the recommendations of the last Cambodia Economic Forum in 2011. Second, agriculture was the only driver of growth that recorded increases (around 5 percent), but as this monitoring study suggests, this sector remains underdeveloped and highly vulnerable to weather. Third, current formal social protection programs have had limited outreach during the crisis, pointing to the need for further improvements. This is not new, but it is particularly relevant as gains made in poverty reduction in recent years may be undermined in the medium term by growth forecasted at lower levels than in the recent past. Finally, the findings also suggest that informal social solidarity in Cambodia has remained strong despite decades of internal conflict. During the economic crisis of 2008–09, the informal mechanisms of mutual support, although weakened and stretched by the strength of the shock, served as one the most important safety nets for poor households in the countryside and as the only one for many rural migrants working in the city (table 3.1).

After this introduction, the chapter consists of five sections, the first of which describes the methodology and scope of the study and the characteristics of the sample. The second section deals with the main changes that affected workers in rural and urban settings between May 2009 and February 2010 in the labor market, income, migration patterns, and inflation and food prices. The third section looks at the main coping strategies identified during the year and their changes over time, and the fourth presents the sources of support that were available to the workers in the sample during the year, both formal and informal. The chapter ends with a summary of the findings.

Table 3.1. Cambodia and the 2008–09 Global Economic Crisis

Population (millions)	13.4	(2008)
Life expectancy at birth (years)	62	(2009)
Percentage of population living below the national poverty line	30.1	(2007)
Under 5 mortality rate per 1,000 live births	88	(2009)
Maternal mortality ratio (national estimate, per 100,000 births)	461	(2008)
Malnutrition prevalence, weight for age (% of children under 5)	28.8	(2008)
Malnutrition prevalence, height for age (% of children under 5)	39.5	(2008)
Adult literacy rate (%)	78	(2008)

Source: World Bank 2010.

The Crisis Monitoring Initiative: Methodology and Scope

The study monitored the evolution of the crisis in four rounds of research spanning a full 12 months at roughly 3-month intervals. It looked at how people were experiencing the impact of the crisis and how they were seeking to cope through individual, household, and collective arrangements. The study aimed to better understand the nature, causes, and scale of changes in individual and household circumstances throughout the year and to identify the various coping strategies undertaken by different vulnerable groups. It also sought to explore potential effects of the use of these strategies over time and to hear the participants' views on the effectiveness and coverage of current social safety nets and how these safety nets were assisting them during the crisis period.

The CDRI has been conducting quarterly surveys of real income and consumption among a sample of 480 vulnerable workers since 1998 (table 3.2). The sample included selected vulnerable worker groups—cyclo drivers, porters, scavengers, and vegetable sellers in Phnom Penh, and motorcycle taxi drivers, skilled and unskilled construction workers, waiters and waitresses, garment workers, and ricefield workers in Kandal and Kompong Speu provinces. In the context of the global economic crisis, in 2009, CDRI extended the survey to cover additional groups—the tourist sector and migrant workers—in Siem Reap and Battambang provinces. By August 2009, it had increased the sample to 560 workers from 12 different occupational groups. CDRI complemented the survey with focus group discussions (FGDs) with participants selected from occupational groups and sites sampled in the vulnerable workers survey, plus FGDs with rural poor households selected from panel data from the longitudinal poverty dynamic study *Moving Out of Poverty* (FitzGerald et al. 2007).[4]

FGDs were conducted with cyclo drivers, skilled and unskilled construction workers, waiters and waitresses, and garment workers in Phnom Penh; workers in the tourism sector in Siem Reap; ricefield workers in Kandal; and cross-border migrants and their families in Battambang province. FGDs with poor and vulnerable rural households were organized in the following: (1) Kampong Tnaot, a coastal village in Kampot province; (2) Trapieng Prey village in the plateau of Kompong Speu province; and (3) Babaong village located in the southwest plains of Prey Veng province. Two separate FGDs were organized in each village, one with male and female household heads, and another with only female heads of household. The aim of these separated FGDs was to trace differentiated effects of the crisis on males and females.[5]

Table 3.2. Sample of Income and Consumption Monitoring and Focus Group Discussions, 2009–10

Group	Vulnerable Workers Survey		Location	Focus Group Discussions (FGDs) on Crisis Impact and Coping	
	Round 1	Rounds 2–4		Round 1	Rounds 2–4
Cyclo driver	40	40	Phnom Penh	1	1
Porter	40	40	Phnom Penh		
Vegetable trader	40	40	Phnom Penh		
Scavenger	40	40	Steung Meanchey dump		
Skilled construction worker	40	40	Phnom Penh	1	1
Unskilled construction worker	40	40	Wat Langka and Steung Meanchey	1	1
Motortaxi driver	40	40	Phnom Penh		
Waitresses and waiters	40	40	Phnom Penh		1
Ricefield workers	40	40	Kandal (Kropeau Troum and Donn Vong villages) Speu (Udam Mony and Peil Heil villages)	1	1
Tourism sector workers	20	40	Siem Reap	2	2
Migrant workers	20	40	Battambang (Andong Trach and Kraisang)	2	2
Garment workers	120	120	Phnom Penh	2	2
			Babaong (Southwest plains)	1	2
			Trapieng Prey (Plateau)	1	2
			Kompong Tnaot (Coastal)	1	2
Total	**520**	**560**		**13**	**17**

Source: Research team.

Major Changes Observed between May 2009 and March 2010

The quarterly monitoring suggests that all of the 12 groups of vulnerable workers participating in the surveys or group discussions between May 2009 and March 2010 were affected by the economic crisis. Garment and tourism workers were initially the most affected by a contracting labor market but started to recover when external demand for Cambodian products rebounded. Informal workers and landless rural households, on the other hand, were strongly affected by the combined effects of reductions in remittances and low demand for their services, and they were taking a longer time to recover.

Urban Low-income Workers

The income and consumption surveys conducted by CDRI suggest that low-income workers were not immediately affected by the economic crisis, but effects trickled down, and, by the first and second quarters of 2009, income declines became evident (Kimsun, Sothy, and Dalis 2009).

By May 2009, the real daily income of most groups in the sample had declined compared with May 2007. The average real daily earnings of waiters and waitresses fell by 25 percent, garment workers by 18 percent, motortaxi drivers by 16 percent, cyclo drivers by 15 percent, porters by 7 percent, and vegetable sellers by 3 percent.

Findings from the focus group discussions confirmed overall reductions in income among groups of vulnerable workers in the cities. A large majority of the urban workers interviewed were domestic migrants from poor rural communities. With lower incomes, most of them were unable to send money to their families in rural areas, as they had barely enough to sustain themselves in the cities.

> "We have been able to work only three to four days a week for only a few weeks this month. The owner told us to take a rest for a week and wait for additional orders. Sometimes we wait more than a week without work, then we get only 50 percent of our monthly salary because there is no work to do."
>
> Garment workers, May 2009

Demand for construction workers, for example, remained low throughout the year. In the sample, by August 2009, unskilled workers were employed between 5 to 7 days per month compared to 10 to 14 working days in May 2009.

"The situation is very bad now! There are very few jobs to do. They give us much less than they used to three months ago for the same type of job with the same amount of work. To gain money we have to do whatever they require. We are very upset now because we do not have money to send back to our families so they will face great difficulty."

Unskilled workers, Phnom Penh, August 2009

Skilled construction workers interviewed in August 2009 had managed to reinsert themselves in the job market by drastically reducing their fees and accepting daily wages that were approximately 30 percent lower than during the same period a year earlier. They found some demand in small-scale construction as people with savings were taking advantage of the cheap labor to renovate their houses.

The August 2009 survey found slight signs of stabilization among the nongarment worker groups and recovery among tourism workers as tourists started to arrive and hotels and restaurants restarted operations, while the situation had further deteriorated for garment workers, whose real daily earnings had continued to fall. Upward trends were finally observed by the fourth quarter of 2009 when some of the garment factories that had closed down were able to relaunch operations and started to recruit.[6] The survey in November 2009 allowed CDRI to categorized the sample into (1) the most affected: cyclo and motortaxi drivers and ricefield workers (figure 3.1); (2) the least affected: skilled and unskilled construction workers; and (3) the recovered groups: garment workers, waitresses and waiters, and tourism workers (figure 3.2). By February 2010, the average daily earnings of garment workers reached $1.81 from $1.44 in May 2009, and 37 percent of workers in the sample were working overtime. The daily income of migrant workers reached $2.22, a 60 percent increase from November 2009.

In May 2008, inflation reached its highest level in three decades at 25.7 percent. The increase was largely driven by the global surge in oil and food prices. After a drop in 2009, inflation returned at a rate of 5.3 percent in December of that year (ADB 2010). Prices for food and other commodities soared. Most of the groups that started earning better incomes by the end of 2009 had been unable to make savings because they were spending more on food as their purchasing power declined.

Poor and Vulnerable Rural Households

For most of 2009, rural areas were negatively affected by multiple shocks including drought, pest outbreaks, low yields, reduced remittances from

Figure 3.1. Real Daily Income for Cyclo Drivers, Motortaxi Drivers, and Ricefield Workers

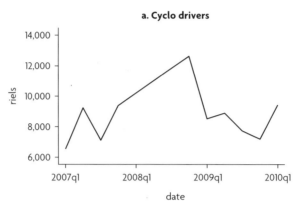

a. Cyclo drivers

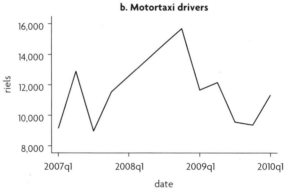

b. Motortaxi drivers

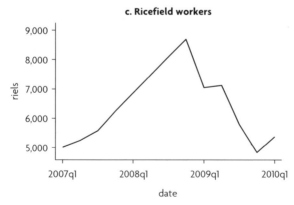

c. Ricefield workers

Source: Kimsun and Dorina 2010.

Figure 3.2. Real Daily Income for Garment Workers, Waitresses, and Tourism Workers

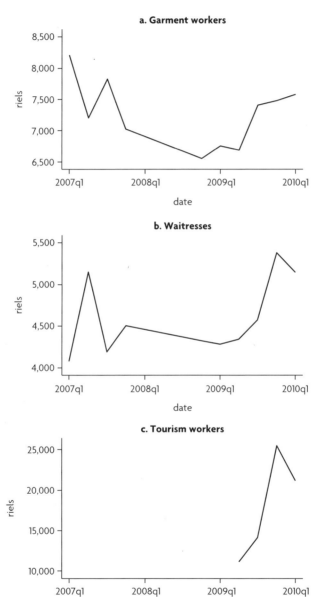

a. Garment workers

b. Waitresses

c. Tourism workers

Source: Kimsun and Dorina 2010.

relatives working in urban areas, and low availability of off-farm work. Farmers feared food shortages due to the magnitude of the agricultural losses and the contraction of the job market. In villages with large numbers of landless farmers, such as Trapieng Prey and Donn Vong, the combined effects were stronger and more dramatic, as people could not even fall back to subsistence agriculture.

Landless Households. Villagers who sold their farming land during the boom in land prices in 2007 (Trapieng Prey and Donn Vong) had invested the money in renovating or building houses for their families, buying productive assets such as motorbikes to be used as taxis, starting small businesses, or financing the migration of family members to urban centers. To cover those investments, many of them also accessed additional credit from microfinance institutions (MFIs), which was widely available at the time. When the economic crisis hit Cambodia, many villagers had outstanding loans and were finding it increasingly difficult to earn enough to cover their daily expenses and meet their debt commitments. They were also having problems selling their labor, as high prices for agricultural inputs (such as fertilizer and pesticides) and low yields had reduced the ability of farmers to hire workers. Finally, and to make things even harder, relatives working in the city had reduced or stopped sending remittances, an important source of additional income for landless households. With no land, no job, and no remittances, some villagers, desperate to service their debt, accessed additional loans from informal moneylenders at 5 percent to 6 percent per month. As the situation deteriorated, many could not managed their debt and ended up losing their houses and their sources of income.

Farmers and Seasonal Migrants. Babaong village produces dry-season rice. After the harvest, villagers usually leave in search of work in adjacent regions or in the cities, so that changes in income are seasonal. In 2009, rice farmers had a difficult season caused by a mix of unusual weather and an outbreak of brown plant hoppers. Farmers indicated losses of around 60 percent to 70 percent of their crop. To control the outbreak, farmers increased the frequency of pesticide spraying up to 10 times during the season, more than twice the usual number of 3 to 4 sprayings. To afford the agricultural inputs, farmers had taken loans from suppliers. The farmers expected to pay in kind (rice) during the harvest season. With low yields and falling rice prices, farmers found themselves with loans they could not pay back.

"Even though I have already cooked my food, I have to tell my children that mummy cannot eat, because I have so many worries due to too much debt."

Participant in Babaong village, May 2009

Poor Coastal Households. Kampong Tnaot (Kampot province) is a fishing village. When the crisis hit, this village was just recovering from a strong shock caused by drought in 2008 that resulted in a loss of 50 percent of the rice yield. The main concern for villagers was that large (and illegal) fishing boats had started operating in their region and were causing sharp declines in fish stocks. When the research team first visited in May 2009, villagers were in the process of selling their boats as artisanal fishing had become unprofitable. Many had started working in the large boats themselves, others had joined crab-processing operations, and the young were migrating in large numbers to cities in search of work.

Main Changes in Rural Poor Households, May 2009–March 2010. During the second quarter of 2009, all poor rural households in the sample were facing grave risks to their food security and general well-being. Drought in August brought further challenges. Transplanting of rice seedlings had been postponed, meaning there were no on-farm jobs in their villages or nearby regions. Jobs in the cities remained scarce. People were desperately searching for jobs in and outside the village to meet their consumption needs and their growing debt commitments.

"Our last hope will fade away if rain does not come within this next two or three weeks. There will be of course a lack of rice to eat, and everybody in the village will face enormous difficulties then. There is almost nothing we can rely on now: not much work to do, our debts have still not been paid back, no remittances from our children in the city, and everything is getting more and more expensive."

Participant in Trapieng Prey village, August 2009

Hope arrived in September when garment factories restarted operations and workers in the city could begin to send remittances back home. Seasonal availability of off-farm work was recorded for all villages in the sample (increased sales of homemade cake and wild foods). Most important, the rain came, and rice workers could benefit from selling their labor, although the demand for their work was markedly lower than in 2008 as landowners had become less able to pay for hired labor.

When the research team returned in March 2010, they found that farmers in most villages had managed to obtain high rice yields. The resulting income had served to repay some outstanding loans and to improve their food consumption.

> *"Rice yield and the prices of rice are better than last year, but we had debts to rice traders or moneylenders; we have repaid our debts by selling our rice and have kept something to eat. Our livelihood did not change, but it is better because our loans have been reduced."*
> Participant in Babaong village, February 2010

Not all regions had been so fortunate. Too much rain and a severe rat infestation in Trapieng Prey had caused devastating rice yield losses. The destruction was estimated at around 30 percent when compared to the harvest obtained in 2008. Doing off-farm paid work together with remittances from family members was seen as the last financial safety net for these villagers, one that remained largely unpredictable due to the fragile economic recovery.

Migration Patterns

Several marked migration patterns were observed between May 2009 and March 2010. When jobs first became scarce, workers remained in the cities waiting for the situation to improve. This phase lasted until people ran out of savings or were finding it increasingly difficult to find additional sources of income.

Domestic Migration. The second assessment, in August, found more movement from and to the village. Many construction workers had left Phnom Penh, searching for work in border areas (Poipet and Malai) or in their villages. At the same time, and despite people being aware of the difficulties, more people started leaving the villages for the cities. The profile of the migrants also seemed to be changing. Prior to the crisis, young people were the main group migrating to cities, but by August, more children were migrating. Girls were sent to work as domestic workers, and boys as laborers on farms or fishing boats.

When garment factories started to rehire in September, a new wave of young people moved to the cities, and older migrants returned to their villages to take part in seasonal on-farm work. FGD participants indicated that by the end of 2009, children who had been sent to cities in search of work had returned to their villages and were going back to school—except in one of the most affected sites in our sample, Kampong Tnaot, where children were still working and contributing to the household income.

Cross-border Migration. Demand for Cambodian workers in Thailand suffered ups and downs during the year. By February 2010, workers in Thailand reported receiving 40 percent lower daily wages than in November 2009. Migrants returned to their villages during rice harvesting in October and mushroom farming in February and when work was scarce in Thailand. In the discussions, cross-border migrants expressed concern about the trend toward mechanized agriculture in Thailand, which threatens their sources of work and income in the medium term.

Responding to Shocks and Crises

To respond to falling incomes, unemployment, loss of crops, and rising food prices, people used multiple strategies. They included reducing consumption of food and nonfood products, pooling resources, and cooperation. The strategies used more often and by most participants are described here. Safety nets are discussed separately in the next section.

Changes in Food Consumption

By May 2009, most FGD participants had reduced their expenditure on food, with changes evident not only in the amount of money spent daily but also in the quality or type of food purchased. People were gradually moving from more expensive products to cheaper ones. By August, fish, beef, and pork had become more expensive than two months earlier. Workers and rural families reported replacing meat with pork fat and consuming more vegetables and eggs. They also had stopped consuming fruit. The one product that people in rural and urban areas had continued consuming was second-quality rice.[7] As the situation worsened, people also started reducing the quantity of food consumed—drastically, as the next quote suggests. Nevertheless, all households indicated that they were trying to maintain the nutrition of young children:

> *"We have reduced our food consumption in recent months, by about 50 to 70 percent. Now we buy pork once a month, about 100–200g only; before we bought pork about five or six times a month, about 300–400g. When we catch fish or crabs from the sea we never eat the big fish now; we eat only*

*the small fish because we sell the big fish and crabs to earn money. We allow
our children to eat a lot though, otherwise they will cry."*

Participant in Kampong Tnaot village, May 2009

*"Although we have reduced our food consumption, our children still eat
as much as before. Only we adults eat little."*

Participant in Donn Vong village, May 2009

The direct effects of this extreme strategy were clear to the people in the
FGDs. Garment and construction workers complained of illness related to
eating less nutritious food.

*"Every month one or two garment workers in Mitona Garment factory
collapse in a faint because they are eating less. We have reduced the quantity and quality of meat due to the high price. The price of fish has also
increased so we are rarely able to buy any for consumption."*

Garment workers, Phnom Penh, February 2010

*"Eating low quality food is not always good for us because our work
takes physical strength . . . before, we would usually have other snacks as
well as our meals, but now we feel more exhausted after work."*

Skilled construction workers in
Phnom Penh, March 2010

By the beginning of 2010, and despite high food prices, reducing food
consumption seemed to have become less common among most groups
(although the quality of purchased products remained low for all). Two
main factors seemed to be making this change possible. First, the rice harvest had started, and villagers were saving stocks of rice for their own
consumption rather than sale. Second, rainfall had increased fish stocks
and other wild foods in common property lands, and families were avidly
collecting these items and using them for their own consumption and for
sale. The FGDs suggest that wild foods were a key safety net for rural
households facing food insecurity and an essential element complementing household nutrition and income during the year. In one village, people
indicated earning more from selling smoked rats (seasonal) than from farm
labor or construction work.

However, the diet of villagers where the harvest had failed, and of cyclo
drivers and construction workers interviewed in the cities, remained poor
or got worse.

*"Within this few months not only did I not have money to send home,
but instead there was not even enough for me, not even for food expenses.*

*Any week that goes by without work to do, my savings having run out,
I eat only one pack of instant noodles instead of three meals per day."*
Unskilled construction workers,
Phnom Penh, February 2010

Reductions in Nonfood Consumption and Health Care

All the people in the sample reduced their expenses on nonessentials such as clothes, alcohol, or cigarettes. In addition, they cut expenses on transport to the minimum, as was the money given to children to go to school. Most urban migrants reported having reduced the frequency of travel to their home villages or not going home at all. People were reducing their expenditures to the minimum by early 2010, although there were indications of increased spending on rent, water, and electricity because of the rising costs of living.

Workers in urban areas indicated they had cut their expenses on health care and were increasing self-treatment using nonprescription medication from private pharmacies. Some opted to return to their villages for care if they came down with a serious illness. Workers in the city mentioned going to health centers only in case of accident or severe illness, with many complaining about the poor service provided at the urban health centers.

Changes in the Labor Allocation within the Family

During the first two quarters of 2009, there were indications of school dropouts in the villages sampled and of children searching for paid jobs, but this did not occur in cities. Most of the young girls from Babaong village had been sent as domestic workers to Phnom Penh. Young boys were working as laborers in farms or in fishing boats, as well as in construction. People in Donn Vong village indicated that, by May 2009, only 5 out of approximately 100 children were still attending the primary school. The others were helping their families with productive activities.

"Our young children now help us earn money. The girls go to get vegetables from the lake and some tree leaves to sell at the market . . . and the money they earn is used to buy rice for daily family consumption. The boys help their father fishing. They need to work more on this because the family does not have anything to eat . . . they have to work harder."
Participant in Donn Vong village, May 2009

During the school holiday months of August and September, children were helping with income-generating activities in villages and in the cities.

By November, signs of economic recovery and the availability of seasonal work influenced changes in labor allocation within families. Adults, male and female, were involved in farm and off-farm work. Their older daughters returned to work in garment factories, and younger boys and girls were going back to work in hotels and restaurants. People mentioned that older children are the human capital of the family and key sources of financial support. Children in rural areas were also back at school but were distributing their time between school and other activities such as housework, looking after animals, and collecting wild foods.

> *"My son goes to school about 10 days in the whole month because I ask him to help me collect crabs and snails to exchange for rice."*
> Participant in Andong Trach village, November 2009

Kampong Tnoat, where, prior to the crisis, child labor and migration were uncommon, was the only village in the sample where some children were still working by February 2010, suggesting that households highly affected in this village were trying to avoid further drops in consumption by keeping children out of school and engaged in productive activities. Recovery in this village was taking longer, perhaps as a result of the cumulative impact of consecutive shocks since 2008: drought, decreasing fish stocks, and a drop in remittances.

Working Longer Hours and Diversifying the Sources of Income

Working more hours had become a common coping strategy for the self-employed in 2009. Traders, cyclo drivers, and *tuk-tuk* (rickshaw) drivers had added a couple of hours to their usual working day and were working on average 12 hours per day, seven days a week. Even with the additional hours, they were earning less than during the same period in 2008. Workers were also trying various types of additional work: some construction workers were working as cyclo drivers, cyclo drivers were working as porters, and tuk-tuk drivers were searching for work in nearby towns.

A large majority of the garment sector workforce (nearly 90 percent) is composed of young female migrants between the ages of 18 and 25. Findings from the FGDs suggest that some of the laid-off female garment workers had taken jobs in the entertainment sector, in karaoke clubs and massage parlors, jobs entailing a high risk of exploitation, abuse, and health-related risks. Studies have revealed long-standing, often cyclical labor flows between the garment sector and direct or indirect forms of sex work in Cambodia (Nishigaya 2002).

Reducing Fees and Prices. As overall consumption fell and competition for the fewer customers increased, the self-employed in the sample reduced their daily fees and prices to a minimum between May and September 2009. This strategy was used by small-scale traders, cyclo and tuk-tuk drivers, farm laborers, and construction workers. In August 2009, construction workers were charging up to 30 percent less for their labor than they had a year earlier.

Pooling and Cooperation. Pooling resources and cooperating with one another are traditional ways of solidarity when rural workers migrate to urban areas in Cambodia. These forms of cooperation continued to be widely practiced during the economic crisis. Construction and garment workers in particular were pooling money or rice sent from the villages and cooking and eating together in large groups. The eating groups kept on growing throughout the year and were still observed in early 2010. Organizing in self-defense groups was another cooperative strategy used by homeless cyclo and tuk-tuk drivers, who usually sleep on the roadside in their vehicles. These drivers explained that crime and violence, present before the crisis, increased in 2009, and that they were being attacked by gangs on a regular basis at night. Later in the year, banding in self-defense groups was also observed among laid-off construction workers, who, after losing their jobs, could no longer sleep at construction sites and had no other choice but to sleep on the street.

Reverse Remittances. Cooperation and solidarity was also observed in the changing direction of remittances and transfers of goods. Reverse remittances were first mentioned in August 2009, when rural households, which prior to the crisis had been receiving remittances, started sending money and food to laid-off relatives who had run out of savings but remained in the cities waiting for the job market to improve. It is telling and an indication of strong bonds of solidarity that despite the extreme hardship experienced by rural households (no remittances, mounting debt, poor harvest), they were still trying to support family members in the cities.

Borrowing. Most FGD participants increased their debt during 2009 to refinance previous loans or pay interest, invest in agricultural inputs, or cover pressing needs (food or medical expenses). The credit market contracted by midyear, and access to loans, either from moneylenders or from

MFIs, became extremely difficult. As already mentioned, farmers also accumulated debt by buying pesticide and fertilizer on credit, expecting to pay it back with rice after the harvest. The team observed that, by August 2009, many farmworkers, especially single female and elderly heads of household, had started purchasing food on credit or borrowing money from neighbors to cover basic expenses. They had borrowed on the promise of repaying with labor at half their usual wage in the future. This drastic strategy was not common in May 2009, when it was still possible to borrow food at no interest from neighbors or traders. The debt situation appeared to have improved during the first quarter of 2010 when good yields allowed farmers to pay back some of their loans.

Sale of Assets. In 2009, selling productive and family assets to pay off debt or to cover basic needs or medical expenses seemed to have been commonly practiced. People sold their houses, their motorbikes, and livestock, which largely reduced household endowments and increased their vulnerability and the potential of falling into poverty (Dercon and Saphiro 2007). In early 2010, asset selling was not as prominent as it had been during the previous year. Either the need for selling assets had lessened or households had nothing left to sell, as was the case in Andong Trach and Donn Vong villages, where eight of the nine participants had already sold their draft animals. New job availability in the garment sector meant some remittances were arriving, and villagers were earning income from seasonal off-farm work.

Safety Nets and Mutual Assistance

Formal Social Protection

Formal social protection in Cambodia is still underdeveloped and characterized by low budget allocation, high dependency on development assistance for funding, and large gaps in coverage, but there are some signs that social protection has started to improve. In 2008, the government established the National Social Safety Fund for the private sector, in which firms with more than eight employees are required to enroll. The fund has three components: (1) employment injury coverage, which has been rolled out since the end of 2008;[8] (2) the health insurance scheme currently in the design stage; and (3) the pension fund expected to be implemented in 2012. Civil servants are covered under the National Social Security Fund for Civil

Servants, operating since May 2009. Around 180,000 civil servants and their families were enrolled in 2010.

Two health programs specifically target poor and informal workers: the Health Equity Fund (HEF) and the community-based health insurance schemes (CBHI). HEF is a mechanism to reimburse health providers for treating patients classified as too poor to pay. This program started in 2004; its second phase will continue until 2013. It is funded by different sources and implemented by government, donors, and nongovernmental organizations (NGOs). By May 2009, it covered 68 percent of the population categorized as poor in 50 out of 70 districts, although actual use is lower. CBHIs are voluntary schemes for the near-poor who can afford a minimal premium for a set package of benefits. Perhaps the need to minimize out-of-pocket health expenses caused the sudden increase in the CBHI's membership from 79,900 members in 2008 to 123,000 in 2009.

Trade unions are still young in Cambodia. They appeared during the late 1990s, and the government formally recognized them in the Labor Code of 1997. Garment workers in the sample indicated seeking the help of unions when facing serious problems with factory management, particularly against unfair dismissals. Unfair termination was a significant problem during 2009 according to a tracking exercise conducted with 2000 garment workers in and around Phnom Penh (CIDS 2010). Garment workers in the sample sought help from unions when assistance with leave requests was needed, when mobilizing to improve working conditions, and to claim holiday pay, but the study provided mixed evidence with regard to the effectiveness of union support.

Formal safety net interventions in Cambodia are mainly food based, such as food for work, school feeding, take-home rations (food scholarships), rice banks, health and nutritional programs, and emergency food assistance. Since 2006, the government has implemented the Scholarship for the Poor Program, which is funded by various donors and reached 21,459 children from poor and very poor families in all provinces except Phnom Penh.[9] All these programs continued to be implemented during the crisis in 2009 and 2010.

Safety Nets in Rural Areas

Vulnerable households in rural areas had indeed benefited from some formal support. School feeding and free health care for the poor at the village level, which included vaccinations and distribution of nutritional supplements for women and children, were very much appreciated, as was the Health Equity Fund, although some users found this mechanism inadequate to treat serious illness.

These forms of support were, however, insufficient to assist rural households with growing debt, mounting food insecurity, imminent agricultural disasters, loss of productive resources, and loss of property. The support of World Vision with an integrated rural development program, and later in the year with emergency food supplies, was therefore considered fundamental in two villages seriously affected by drought.

Beyond these examples and for most of the groups in the sample, both in rural and urban settings, informal safety nets were the only mechanisms available for people trying to manage their increasing vulnerability. Informal forms of mutual support included social practices of reciprocity, informal credit arrangements, community pooling and contributions, and informal transfers of food to the destitute. The protracted and covariate nature of the shock weakened these mechanisms. For example, borrowing small amounts of money in informal credit arrangements without interest from relatives and neighbors had been a common and essential strategy to deal with sudden liquidity shortages, but became more difficult as the year went by, with people restricting lending to close relatives as they did not have enough to share with a wider group.

> "Now there is no mutual assistance. Rural people are like city people now: we sell everything, even wild vegetables growing on our fences or just young tamarind leaves. Everyone is looking out for themselves. Each household has to look after its own."
>
> Participant in Trapieng Prey village, May 2009

> "How can we help and take care of each other like we used to in our village? Every family is facing its own difficulties. We struggle to survive ourselves, so how can we help other people when we can barely help ourselves?"
>
> Participant in Donn Vong village, May 2009

Other forms of social solidarity also suffered and were undermined during the crisis. One example is the communal practice of *provas dai* (literally, exchange of hands) in which neighbors cooperate with one another, mostly on agricultural activities, by sharing productive resources. The use of a plowing animal during planting would be reciprocated by labor during harvest. Participants mentioned that in the past years, a process of transformation has been taken place with provas dai gradually being monetized. They also observed that this transformation accelerated during the difficult years of 2008 and 2009.

"I provas my cattle to my brother. . . . Sometimes I allow him to use the cattle to plough the land although I would charge people in the village 10,000 riel to rent my cattle for a whole morning."
Participant in Trapieng Prey village, May 2009

Findings of the study, however, suggest that the informal mechanisms are extremely resilient and very long term, and, despite being stretched and weakened by covariate and extended shocks, such as decades of conflict, they remain in place and are used as coping mechanisms and to prevent outright starvation. In many of the villages visited, people affirmed that they would not let anyone die of hunger, and food support for the destitute continued to be practiced throughout 2009–10.

"We help only elderly people who have nobody (no children and no relatives) to look after them—giving them food or anything they need to survive. If elderly people have children or relatives, we do not help them, because we are also poor and have to take care of ourselves as well. But we will not allow any people to die from hunger in our village."
Participant in Babaong village, May 2009

Buddhist temples sustained through donations suffered important reductions in contributions during the crisis but continued their support to poor households with a restricted scope to the poorest and the elderly who were sick or in extreme difficulty. Community-wide support during funerals was also maintained in *all* the villages visited. People were still receiving money, in-kind support, or labor to cover funeral costs, either from individuals in an informal manner, or in some villages from established community-based funeral insurance systems. This practice seems to be an integral part of the social fabric, and communities continued providing their support for those worse-off suffering a strong idiosyncratic shock in addition to the covariate shock.

Safety Nets in Urban Areas

Formal support systems were largely unavailable for urban workers in the sample, with a few exceptions: garment workers mentioned having had tetanus vaccinations and HIV awareness workshops, and cyclo drivers mentioned life-skills programs. Beyond this type of support, these workers relied mostly on their own ability to make ends meet and on informal safety nets that included mutual support, sharing resources, and self-help groups. As the workers in the sample are quite poor, what they can share with each other is limited from the outset, yet their social network appeared strong. The study found that urban workers, a majority of whom are domestic migrants, identify strongly not only with people from the same region or village, but also with people working in the same trade. The workers in the sample expressed strong bonds of solidarity and high levels of mutual support, which is basically all they have to fall back on in times of crisis.

> *"We depend mainly on ourselves and the people around who come to work in the city like us. We are now very close to each other, helping the people next to us when they need help and treating one another just like brother and sister."*
>
> Unskilled construction workers,
> Phnom Penh, May 2009

The informal mechanisms used in the cities resemble in some way those observed in rural areas, adapted in some cases in response to the particular challenges experienced in urban settings. Cooperation was observed among all groups of workers who were helping each other in times of need, taking people to hospital in case of sickness and banding together to prevent robbery (construction workers and cyclo drivers).

> *"People like each other. We never have any violence in the group or towards other cyclo drivers, but instead we try to help each other during hardships like sickness or other difficult circumstances. . . . We all come from rural areas. . . . Nobody can understand us and assist us beside ourselves and our friends."*
>
> Cyclo drivers, Phnom Penh, May 2009

Sharing resources was also widely practiced by the workers in the sample, in particular, food, information, and skills. It is interesting to note that despite strong competition, construction workers were still exchanging information on work opportunities and continued sharing their skills with relatives and close friends from the same villages or commune, indicating a way of preserving rural social capital. Sharing became more difficult for all as the economic situation worsened, but it did not completely disappear.

> *"We do feel pity for them* [cyclo drivers skipping meals] *but we also have nothing to offer because we have to think of ourselves first. It is not easy to make an income now. If they come by at the time we eat we can share some food with them."*
>
> Cyclo drivers in Phnom Penh, August 2009

Conclusion

This chapter has presented the results of a year-long monitoring of the effects of the economic crisis on a diverse range of vulnerable workers in Cambodia. The study indicates that all groups of workers in the sample were affected in one way or another and suffered high levels of hardship by the combined effects of the crisis, rising food prices, variable weather conditions, and seasonal livelihood changes. Decreases in employment, hours, and wages affected workers in the formal sector, particularly garments and construction; the informal sector was affected by the movement of workers from formal to informal sectors, the consequent rise in competition, and low demand for their services. In rural areas, the study found evidence of households experiencing reductions in remittances, which caused liquidity shortfalls and affected the ability of poor and landless households to cover basic expenses and to service their debt commitments. A credit crunch and decreases in seasonal employment coupled with low harvests further reduced the capacity of the rural poor to pay their debts, and many people ended up losing assets such as houses, draft animals, or land.

The economic shock triggered multiple coping responses—some with potentially high costs on household welfare in the medium and long term. Vulnerable workers searched for alternative work; worked additional jobs and longer hours; pawned assets; and borrowed from moneylenders, friends, and family. As the situation worsened, many poor rural households sold productive assets (draft animals) and pulled their children out of school so they could work and contribute to the household income. Many poor households in rural areas and vulnerable workers in the cities went to the extreme of reducing their food consumption, in the worst cases up to 70 percent, although all participants indicated protecting the nutrition of children.

The formal safety nets available were insufficient to absorb the strong systemwide shock. Focus group discussion participants appreciated the free health care program, school feeding, and the emergency food support from NGOs, but gaps were evident. People needed mechanisms to better manage weather risks to ensure production and avoid loss of harvest, income generation programs, loan refinancing assistance to prevent loss of essential livelihood assets, and access to credit to purchase agricultural inputs. These were the overarching concerns voiced by FGD participants. The assessments showed that in the absence of formal mechanisms for risk mitigation, vulnerable workers relied primarily on informal forms of mutual support. In fact, for the most part, informal safety nets were the only mechanisms available to them, particularly among informal urban workers. These informal risk management mechanisms proved to be extremely dynamic, resilient, and long term. They remained in place, even if stretched and weakened by the strength, length, and covariate nature of the shock.

Notes

1. According to the Cambodian Millennium Development Goals (CMDG) Update Report for 2010, some of the MDG elements that are seriously off-track include equity in growth, food poverty, child labor, use of contraception, access to emergency obstetric care, protection of natural resources, and land titling. Ministry of Planning Cambodia, *Achieving Cambodia's Millennium Development Goals—Update 2010* (Phnom Penh: Royal Government of Cambodia, 2010).
2. The United States accounts for 70 percent of total garment exports from Cambodia. *Asian Development Outlook 2010* (Manila: Asian Development Bank, 2010).
3. According to the Cambodian Ministry of Labour and Vocational Training (MoLVT).
4. The *Moving Out of Poverty* study explored trends in community well-being and household mobility in nine Cambodian villages over the decade from 1993 to 2004–05, roughly coinciding with the national socioeconomic surveys: the Socio-Economic Survey of Cambodia 1993–94 (SESC) and the Cambodia Socio-Economic Survey 2004 (CSES).
5. For detailed data on the real income and consumption surveys, see Kimsun, Sothy, and Dalis 2009 and Kimsun and Dorina 2009a, 2009b, 2010. Detailed findings from the qualitative focus group discussions and interviews can be found in CDRI 2009a, 2009b, 2010; and Vuthy and Sothorn 2009.
6. Garment exports in November 2009 reached almost $250 million compared to $60 million in September 2009. *Economic and Monetary Statistics,* National Bank of Cambodia.
7. First-quality rice is *Neang Minh* and *Phkar Knhei* (export rice); second-quality rice is IR66 high-yield variety; and third-quality rice is broken rice, commonly referred as rice offered to soldiers.
8. The fund covers medical costs and 70 percent of the worker's salary while in treatment. Employers make a monthly contribution equal to 0.8 percent of the worker's salary. By February 2009, 400 firms had enrolled and were covering

roughly 300,000 workers. Responding to the crisis, in 2009 the government decided to subsidize 0.3 percent of the firm's contribution for two years.

9. At primary school, all eligible children receive $30 per year. At lower secondary, a very poor family would get $60 for a year, and a family considered medium poor would receive $45.

References

ADB (Asian Development Bank). 2010. *Asian Development Outlook 2010.* Manila: ADB.

Braithwaite, J., L. Bruni, T. Conway, J. Larrison, and J. Rigolini. 2009. "Safety Nets in Cambodia." Concept Note and Inventory, World Bank East Asia Unit, the Council for Agriculture and Rural Development, and the World Food Programme, Washington, DC.

CDRI (Cambodia Development Resource Institute). 2008. *Annual Development Review 2008/2009.* Phnom Penh: CDRI.

———. 2009a. *Rapid Assessment of the Impacts of the Economic Crisis on Cambodian Households and Vulnerable Workers.* Round 2. Phnom Penh: CDRI.

———. 2009b. *Rapid Assessment of the Impacts of the Economic Crisis on Cambodian Households and Vulnerable Workers: Road to Recovery.* Round 3, December. Phnom Penh: CDRI.

———. 2010. *Rapid Assessment of the Impacts of the Economic Crisis on Cambodian Household and Vulnerable Workers.* Round 4, May. Phnom Penh: CDRI.

CIDS (Combodia Institute of Development Study). 2010. *Tracking Study of Cambodian Garment Sector Workers Affected by the Global Economic Crisis.* Benchmarking Survey Report, March 2010. Phnom Penh: CIDS.

Dercon, S., and J. Saphiro. 2007. *Moving On, Staying Behind, Getting Lost: Lessons on Poverty Mobility from Longitudinal Data.* Global Poverty Research Group, GPRG-WPS-075, Economic and Social Research Council, Oxford, U.K.

FitzGerald, I., S. Sovannarith, C. Sophal, K. Sithen, and T. Sokphally. 2007. *Moving Out of Poverty? Trends in Community Well-Being and Household Mobility in Nine Cambodian Villages.* Phnom Penh: Cambodia Development Resource Institute.

Kimsun, T., and P. Dorina. 2009a. *Vulnerable Workers Survey in Phnom Penh, Kandal, Kompong Speu, Siem Reap, and Battambang.* Round 2, September. Phnom Penh: Cambodia Development Resource Institute.

———. 2009b. *Vulnerable Workers Survey in Phnom Penh, Kandal, Kompong Speu, Siem Reap, and Battambang.* Round 3, December. Phnom Penh: Cambodia Development Resource Institute.

————. 2010. *Vulnerable Workers Survey in Phnom Penh, Kandal, Kompong Speu, Siem Reap, and Battambang.* Round 4, May. Phnom Penh: Cambodia Development Resource Institute.

Kimsun, T., K. Sothy and P. Dalis. 2009. *Vulnerable Workers Survey in Phnom Penh, Kandal, Kompong Speu, Siem Reap, and Battambang.* Round 1, August. Phnom Penh: Cambodia Development Resource Institute.

MoP (Cambodian Ministry of Planning). 2010. *Achieving Cambodia's Millennium Development Goals—Update 2010.* Phnom Penh: Royal Government of Cambodia.

Nishigaya, K. 2002. "Female Garment Factory Workers in Cambodia: Migration, Sex Work and HIV/AIDS." *Women and Health* 35 (4): 27–42.

UNICEF (United Nations Children's Fund). 2010. http://www.unicef.org/infoby country/cambodia_statistics.html.

Vuthy, T., and K. Sothorn. 2009. *Rapid Assessment of the Impacts of the Economic Crisis on Cambodian Households: Component 3 Focus Group Discussions with Vulnerable Workers and Rural Households.* Round 1, May. Phnom Penh: Cambodia Development Resource Institute.

World Bank. 2006. "Managing Risk and Vulnerability in Cambodia: An Assessment and Strategy for Social Protection." June. Policy Note, World Bank, Washington, DC.

————. 2007. *Sharing Growth: Equity and Development in Cambodia.* Equity Report 2007, East Asia and the Pacific Region. Washington, DC: World Bank.

————. 2009a. "Cambodia Country Economic Memorandum." World Bank, Washington, DC.

————. 2009b. *Poverty Profile and Trends in Cambodia 2007.* Washington, DC: World Bank.

————. 2010a. *World Development Indicators.* Washington, DC: World Bank.

————. 2010b. "Cambodia." In *Country Pages and Key Indicators, East Asia and the Pacific Update,* 41–46. Washington, DC: World Bank.

————. 2011. *Cambodia Recent Economic Developments: Cambodia Economic Monitor,* 7th ed. World Bank Cambodia Country Office. http:// siteresources.worldbank.org/CAMBODIAEXTN/Resources/KH_Econ _Monitor_Feb2011.pdf.

CHAPTER 4

Impact of the Economic Crisis in the Central African Republic: Quantitative and Qualitative Assessments

Lea Salmon, Josias Tebero, and Quentin Wodon

Introduction

The food, fuel, and financial crisis that took place during much of 2008–10 had a large negative impact on the welfare of the population of many African countries. On the basis of household survey data, it has been estimated that in a dozen West and Central African countries, the increase in food prices alone, especially in 2008, led to an increase in the share of the population in poverty of several percentage points on average. Even more important, about 80 percent of the poverty impact of the higher food prices increased the depth of poverty among those households that were already poor before the crisis.

The objective of this chapter is to provide an assessment of the likely impact of the economic crisis on the poor in the Central African Republic (CAR), as well as the strategies used by the population to cope with the crisis. The assessment is reached by combining data from the country's latest (2008) nationally representative household survey with results from qualitative work using focus groups undertaken at two different times, January–February 2010 and July 2010, in a few areas of the country that were deemed to be more significantly affected by the crisis.

The Central African Republic is a postconflict country, vast but with low population density, struggling to complete its transition from successive periods of instability to steady growth and development. Since the end of the conflict in 2003, the government has pursued prudent macroeconomic policies and implemented structural reforms, but these measures have led to only a modest recovery of growth that, given the current population growth rate, barely keeps per capita income levels constant, and real gross domestic product (GDP) growth has averaged only 2.5 percent per year since 2003).[1] Although the Central African Republic's government has shown its commitment to sustaining economic and governance reforms and improving service delivery, the country is unlikely to meet any of the Millennium Development Goals by 2015. Social indicators place the Central African Republic among the least developed countries in the world: its Human Development Index ranks 159th out of 169 countries (UNDP 2010).

The 2008 household survey suggests that 62.0 percent of the population lived below the poverty line that year, with the share of the population in poverty at 69.4 percent in rural areas, where close to two-thirds of the population lives (Backiny-Yetna and Wodon 2011). Although good data are not available to assess the trends of well-being and human development outcome indicators, life expectancy has fallen from 50 years in the early 1990s to 47 years in 2008; maternal mortality, estimated at 850 per 100,000 live births in 2008, remains high. Furthermore, maternal and infant mortality rates have increased over the past two decades (table 4.1).

What about the impact of the crisis?[2] One might be tempted to assume that in a country as poor and isolated as the Central African Republic, the impact of the crisis may have been significantly smaller than in other countries because the country's population is mostly rural, with many households involved in subsistence agriculture and therefore less exposed to changes in the world prices of staple foods and fuels. The weight of such imported goods in the consumption basket of the population is much smaller in the Central African Republic than in other countries. Actually, the inflation

Table 4.1. Central African Republic: Development Indicators

Population (in millions)	4.3	(2008)
Population growth (annual %)	1.9	(2007–08)
Population ages 0–14 (% of total)	40.9	(2008)
Life expectancy at birth (years)	47	(2008)
Percentage of population living below the national poverty line	62	(2008)
Adult literacy rate (%)	54.6	(2008)
Percentage male and female pupils completing grade 5	53.1	
Under 5 mortality rate per 1,000 live births	172.3	
Maternal mortality ratio (per 100,000 births)	850	

Source: World Bank 2010.

rate rose sharply to 9.3 percent in 2008, but the increase was of short duration, and inflation has been reduced to 1.8 percent since then. Furthermore,
the inflation rate, given the way it is measured, reflects more of the situation
in the capital city of Bangui than in the country as a whole.

Other channels of transmission for the impact of the global economic
crisis also suggest that the impact may have been limited. For example, emigration from the Central African Republic to other countries
is rather limited, so it is unlikely that many households would have
been affected by a reduction in international remittances. Similarly,
the Central African Republic's participation in the world economy is
also limited, so the reduction in demand for various export products
would have only a limited impact on the population.

As will be shown in this chapter, simulations-based quantitative analysis of available household survey data indeed suggests that the impact of
the crisis on the population is likely to have been small, at least for the
increases in food and fuel prices. Such a view could be misleading, however. Although it is correct that many households live in quasi-autarky,
especially in rural areas, a number of people are involved in trading
activities that may have been affected by the crisis. Furthermore, several
segments of the economy are vulnerable to a variety of shocks, especially
in terms of the external demand for the country's two main exports, timber and diamonds. Both sectors contracted sharply, which contributed
to a reduction in the growth rate of real gross domestic product from
3.7 percent in 2007 to 1.7 percent in 2009 (IMF 2010). The breakdown of
the hydro plant used for electricity generation and the crisis in the telecom
sector also had negative impacts.

The government budget is also likely to have been affected, if only in
terms of a reduction in revenues from exports, which limited further the
authorities' already weak ability to respond to the crisis through investments, safety nets, or other programs. In response, fiscal policy was geared
to supporting aggregate demand with a focus on expanding public investment. But limited availability of grants from donors, weak domestic
resource mobilization (the domestic revenue to GDP ratio was 10.8 percent
in 2009, versus 17.4 percent on average for fragile countries and 22.7 for
Sub-Saharan Africa), as well as weak implementation capacities made it
difficult for the government to maintain and expand priority spending programs in areas such as education, health, agriculture, social welfare, and
infrastructure. Government support for households affected by the crisis is
likely to have been limited, so that even if the slowdown in growth and the

increase in the prices of basic food staples and fuel may have had a smaller negative welfare impact on the population as a whole than in other countries, in the absence of safety nets, the impact on specific groups is likely to have been significant.

Lessons from past crises suggest that one might expect at least two rounds of impacts, the first reflecting the initial shocks to household incomes and purchasing powers, livelihoods, and food security, and the second relating to the potential medium- or long-term consequences of the mechanisms used by households to cope with first-round shocks by, for example, selling assets or reducing children's time in school.

In terms of the first round of impacts, the increase in prices for food and fuel is likely to have affected a large number of households. Despite the reliance on subsistence agriculture in rural areas, many households remain net purchasers of basic foods and fuels. Furthermore, specific household groups are also likely to have been affected by the reduction in economic activities, especially in export-oriented sectors. Finally, a smaller subset of households may have been affected by reductions in international remittances and in the availability of credit. Finally, the inability of the government to provide adequate safety nets and to increase access to basic public services was likely to have affected a majority of households.

The impact of the second-round effects is more difficult to assess. Coping strategies adopted by vulnerable households may generate lasting negative impacts on well-being and food security (increased indebtedness, sale of productive assets, or curtailed investment in human capital). There may also be community-level effects: the stress brought about by the crisis leading to losses in social capital and social cohesion.

After this brief discussion of context and background, the chapter is divided into four sections and a conclusion. The second section describes the methodology used for data collection and analysis, relying both on the latest nationally representative survey and on a number of focus group surveys implemented in specific areas of the country most likely to have been affected by the crisis. The third section provides a summary of quantitative results regarding the potential impact of some aspects of the crisis, as well as the coping mechanisms households were likely to have used to deal with it. The fourth section discusses the results of the qualitative work, with a focus on specific groups of affected workers, again both in terms of the shocks incurred and the coping strategies used.

Data and Methodology

It is especially difficult in a country such as the Central African Republic to rapidly assess the impact of a crisis because of the lack of reliable data. For many years, partly due to the conflict, the country did not implement national household surveys. When such surveys were implemented, they were often of poor quality due to limited capacity of the National Statistical Office. Fortunately, a new, nationally representative, and good quality survey is available: Central African Survey for Welfare Monitoring and Evaluation *(Enquête Centrafricaine pour le Suivi-Évaluation du Bien-être* [ECASEB]) was implemented by the National Statistical Office *(Institut Centrafricain des Statistiques et des Etudes Economiques et Sociales* [ICASEES]) in 2008, with a sample of 7,000 households. The first part of the questionnaire of the survey was based on the QUIBB *(Questionnaire Unifié sur les Indicateurs de Base du Bien-être* [Unifiéd Questionnaire on Main Welfare Indicators]) design and technology, which collects basic data on the sociodemographic characteristics of households (composition of the household, employment, education, and health); housing characteristics; access to basic infrastructure; and perceptions about poverty. In addition, a second part in the questionnaire collected data on consumption and income sources, including transfers between households, as well as some other topics such as shocks to households and their coping mechanisms.

Because no subsequent surveys were implemented to assess the impact of the crisis as it unfolded, the data from the 2008 survey are the only data available to conduct simulations (as opposed to ex post estimations) on the likely impact of the crisis, with a focus on the increase in food prices. In addition, the survey can also be used to analyze the shocks to which households were confronted over the five years preceding the survey, which is also instructive, as responses to previous shocks are likely to be similar to the strategies used to cope with the crisis itself. Thus, although the 2008 survey cannot be used to measure the direct impact of the crisis itself (both because it was implemented in the early stages of the crisis and because no other comparable surveys are available to make comparisons over time), it does still provide valuable information as to the potential impact of the crisis and the coping mechanisms.

In addition to the survey, we also rely on qualitative data collection implemented in January–February 2010 and June–August 2010 in the capital city of Bangui and its outlying areas, as well as in the Mbaïki sub-prefecture in Lobaye (Tebero, Dimanche, and Bonder 2010a, 2010b). In the second round of data collection, owing to the climate of insecurity during the preelectoral period, the focus was maintained on the same groups but with further emphasis on those groups living in the city of Bangui and its outlying areas, using the same selection criteria and variables, such as urban/rural areas, public sector/private sector workers, and the formal/informal sectors. The qualitative data collection tools were specifically designed to monitor, as much as can be done through such qualitative data, the impact of the crisis. The exercise was carried out by the World Bank with support from the Ministry of Planning and Development, and it aimed specifically to investigate the following questions:

- Who is being affected and through which channels? How do impacts differ for different groups and individuals? How are impacts distributed within the household and between households? Are there particular impacts on women or children?
- How do people respond to price and labor market shocks? Which formal and informal institutions do they turn to for help? Have these sources of assistance—and, in the case of informal assistance, the terms of such support—changed over the past year? If so, how? Within a household, do men and women turn to different coping strategies or different sources of support?
- Can the implemented coping strategies eventually cause harm in the longer term, and how can such harm be prevented?

Specific vulnerable groups were selected for participation in focus groups to analyze how these groups were affected in one way or another by changes in world market conditions, and to what extent they were vulnerable to the crisis. The groups were chosen according to a number of likely channels of transmission of the global crisis into changes in local conditions within the Central African Republic. These channels of transmission included labor market adjustments likely to affect public sector workers (resulting in reduced earnings and increased income instability) and informal sector workers in urban areas (who tend to depend on domestic demand for goods and services and therefore were also likely to face reduced earnings and increased income insecurity). A second channel identified as a potential source of shocks was remittances from overseas. The third channel was commodity price movements, which could affect workers in the agricultural sector (who represent 80 percent of the population), and workers in export-oriented industries (especially the timber and diamond industries, which account, respectively, for 16 percent and 40 percent of the country's export earnings).

In total, 20 focus group discussions (FGD) were held in each of two rounds of data collection (in January–February and in June–August 2010), which provided data from 403 participants. On average, each FGD included 8 to 12 participants. The locations included the capital and its surroundings (Bangui), the Lobaye district (Batalimo, Bangandou-Lobaye, Bolema Ndolobo), and the Ombela-Mpoko district (locations on Damara road). This sample was more urban than the nationally representative quantitative survey and may overstate certain crisis impacts, particularly those on the formal sector. Most FGDs included mixed groups of men and women, although four FGDs were mostly or exclusively composed of women, for example, households headed by widows and women in rural areas.

Quantitative Analysis

Simulated Impact of the Increase in Food and Fuel Prices

In this section, we use simple simulations to assess the likely short-term impact on poverty of the increase in the price of selected food and fuel items in the Central African Republic. For the sake of simplicity, we use a number of assumptions. First, we assume that the cost of an increase in food or fuel prices for a household translates into an equivalent reduction of its consumption in real terms. This means that we do not take into account the price elasticity of demand, which may lead to substitution effects and thereby help offset part of the negative effect of higher prices for certain items (with substitution, the effects would be marginally lower). It should be also noted that the ECASEB data does not provide detailed information on the production by households of food items that are likely to have been affected by the increase in world food prices. The questionnaire has information only on the production of a dozen crops, mostly vegetables, none of which is closely related to the crops for which international prices increased during the crisis. Therefore, we assume no potential positive impacts of the increase in world prices for basic staples on the side of producers, and we look only at the potential negative impact on the side of consumers of the increase in food prices. Similarly, fuel prices are assumed to have only negative impacts on households consuming those fuels.

We do however take into account information on food that is autoconsumed by households. Such information is available in the survey, but it is not factored into the simulations because changes in prices do not affect households when food is autoconsumed. Poverty measures obtained after the increase in prices are then compared to baseline poverty measures at the time of the survey to assess impacts. We do not take into account the potential spillover or multiplier effects of the increase in food or fuel prices through the economy as a whole.

Table 4.2 provides estimates of the impact of a 25 percent and 50 percent increase in selected food and fuel prices on the headcount index of poverty (the share of the population in poverty), the poverty gap (the product of the headcount and the distance separating the poor from the poverty line as a proportion of that line), and the squared poverty gap (which in addition takes into account for the poor the square of the distance from the poverty line as a proportion of that line). It is striking that most impacts are very low, but the reason is that only a small part of the population consumes the various items listed. Moreover, the consumption of those items represents a small share of the total consumption of households simply because many households tend to rely on locally produced food, or they consume only small amounts of the items, as is the case for kerosene (other fuels were considered in the analysis, but the impact on poverty of an increase in gas prices was very small, given that few households consume gas). The only good in the list in table 4.2 that represents a sizable proportion of household total consumption is manioc (cassava), but most of the manioc consumed is autoproduced by households and therefore not subject to price variations that affect household welfare directly. Note that a simulation for all the goods taken together would yield a total impact slightly different than the sum of the impacts for the various goods (given nonlinearities in poverty measures), but the overall impact would still be limited in comparison to other countries.

Although the impact of higher food and fuel prices on poverty is likely negative, and although this impact should not be neglected given the already high level of poverty encountered in the country, this impact seems to be relatively small, at least as compared to the results of similar simulations in other countries (for such results, see Wodon et al. 2008). The relative

Table 4.2. Impact on Poverty of an Increase in Selected Food and Fuel Prices, 2008 (%)

	Base			25% Increase			50% Increase		
	Headcount	Poverty gap	Squared poverty gap	Headcount	Poverty gap	Squared poverty gap	Headcount	Poverty gap	Squared poverty gap
Rice									
Urban	49.6	19.8	10.5	49.7	19.9	10.6	49.9	19.9	10.6
Rural	69.4	34.4	20.9	69.6	34.5	20.9	69.6	34.5	21.0
All	62.0	29.0	17.0	62.2	29.0	17.1	62.3	29.1	17.1
Manioc									
Urban	49.6	19.8	10.5	50.3	20.2	10.8	51.1	20.6	11.1
Rural	69.4	34.4	20.9	69.5	34.6	21.1	69.9	34.9	21.3
All	62.0	29.0	17.0	62.4	29.3	17.2	62.9	29.6	17.5
Maize									
Urban	49.6	19.8	10.5	49.6	19.8	10.5	49.8	19.9	10.6
Rural	69.4	34.4	20.9	69.4	34.4	20.9	69.4	34.5	20.9
All	62.0	29.0	17.0	62.1	29.0	17.0	62.1	29.0	17.1
Bread									
Urban	49.6	19.8	10.5	49.6	19.9	10.6	49.9	20.0	10.6
Rural	69.4	34.4	20.9	69.4	34.4	20.9	69.5	34.4	20.9
All	62.0	29.0	17.0	62.1	29.0	17.0	62.2	29.1	17.1
Sugar									
Urban	49.6	19.8	10.5	49.9	19.9	10.6	50.1	20.1	10.7
Rural	69.4	34.4	20.9	69.6	34.6	21.1	69.8	34.9	21.2
All	62.0	29.0	17.0	62.3	29.2	17.2	62.4	29.4	17.3

(continued next page)

Table 4.2. Impact on Poverty of an Increase in Selected Food and Fuel Prices, 2008 (%) *(continued)*

	Base			25% increase			50% increase		
	Headcount	Poverty gap	Squared poverty gap	Headcount	Poverty gap	Squared poverty gap	Headcount	Poverty gap	Squared poverty gap
Palm oil									
Urban	49.6	19.8	10.5	49.7	19.9	10.6	49.8	20.1	10.7
Rural	69.4	34.4	20.9	69.5	34.6	21.0	69.6	34.7	21.1
All	62.0	29.0	17.0	62.1	29.1	17.1	62.2	29.3	17.2
Vegetable oil									
Urban	49.6	19.8	10.5	49.8	19.9	10.6	49.9	20.0	10.6
Rural	69.4	34.4	20.9	69.4	34.5	20.9	69.5	34.6	21.0
All	62.0	29.0	17.0	62.1	29.1	17.1	62.2	29.1	17.1
Kerosene									
Urban	49.6	19.8	10.5	49.7	19.9	10.6	49.9	20.1	10.7
Rural	69.4	34.4	20.9	69.5	34.5	21.0	69.7	34.6	21.1
All	62.0	29.0	17.0	62.1	29.1	17.1	62.3	29.2	17.2

Source: Authors' estimation from 2008 ECASEB survey.

autarky of many households and their lack of consumption of globally traded food products clearly helped to protect them from commodity price shocks that took place in 2008–10.

This finding does not mean, however, that the crisis had no other impact on the population. As noted in the introduction, specific groups of households, such as the export-oriented sectors, were affected. The survey data makes it difficult to conduct a detailed assessment of the likely effect of the crisis on such groups because they tend to be small and concentrated in the capital, so that only few households in the survey can be identified as especially vulnerable to the crisis in terms of their employment status. The section on qualitative analysis provides an assessment from the subjective perspective of households belonging to certain vulnerable groups as to the impact of the crisis on their livelihoods. First, however, another component of the survey data can be used to assess the extent to which households are able to cope with shocks through existing solidarity mechanisms, and it is to this that we turn next.

Shocks and Coping Mechanisms

Here, we look at the types of shocks that affect households, as well as the mechanisms of solidarity that households can count on to cope with shocks. The analysis is based on a set of questions in the 2008 ECASEB survey, in which people are asked if over the past 12 months their household suffered from various shocks, and what support they obtained in dealing with the shocks. Two main findings emerge from the analysis. First, the majority of households are affected by at least one important shock over a one-year period, and, second, the mechanisms of solidarity on which households can rely to cope with shocks are fairly limited.

Table 4.3 indicates that 64.5 percent of all households were affected over the 12-month period by at least one type of shock. The most common is a reduction in income, which affects almost one in three households. Having less income could represent the early impact of the crisis (given that the survey was implemented in 2008) as well as other factors. Indeed, due in part to the high level of informality in the economy, many households have income sources that vary over time, so that losses in income are frequent. One in four households was affected by a severe illness, which is not surprising given the lack of access to affordable health care in much of the country. A death (most likely in the family), bankruptcy (which need not relate to formal businesses, and is most likely

Table 4.3. Share of Households Exposed to Different Types of Shocks (%)

	Location		Quintiles of consumption per equivalent adult					All
	Urban	Rural	Q1	Q2	Q3	Q4	Q5	Total
Death	18.0	20.1	24.5	19.2	18.0	20.4	16.7	19.4
Severe illness	24.4	28.2	32.9	26.2	26.6	27.4	23.5	26.9
Loss of employment	5.2	0.9	1.1	1.7	2.3	3.0	3.2	2.4
Bankruptcy	15.8	5.6	5.3	9.5	7.9	9.8	11.3	9.0
Loss of crops	15.1	33.3	41.4	33.7	27.0	25.0	15.6	27.2
Loss of livestock	6.9	16.7	19.5	15.5	14.5	11.1	9.2	13.4
Loss in income	30.0	33.0	39.1	33.3	31.9	31.2	27.1	32.0
Loss of housing	5.1	9.7	13.4	8.4	7.2	7.1	6.3	8.2
Any shock	60.1	66.7	73.1	67.1	64.9	64.0	57.3	64.5

Source: Authors' estimation from 2008 ECASEB survey.
Note: The shares indicate the households that suffered from any specific type of shock and may add to more than 100 percent.

to apply here to small informal trades), and the loss of crops are also frequent, affecting close to one in six households. Other shocks were less frequent, including loss of employment, loss of livestock, and loss of housing. Still, the data suggest that the Central African Republic's population, especially the poorest quintiles of the population, is exposed to frequent and various shocks with the exception of bankruptcy, which by nature affects better-off households because it implies running a small business. In the poorest quintiles, 41.4 percent of households are affected by losses in crops.

The mechanisms of solidarity on which households can rely to cope with shocks appear to be limited to informal support from friends and family and some support from NGOs and faith-based organizations (FBOs). Most often, such mechanisms of support tend to be provided when there is a death or a severe illness affecting households. In such cases, as shown in table 4.4, most of the support is obtained from family and friends, and in many cases, the poor are less likely to be able to benefit from support than other population groups. Among organizations, faith-based organizations are more likely to provide support than NGOs or the government. However, for losses of crops, livestock, income, or housing—some of which are more prevalent among the poor—the likelihood of support is very limited.

Table 4.4. Share of Households Benefiting from Outside Support in Case of Shocks (%)

	Location		Quintiles of consumption per equivalent adult					All
	Urban	Rural	Q1	Q2	Q3	Q4	Q5	Total
Death								
Family and friends	61.7	54.7	53.6	53.9	55.8	58.7	61.2	56.8
Government	1.2	0.8	0.6	0.8	1.5	0.6	1.1	0.9
NGO	1.1	1.4	1.1	1.5	1.5	1.1	1.4	1.3
FBO	36.5	35.4	38.7	35.2	32.6	36.8	34.7	35.7
Associations	4.9	3.2	2.9	1.5	4.1	4.0	5.6	3.7
Any help	70.9	66.3	65.0	66.7	65.3	68.4	72.3	67.7
Severe illness								
Family and friends	39.6	35.4	27.8	37.7	31.7	43.6	41.1	36.7
Government	2.0	1.1	0.9	1.6	2.8	0.7	1.0	1.3
NGO	3.3	2.0	2.8	1.5	4.0	1.8	2.0	2.4
FBO	10.6	10.1	9.5	11.5	7.5	11.4	11.2	10.3
Associations	2.3	0.6	0.1	1.7	0.7	0.9	2.2	1.2
Any help	48.8	42.4	34.7	46.2	42.2	50.9	46.9	44.4
Loss of employment								
Family and friends	27.8	22.7	21.9	4.3	32.3	27.9	31.7	26.5
Government	0.9	0.0	0.0	0.0	1.5	1.0	0.3	0.7
NGO	0.4	0.0	0.0	0.0	0.0	1.0	0.0	0.3
FBO	6.3	7.3	11.5	5.3	16.0	3.5	3.3	6.6
Associations	0.0	3.2	0.0	0.0	0.0	3.1	0.0	0.8
Any help	33.6	26.7	21.9	6.9	49.8	30.0	35.3	31.8
Bankruptcy								
Family and friends	19.4	12.2	2.6	13.9	20.8	10.7	23.8	16.4
Government	0.3	1.2	0.0	1.3	0.6	0.4	0.8	0.7
NGO	0.0	0.0	0.0	0.0	0.0	0.0	0.0	0.0
FBO	1.4	0.6	0.7	2.8	0.6	1.3	0.1	1.0
Associations	0.5	0.0	0.4	0.0	0.6	0.2	0.4	0.3
Any help	21.0	13.4	3.7	16.4	21.4	12.1	25.1	17.8
Loss of crop								
Family and friends	7.6	4.8	3.8	3.9	6.5	5.4	8.2	5.3
Government	0.2	0.4	0.0	0.7	0.5	0.5	0.0	0.3
NGO	1.0	0.8	1.3	0.1	0.1	0.4	2.6	0.8
FBO	1.1	0.8	1.6	0.5	0.5	0.5	1.1	0.9
Associations	0.2	0.3	0.0	0.4	0.4	0.5	0.0	0.3
Any help	9.5	6.6	5.8	5.1	7.9	6.8	11.8	7.1

(continued next page)

Table 4.4. Share of Households Benefiting from Outside Support in Case of Shocks (%) (continued)

	Location		Quintiles of consumption per equivalent adult					All
	Urban	Rural	Q1	Q2	Q3	Q4	Q5	Total
Loss of livestock								
Family and friends	5.8	1.4	1.5	2.2	3.6	2.1	1.4	2.2
Government	0.9	0.4	0.0	0.0	0.8	0.7	1.1	0.5
NGO	1.0	0.0	0.7	0.0	0.0	0.0	0.0	0.2
FBO	0.8	1.0	0.0	0.3	1.0	0.9	2.8	0.9
Associations	0.3	0.0	0.0	0.0	0.0	0.2	0.2	0.1
Any help	7.3	2.6	1.5	2.5	5.2	3.7	4.4	3.4
Loss of income								
Family and friends	14.7	6.0	3.7	6.7	8.5	10.6	13.5	8.7
Government	0.5	0.2	0.3	0.0	0.5	0.6	0.0	0.3
NGO	0.4	1.3	3.3	0.4	0.9	0.0	0.4	1.0
FBO	3.1	0.8	0.9	1.8	1.3	0.8	2.6	1.5
Associations	0.2	0.1	0.0	0.0	0.0	0.2	0.4	0.1
Any help	16.9	7.8	7.5	8.1	10.5	11.3	15.4	10.7
Loss of housing								
Family and friends	12.5	3.8	4.5	9.6	2.7	7.7	3.7	5.6
Government	0.5	0.0	0.0	0.0	0.0	0.4	0.2	0.1
NGO	2.6	4.2	7.8	3.4	3.1	0.6	2.7	3.9
FBO	1.1	4.6	7.1	4.2	3.9	0.2	2.5	3.8
Associations	0.0	0.0	0.0	0.0	0.0	0.0	0.0	0.0
Any help	16.6	8.8	13.5	13.0	6.6	8.1	9.1	10.4

Source. Authors' calculations using data from the ECASEB.
Note: The shares indicate the households who benefited from any specific form of help and may add to more than 100 percent.

Qualitative Analysis

Perceptions of Well-Being

In the qualitative work and FGDs, well-being was defined for the groups interviewed as: "The condition of a person who has enough money to feed himself, to dress up, to find a decent place to live, to be educated, and to care about his own." In other words, well-being is the possibility for someone to satisfy his or her basic needs and be able to provide support to the household either partially or in full. In practice, a scale of well-being was shown to participants of FGDs to help them to position themselves on the scale. The values ranged from one to five, with one corresponding to the level of extreme poverty, three being an average level, and five corresponding to wealth. Not surprisingly, in the two rounds, most participants considered themselves at the lowest level, that of extreme poverty. Participants repeatedly emphasized their lack of "access to money."

Three-fourths of the participants interviewed in the summer of 2010 said that their situation had not changed since January–February, even though the crisis had tempered somewhat, at least in terms of the level of the prices of basic commodities. Some of the participants who had a relatively high level of perceived well-being (not poor) declared that they had slipped to lower levels (poor or extremely poor). The perception was that living conditions had deteriorated, especially among poor and vulnerable households. The majority of participants expressed little excitement over promises made by donors and the government. Many were not aware of the causes of the global crisis, and in most instances attributed their difficulties to internal problems (armed conflict, insecurity, and the like) and poor management of the national economy by the country's leaders. Overall, the results signaled the persistence of a difficult situation in the Central African Republic with the existence of two distinct groups of individuals. The first group— including widows, rural women, and gardeners—experienced perhaps less change in their situation over time, but that situation itself was already very difficult at the start of the year. The second group—including public sector employees, artisans, and retailers—was more likely to see a deterioration of their situation, but remained better off than the first group.

In terms of the shocks incurred, regardless of whether they lived in the urban or rural areas, participants identified three main types of shocks: lower income (bad harvest for small farmers, slump in product sales for small businesses, and job losses for employed workers); illness (problems with access to health centers, not only because of distance but also because of the cost of medical consultations and high prices of medicines); and death (of the 12 persons interviewed as part of a focus group, 7 or 8 indicated that they had lost a close relative). These results match the quantitative evidence already cited.

With respect to wages and incomes, a typical statement was, *"Our income has declined owing to the fact that wages are not paid on a regular basis. Furthermore, the slump in product sales has left us with less money."* Some participants referred to irregular payment of wages paid by the state to government workers with back pay of up to six to seven months owed for the years 2008 and 2009, a problem that predated the international financial crisis but was aggravated by it.

More generally, participants stressed that financial insecurity had grown and prevented them from meeting their basic needs for health care and food. Such situations *"engender feelings of resignation, and people look on powerlessly as their relatives die,"* stated one participant. Some participants mentioned positive news such as the birth of a baby, a wedding, or the acquisition of new tools. In the long run, however, participants were aware that such events also translate into financial commitments that are difficult to meet. One group only, the Mboko-Landja planters who were provided with parcels of land paid for by Libyan assistance, was able to identify a clear positive event, but it was a special case.

Even if the crisis was expected to, and indeed appeared to, have affected urban areas and the members of the second group more than rural areas and members of the first group, the situation was also difficult in rural areas, where participants declared having trouble selling their agricultural products despite yields that were on the low side in the wake of a small drought that followed the planting period in May and June. When farmers did manage to sell their products, their sales were small, and the prices paid were apparently low with the resources obtained being enough only *"to buy salt, milk, and soap"*—the most basic necessities.

Access to basic services such as health centers for basic care, schools, roads, potable water, and electricity remains limited, especially in rural areas. When health centers and schools do exist, they fall far short of providing the expected services in terms of quality, owing to a lack of qualified staff and resources. Maintenance problems prevent donor-financed water supply programs from providing safe drinking water (this was the case in two villages). Although rural electrification is the subject of politicians' slogans, the service does not reach the poor, who are quick to say that *"electricity passes over our heads, but we do not see it,"* in reference to the high-voltage line powered by hydroelectric dams that provides the capital with intermittent electricity. Participants also raised the issue of the deterioration of neglected secondary roads. Rural roads are *"rarely traveled by haulers, which impede the access of agricultural products to markets, as well as their movement between villages and from towns to the countryside."* As expected, the situation did not change much between early 2010 and mid-2010, and it has serious implications for the well-being of the population, as summarized by the following comment from a rural woman: *"There are times when patients die at home or on the way to the hospital. The public school is far away. Our children walk 5 km before they reach it. Younger cannot walk that distance. That is why we enroll them in school when they are 7 or 8 years old."*

Income and Consumption

For most participants, income sources remain unstable. Most respondents did not have a salaried job and therefore did not benefit from a steady flow of revenues. Participants who work in the informal sector (retail merchants, market gardeners, artisans, and miners) earn a livelihood from the daily activities they undertake, and their earnings go directly toward daily consumption during the rainy season when food is in short supply. The participants noted that they could not think in terms of profit or daily income, but rather in terms of *"infrequent and uncertain scraps received"* to meet their basic needs, which is why it is difficult for them to keep a record and provide an account of their earnings at the end of a given season. When asked, a common response would usually be along the lines of, *"We cannot tell you how much we earn on a daily or monthly basis. We live on a day-to-day basis. Gone are the days when we would speak of profit at the end of the coffee or groundnut seasons."*

Farmers sometimes manage to secure temporary jobs with their neighbors or landowners. A day's pay varies from one employer to the next, but the average seems to be around CFAF 1,000, the equivalent to about $2. Most participants did not benefit from external sources of funds such as remittances. Indeed, only a few participants indicated that they receive assistance from friends or relatives living in other African countries or countries belonging to the Organisation for Economic Co-operation and Development (OECD). This assistance is often provided for a specific purpose, and the funds are transferred once a year at the request of the recipients to address specific issues, such as school fees or the purchase of a parcel of arable land.

For those employed in the formal or semi-formal sector (forestry and telecommunications companies, agribusinesses, state-owned enterprises), the main source of income is their wages, but participants at all levels indicated that their incomes had shrunk as a result of job losses (technical unemployment) or the slashing of their incomes (as was the case of employees of the telephone company SOCATEL, which is struggling with ongoing strikes that have spawned a crisis with no end in sight as of mid-2010). As a result, workers turned to other, mostly informal activities such as running a small business, farming, or livestock production *"to keep their households afloat."*

In addition to income instability, most participants have a low or very low income that does not allow them to build up savings or face family obligations. To cope with this constraint, many—with the exception of widows—have a secondary income-generating activity on a small scale, such as agriculture, pig breeding, selling pharmaceuticals, or running a small restaurant.

In such a context, households seek to meet minimum calorie requirements by attending to the quantity of food with little regard to its quality. The focus is on meals of lesser cost, notably manioc and leaves: *"Before the crisis we had enough to eat, but today it is difficult to eat properly. In fact, the quality of food consumed is not good; we eat the same food every day."* Reported vegetable consumption (as opposed to meat) increased significantly in June–August 2010, as compared to the level observed in early 2010 during the first round of the FGDs. As one participant explained: *"The milk and the bread are suspended and are replaced by the prepared bean with oil of palm* (gbari) *for its consistency that can allow going beyond 12 pm."* Another participant said, *"The breakfast is divided by everyone, the lunch (the remainders of the meal of the day before) is offered only to the children. The dinner constitutes the big meal that is shared by the whole family at 4 pm."*

For a poor family of seven persons, daily food expenditures in January 2010 might have amounted to only CFAF 1,000 for manioc/cassava powder, leaf, palm oil, salt, and wood or charcoal for cooking. This amount is equivalent to CFAF 143 ($0.30) of daily expenditure per person. According to participants, in some locations, price increases over a six-month period pushed up the minimum amount required by a household to purchase the same goods to CFAF 1,200 or by 20 percent (recorded inflation was much lower at the national level in 2010, but it reached close to 10 percent in 2009 and was driven by prices of basic foods and other necessities). Consequently, many households were forced to reduce further their food consumption to dangerously low levels. In 2007, according to a United Nations Development Programme (UNDP) study, 43 percent of the population in the Central African Republic was unable to satisfy its essential needs. The same study estimated that 60 percent of the rural population was not able to meet its basic food needs (2,400 kilocalories per day and equivalent adult). The situation was likely to have deteriorated further by the summer of 2010. Most households got by with a breakfast and a dinner in the evening, with only young children having one or two more meals depending on the ability of parents to pay for it.

Household Responses

According to the majority of participants, those most affected by shocks are usually women and children and sometimes the elderly. In case of death or loss of employment by the head of the household, women and children are likely to be especially affected. Two effects are at play: the direct impact of the loss of income and a reallocation in time use. A loss of income may lead to inadequate nutrition, which in turn may affect the normal development of children. As for women, a loss of income for the husband often implies an increase in time worked apart from the domestic chores that still need to be performed. Moreover, the income from the women's labor often does not compensate for the loss of income incurred by their husbands.

The traditional division of labor in the household remains the same, especially in rural areas. The man is responsible for field work deemed difficult, and the woman is entrusted with weeding and harvesting duties. Children under the age of 12 are responsible for collecting water and watching over the younger ones. Elderly persons who lack the physical ability to travel to the plantations located over five kilometers away take care of the household farm crops, which are grown using a crop rotation system and are for household consumption only. During the harvest, the woman travels to the city two or three times a week to sell the produce from the fields (sweet potatoes, bananas, oranges, and cassava leaves and roots), and she uses the earnings to purchase salt, oil, and soap. But at times of crisis, the burden borne by the woman often increases with the need to get any income possible. Female participants from the MBAYE VERT Association noted: "*Those who live in the outlying areas (20–25 kilometers) travel the distance on foot, carrying heavy loads on their heads. They leave home at 4:30 a.m. and arrive at the city market at 7 a.m. or 8 a.m. After they have sold their produce, they take the same route for the return trip home. Others travel to the city in a* taxi-brousse *(bush taxi) in extremely appalling conditions. We have no choice but to get into these caskets on wheels. We always ask God to protect us.*" In nearly all FGDs, participants believed that women worked much longer hours than men; men reportedly worked 8–12 hours a day, and women worked 16–18 hours.

In times of crisis, households are forced to reduce their expenditures (trading quantity for quality in terms of food, removing children from school, cutting nonessential expenses) while trying to diversify and expand their sources of income. Many rejoin agricultural activities (especially former workers in mining and forestry companies who migrated to the capital), try to go into small informal businesses, agriculture and livestock production, or temporary work. Most individuals increase the time spent working, even though the low-productivity activities do not generate significant income. As a market gardener put it: "We *take temporary jobs from our friends or other individuals. We also increase our working time in the garden. Instead of 12 hours daily, we work 14 hours or 15 hours.*"

For women, the necessity to work additional hours implies less time to care for their children, which also may have negative long-term effects. Mothers in urban areas may have to conduct informal trade at markets for hours, leaving young children in the care of older siblings or elderly members of the households. Parents in rural areas who must go to fields or small workshops also leave their children for hours with older siblings or the elders, with the children being fed only wild fruits and grains of palms until the parents return. As a result, in both urban and rural areas, children may be victims of diseases such as *marasme* (mild retardation) or kwashiorkor (severe protein malnutrition), or may even die at an early age. These conditions can be exacerbated by a crisis, and they tend to worsen in summer, when they await "*the new harvests that unfortunately will not be abundant owing to the drought.*" The need for men to find work may also take them far away from the household for substantial periods of time, as is the case when they migrate temporarily to work on mining sites. Sometimes, spouses come back after six or seven months without any resources due to the crisis.

According to the FGDs held in early 2010, most households were trying to keep children at school, but doing so proved difficult, and a few reported removing their children from school because of the financial burden. The fees per child in the public school were at least CFAF 1.25 per month in early 2010 according to participants. By mid-2010 a change in schooling strategy by households seemed to have taken place, as accessing school was difficult (because of distances in rural areas, the low quality of public schools, and cost of private schools in urban areas) and returns on education were low given the state of the labor market. Many parents who were trying to keep their children in school in early 2010 seemed to have decided to use them for work on small farms to try to generate additional family income. As a result, a number of parents indicated that their children had left school, which may lead to the reproduction of poverty over time. A child from a poor family who is unable to attend school is likely to simply accompany his father or mother to the fields or the workshop and have no prospects of pursuing occupations different from those undertaken by his parents.

Access to credit could soften the impact of a crisis, but participants who represented many different trades indicated that the ability to borrow remained problematic throughout 2010. Access to credit depends narrowly on the availability of savings and having a bank account. As many activities that could be undertaken through access to credit would still "*not give them any consequent income, no bank structure can grant them confidence.*" In rural areas, where building savings is even more difficult (owing to the disappearance of cash crops such as coffee, cotton, and tobacco, the sole sources of annual steady incomes), access to credit is simply considered "*a luxury*" for poor farmers.

Community Responses

In times of difficulty or emergency, the majority of participants claim that they rely primarily on themselves because help from others is no longer as readily available as before the crisis. A forestry worker explained: "*When I was working and things were going well, relatives would visit me all the time, especially at the end of the month. I would give them gifts and money for their wives. Today, there is no one at my side. I struggle to survive. My children cannot go to school. The eldest don't have guardians in the town with whom they can stay. So they cope as best they can at the homes of friends.*" Statements such as: "*I rely on myself,*" "*I sell my belongings to deal with the problems,*" or even, "*I borrow at exorbitant interest rates*" and, "*In times of crisis, who can help you? You have to depend on yourself,*" recur throughout. These sentiments attest to the social impact of the crisis and, more generally, of the risk of a gradual decay of the traditional African support networks, the prized feature of the large family.

More than 85 percent of respondents who experienced an emergency or difficulties during the previous six months stated that they did not receive assistance and had to rely solely on their own efforts to cope—a higher proportion than observed in the quantitative survey. Some occasionally receive support from relatives, friends, or members of their faith community in the form of small sums collected from parishioners and donations in-kind after a spell of misfortune or sickness. Informal support structures do exist, but their activities fall far short of the needs to be met. Cases of poor management of community activities and misappropriation of public goods are also rampant, which impedes the formation of production and support associations in the villages surveyed. Formal aid networks exist in some areas, but they are often not functional because they lack resources. Overall, very few formal or informal aid networks are available to help disadvantaged population groups in times of crisis. The best known are religious groups and family associations, whose help takes the form of quarterly or monthly financial contributions (ranging from CFAF 200 to CFAF 500) available to members on a rotating basis. But again this assistance docs not mcct the magnitude of needs.

To survive when all else fails, the only alternative for most households is to turn to religious communities not only for material support, but also to transcend their difficulties and *"forget their concerns by moral consolations from others, as well as have the possibility to find a material solution through prayers."* Lack of other support institutions could partially explain a greater dependence on faith-based organizations in the Central African Republic than in other countries surveyed in this book. Religious communities often provided support and assistance to their members in case of a disaster or important life events (childbirth, death of a family member, or illness), and reliance on faith-based organizations reportedly increased as economic conditions worsened. Assistance was never guaranteed, however. As noted by a participant: *"I am deaconess (adviser) in my church. It has been two months that my two children were admitted to the hospital. I spent nights and days at their bedsides, but neither my pastor nor my sisters and brothers in Christ visited me."*

Most professional organizations, such as the Miners and Forestry Corporation, remain embryonic, but participants nevertheless express their desire to organize themselves in groups. To alleviate formal credit constraints, communities organize *tontines,* which are rotating savings and credit groups that allow members to benefit from small loans (CFAF 200–500) or establish mutual assistance facilities for production works (agricultural, artisanal). *Tontines* tend to be more prevalent in urban areas, while in rural areas, support systems are manifested more through moral support (through one's presence or visits) and especially through mutual assistance when engaged in farm work.

Conclusion

The aim of this chapter was to provide an assessment of at least some of the impacts of the food, fuel, and financial crisis on household well-being in the Central African Republic, as well as to discuss the strategies that households have used to cope with the shocks brought about by the crisis. We have relied on both quantitative and qualitative data for the analysis. The results of the analysis of the household survey are nationally representative, but the qualitative work was intentionally focused on groups of households that were more likely to be affected by the crisis. The work on the household survey is based on data for 2008, and the qualitative work was implemented two years later, in 2010. It should therefore not be too surprising that at least some of the conclusions of the analysis would differ depending on the type of data used, although there are also areas of convergence.

Three main conclusions can be drawn from the quantitative analysis. First, under the assumptions of the simulations, the impact of the increase in food and fuel prices is likely to have had only a limited impact on most households, essentially because much of the Central African Republic's population does not consume large amounts of the commodities whose prices increased substantially in world markets over 2008–10. On the other hand, the data show that many households tend to be affected by other types of shocks. Finally, the mechanisms of solidarity on which households can rely to cope with various shocks appear to be fairly limited. Family and friends provide some help, especially in cases of death or serious illness, and faith-based organizations are also active, but external support to cope with most of the shocks affecting households remains severely limited.

The qualitative work suggests a somewhat different picture regarding the impact of the crisis, with participants in the FGDs suggesting that the crisis has a strong negative impact on them. What might be the sources of such differences between the findings from the quantitative and qualitative work? First, it seems that some of the hardships revealed in the focus groups and household interviews tend to be related to the chronic poverty of some households rather than the crisis per se. Second, the FGDs intentionally were carried out among groups that were most likely to be affected by the crisis, and it was to be expected that we would find more evidence of impacts in the qualitative work than in the quantitative work. Third, it could be that in a country as poor as the Central African Republic, changes in poverty that may appear small when observed through quantitative survey-based measures actually may have a significant negative impact on households because the sacrifices that households must make to cope with a crisis cut further into livelihoods that are already very precarious. Said differently, when one is already living in survival mode, a crisis cuts to the bone. This would suggest that in environments characterized by deep and chronic poverty, beyond quantitative methods of evaluation, it is also important to conduct qualitative work to reflect more in-depth on the hardships endured by population.

At the same time, in terms of partition into categories of households, the FGDs suggest that some of the people who were already very poor before the crisis (including widows, rural women, and farmers) were perhaps less affected by the crisis because they tended to be less connected through their income sources or consumption patterns to world markets. By contrast, a second group, which includes public sector and export-oriented workers, artisans, and traders, seemed to have been affected more severely. Nevertheless, both groups felt that their situation was deteriorating over time. Independent of the economic crises, the lack of rain contributed to the deterioration: weak harvests and the scarcity of edible products that can normally be obtained freely (caterpillars, mushrooms, winged termites, and the like). When combined with increases in food prices, the weather, according to the FGDs, made food consumption, typically already based on the cheapest products available, more problematic over time in quality and nutritional value, which led to increased health risks, especially for children and the elderly.

Finally, the FGDs confirmed the results of the quantitative analysis of the weakness of solidarity mechanisms on which households can rely. In addition, most households do not have access to credit; although informal *tontines* exist, they can provide only small amounts of cash to those who need help. Local communities, and especially churches and faith-based organizations, try to provide informal safety nets of last resort, but even this aid is limited in scope. Even if it may be correct that the impact of the crisis on the population as a whole—especially the increase in food and fuel prices—may have been quantitatively less profound than in some other countries, the fact that much of the population was already extremely poor and that households cannot count on strong informal safety nets suggest that for those who have been affected, the negative impact of the crisis on their well-being was significant.

Notes

The paper was prepared with support from the Trust Fund for Environmentally and Socially Sustainable Development housed at the World Bank and funded by the governments of Norway and Finland. Comments on the paper from Rasmus Heltberg are gratefully acknowledged. The opinions and analysis presented in the paper are those of the authors only and need not reflect those of the World Bank, its executive directors, or the countries they represent. Assistance for qualitative data collection in the field by Josias Tebero, Dimanche Nabena, and Paul Bonder is gratefully acknowledged.

1. As noted in World Bank (2011), since the end of conflict in 2003, economic growth has remained at an average of 2.5 percent per annum. In addition to a still precarious security situation, low public investment in physical and social infrastructure and an unfriendly business climate remain major impediments to sustained growth. In addition to the economic crisis, the breakdown of the major hydropower plant led to a reduction in real GDP by 1.5 percentage points in 2008 as compared to the period 2006–08. Estimates suggest a recovery in 2010 with real GDP growth of 3.3 percent, but this is not sufficiently high to make a significant dent in the levels of poverty.
2. On the crisis in the Central African Republic, see Charny and Woodfork (2007), IMF (2010), Jauer (2009), Keller (2010), and Mercy Corps (2010).

References

Backiny-Yetna, P., and Q. Wodon. 2011. "Profil et corrélats de la pauvreté en République Centrafricaine en 2008." *Perspective Afrique 5* (1–3): article 7.

Charny, J., and J. C. Woodfork. 2007. *The Central African Republic: Worsening Crisis in a Troubled Region.* Washington, DC: United State Institute of Peace.

IMF. 2010. *Central African Republic: Sixth Review Under the Arrangement Under the Extended Credit Facility and Financing Assurances Review,* Staff Report No. 10/332, International Monetary Fund, Washington, DC.

Jauer, K. 2009. *Economic Crisis Hits Central African Republic.* Bangui: Humanitarian and Development Partnership Team.

Keller, W. 2010. *Central African Republic's Reforms Enter Crucial Phase.* African Department, IMF Survey, Washington, DC.

Mercy Corps. 2010. *Coping with the Economic Crisis.* Bangui: Mercy Corps.

Tebero, J., N. Dimanche, and P. Bonder. 2010a. *Rapid Assessment of the Impact of the Economic Crisis on Poor Households in Central Africa Republic.* Round 1, February. Bangui.

———. 2010b. *Rapid Assessment of the Impact of the Economic Crisis on Poor Households in Central Africa Republic.* Round 2, September. Bangui.

UNDP (United Nations Development Programme). 2010. *World Development Indicators 2010.*

Wodon, Q., C. Tsimpo, P. Backiny-Yetna, G. Joseph, F. Adoho, and H. Coulombe. 2008. "Potential Impact of Higher Food Prices on Poverty: Summary Estimates for a Dozen West and Central African Countries." Policy Research Working Paper 4745. World Bank, Washington, DC.

World Bank. 2010. *World Development Indicators*. Washington, DC: World Bank.

———. 2011. "Country Partnership Strategy Progress Report for the Central African Republic." Report 59874-CF, World Bank, Washington, DC.

CHAPTER 5

Risk and Resilience: Summary of Rapid Qualitative Assessments of Social Impacts of the Economic Crisis in Kazakhstan

Sandra Schlossar, with Carolyn Turk

Kazakhstan enjoyed high economic performance and rising living standards during most of the 2000s, but the global financial crisis struck a heavy blow to the republic in 2008 and 2009. Between June and September 2010, almost 50 percent of all focus groups' participants in all regions indicated that they had observed negative impacts on individual, household, or public well-being as a result of the crisis. In response to price shocks and anticipated labor market impacts, the government introduced a crisis response package, the Road Map program.[1] In 2010, the SANGE Research Center, in collaboration with the World Bank, carried out a sequence of two qualitative studies to assess the consequences of economic contraction for vulnerable people in Kazakhstan, to explore the range of coping strategies deployed to mitigate the impacts of the crisis, and to document perceptions of poor and vulnerable groups regarding the effectiveness of the government response.

This chapter presents the results of these rapid qualitative assessments. The chapter starts with a brief portrayal of the economic impacts of the financial crisis on Kazakhstan and describes the main elements of the government's support package: the Road Map program, introduced to assist the people who lost their jobs due to the crisis. This program was not the only government-funded support scheme available in Kazakhstan. The population traditionally has access to old-age and disability pensions, targeted social assistance transfers for low-income people, child allowances, free schooling, and subsidized health care. Most of these support schemes have existed for decades, and their outreach and effectiveness are not the subject of this research. The study focuses on the analysis of the activities of the first phase of the Road Map program's "Employment and Retraining Strategy" (employment strategy), which was designed as a temporary intervention to mitigate the impact of the global economic crisis.[2] The second and third sections elaborate on the study setting and its findings regarding crisis impacts on vulnerable people. We then continue in the fourth section to analyze people's coping strategies, and in the fifth section to elaborate on the government's short-term crisis response measures under the employment strategy. The conclusion offers some views on policy.

Summarizing the main findings, participants of the two assessment rounds in Kazakhstan reported that the impacts of the crisis resulted in significant hardships in the form of unemployment, food insecurity, and a decrease of social and psychological well-being. The crisis was regarded as having intensified existing problems that were traced to labor market impacts, including job loss, reduction in working hours, and price shocks, as the costs of food, education, and communal services increased significantly. Respondents reported a multitude of strategies for coping with the crisis: eating less or cheaper food, borrowing money, or growing food to eat and sell. The most common strategy was to cut consumption and seek help through social networks. Kazakhstan's government attempted to mitigate adverse crisis impacts by starting the Road Map program as a temporary measure to support especially those who lost their jobs due to the crisis and had no further means to support themselves. Through the activities of the Road Map program's employment strategy, many unemployed people received short-term employment and training-based support resulting in temporary relief. The government's response addressed well the population's most important concerns during the financial crisis. Nevertheless, research respondents mentioned some shortcomings of the employment strategy, which included difficulties in accessing the activities, corruption, lack of transparency in program implementation, and the insufficient outreach and scale of benefits. It is worth noting that both the coverage and the generosity of benefits were much higher in Kazakhstan than in other country case studies presented in this book. Criticism of the government support programs could be partially explained by people's higher expectations of the government. Kazakhstan's population still has memories of free public services, job security, long-term employment guaranteed by the state, and the relatively generous pensions and social assistance programs that existed during the Soviet regime.

Economic Impacts and Government Response

Between 2000 and 2007, the economy of Kazakhstan achieved very rapid growth, generated largely by the combination of high natural resource prices and the implementation of the government's strong market reform agenda. In this period, the country was one of the fastest growing economies in the world, averaging annual gross domestic product (GDP) growth rates of 10 percent. Average real incomes more than doubled along with GDP, transforming Kazakhstan into an upper-middle-income country. Poverty reduced dramatically, with the estimated share of the population living below the official poverty line declining from 46 percent in 2001 to 12 percent by 2008. Disparities remain, however, with growth and value-added concentrated in resource-rich regions and larger cities. Although the poverty headcount has declined to under 10 percent in urban areas, it has remained higher than 20 percent in rural areas. Certain rural areas, particularly in the south, remain disadvantaged (Bertelsmann Stiftung 2010).

Starting in 2008, the global financial crisis and associated sharp decline in commodity prices had a severe impact on macroeconomic performance. Monthly export revenues fell from $3–5 billion in the first 11 months of 2008 to less than $1.5 billion at the beginning of 2009, when the financial crisis deepened, the economy dived into recession, and the currency depreciated (World Bank 2011a). Together with a weak capital account, these events placed the tenge (T), the national currency, under significant pressure. Kazakhstani banks lost virtually all access to rollover opportunities on world financial markets. Lower commodity prices had an immediate and highly negative impact on investment and on the overall economic outlook. A 20 percent devaluation of the tenge followed in the first quarter of 2010 (World Bank 2011a). The Kazakhstan government tapped into its fiscal reserve national fund to finance an anticrisis stimulus package of $10 billion. A large share of this package ($3.2 billion) was devoted to the recapitalization of the four largest commercial banks. The remaining funds financed economic stimulus programs for construction, agriculture, real estate, small business, and infrastructure projects.

The contraction in demand for labor was the main transmission channel of the crisis to households across the Central Asia region as firms laid off workers, halted hiring, and reduced their wage outlay (World Bank 2011b). Official statistics suggest that Kazakhstan did not witness a major increase in unemployment as did some of the neighboring countries. Given the deepening of the economic crisis and the slow-down of economic activities, the government had predicted that 350,000 would join the ranks of the unemployed during 2009.[3] Official data suggest, however, that unemployment rates held steady at 6.6 percent in 2009 and decreased slightly in 2010 to 5.8 percent.[4]

In spring 2009, the government introduced a number of short-term measures as a response to the negative social consequences of the financial crisis, all of them implemented through the national Road Map program.[5] The government allocated T 191.50 billion in 2009 and T 151.20 billion in 2010 (altogether the equivalent of $2.35 billion) to the implementation of this program. The program had two objectives: (1) the maintenance of employment and prevention of significant further growth in unemployment, and (2) the creation of conditions for sustainable postcrisis development. To achieve these specified objectives, the government concentrated its efforts on three programs: the Employment and Retraining Strategy (employment strategy), the Agro-Industry Program, and the Industry and Infrastructure Projects Implementation.[6] The present study concentrates on the employment strategy, which was implemented between 2009 and 2010 and involved special budgetary transfers to local authorities. Its activities were subdivided into four components: investment projects, social jobs, youth internships, and vocational training. A large portion of the Road Map program's funding was spent for the investment projects to reduce crisis-related unemployment; the government expected that jobs will come back once the economic conditions normalize. The other components were considerably smaller and focused especially on the poorest and marginalized. The third section of this chapter elaborates further on the details of these four components as activities of the Road Map's employment strategy.

The Study Setting

Between June and September 2010, the SANGE research team conducted two rounds of qualitative focus group discussions (FGDs) and semistructured interviews with approximately 250 vulnerable people in urban and rural areas of Akmola, Almaty, East Kazakhstan, Kyzylorda, and West Kazakhstan oblasts. Focus group participants were selected to capture groups that were expected to be particularly vulnerable to the impacts of the crisis.

Participants included poor and very poor people and unemployed persons registered at the national Employment Department. Focus groups also included individuals who were eligible to benefit from or were specifically targeted by the employment strategy's activities of the Road Map program; they were mostly low-income people. Targeted beneficiaries included youth, families with many children, people with disability, *oralmans* (ethnic Kazakh immigrants coming primarily from China, Mongolia, and Central Asian states), public workers, people close to retirement age, and rural women. Interviews, as opposed to focus groups, were directed mainly at gathering the views of more than 20 public and nongovernmental organization (NGO) employees. The design of this study was different from most other case studies presented in this book in that it did not include workers of export-oriented enterprises and other occupational groups that were relatively well-off before the crisis. In Kazakhstan, the study focused mostly on people who had low or unstable incomes even before the global economic recession. Therefore, research findings may overestimate the impacts of the crisis relevant to the whole population.

Sixty percent of the first-round participants took also part in the second round, and 62 percent of participants of the second round participated in activities of the Road Map program's employment strategy.

The Financial Crisis and Its Impacts on Vulnerable People

Focus group participants sometimes emphasized the difficulty in isolating the impacts of the crisis from preexisting hardships. As a farmer from Kyzylorda oblast said, "*Life is a permanent crisis.*" Respondents across all five regions prioritized five core hardships and problems, which people described as a regular feature of their lives, crisis or no crisis. Several of these troubles intensified as a result of the crisis.

• The increase in public utility tariffs, introduced ahead of the onset of the crisis, was described as the most important precrisis problem for poor families, families with children, and pensioners. It represented a shock at the time of introduction and was still described as "very important" in terms of generating hardship after the crisis—from all groups of respondents, including wealthier people.

- The lack of public kindergartens, which forced mothers to stay at home with their children and reduced the family income, was "important" for families with children and single mothers before the crisis. It was perceived as aggravated and as a high priority problem by the same group of people after the crisis, limiting the possibility of adding family members to the workforce as primary sources of income declined.

- The lack of one's own housing and unaffordable prices for purchasing flats or houses was categorized as "important" by respondents living in cities—both before and after the crisis.

- The rising cost and decreased quality of medicines and health care services and the decreased accessibility of medical services in rural areas were perceived as "important" before the crisis by all groups of respondents. It became "very important" after the crisis, as health care consumption became more constrained.

- The prohibitively high costs of quality higher education following an increase in university tuition fees shifted in importance as poor families with children older than 15 years mentioned it as "not very important" before the crisis; however, they and unemployed young respondents rated it as "very important" after the crisis.

Half of all respondents in all five target regions confirmed that these preexisting problems worsened as a result of the crisis and that it had become even harder to make ends meet in the postcrisis circumstances. In the words of many respondents, the crisis intensified existing problems to such an extent that they no longer knew how to cover the higher education of their children, how to feed the family, or where to find a job. Families and young respondents in every region where the research was conducted believed that children's lives had deteriorated due to the constrained material conditions of families, and they described the impacts on children's physical and mental conditions. In an FGD in Almaty oblast, one participant mentioned, *"They* [children] *study all day long without having eaten anything since there is not enough money. Sometimes there is even no money to buy notebooks."* These circumstances caused stress and discomfort for parents as they became unable to provide a decent standard of living for their children.

These severe problems, which respondents—particularly poor people—experienced in their postcrisis everyday lives in Kazakhstan, were traced to two main transmission channels: labor market shocks and price shocks.

Labor Market Shocks

The labor market shocks reported by respondents included job loss, a reduction in working hours, and the consequent lack of income. Initially, employed respondents, elderly and rural people, and young graduates in the five target regions reported negative impacts in the labor market as "very severe." The closure of enterprises and consequent job cuts led to increases in unemployment among vulnerable segments of the labor force. A 54-year-old mother from a rural area told the research team, *"In 2008, both my 55-year-old husband and I were laid off. Our income went down dramatically, and we were left without any means for survival."* During one FGD with young people from the East Kazakhstan oblast, participants explained the sudden nature of the layoffs. *"The employer will just say, 'Sorry, we're having job cuts' and will lay him or her off."*

Unemployment was associated with an abrupt fall in household income. Focus group discussions suggested that workers in the construction and export-oriented industries were particularly hard hit. Participants were asked to identify groups that might have been most affected by the reduction in demand for labor. Young people, those close to retirement age, unskilled workers, construction workers, petty traders, migrant workers, and people—living in rural areas—particularly the youth were described as particularly vulnerable. Older workers also felt disadvantaged; more than 50 percent of respondents close to retirement age said they were depressed or anxious because they felt their age was hurting their chances of finding more work.

Those respondents who were still employed described deterioration in workplace conditions, including a reduction in wages (often for the same amount of work) and the loss of benefits. People also reported late payments of wages and, in some instances, nonpayment. *"They cheat at work and do not pay wages"* was expressed in nearly every FGD.

Price Shocks

Respondents explained that the impacts of labor market shocks were accentuated by price shocks, which they classified as "severe." The unemployed, families with children, and rural residents reported that prices for food, clothes, livestock fodder and hay, medical products, private medical services, professional education costs, and communal services had all increased. Participating families with children and young people rated the increase of professional education costs as "very severe." One construction worker in Almaty oblast noted the erosion of purchasing power in the households. *"Earnings do not increase, but the prices for products keep steadily growing."*

The impact of these price rises was particularly severe in households that had also seen a reduction in earnings as a result of the labor market shocks. The lack of income—whether its absence or insufficiency—compounded the price shocks as very often the money earned was not enough.

Whether shocks resulted from labor market changes, adverse price movements, or a combination, participants emphasized the consequences for social and psychological well-being. Women, the young, and unemployed respondents reported that pressure conveyed in the messages from mass media and other information sources played a "severe" part in contributing to their depression, anxiety, unrest, and uncertainty about their future. The barrage of negative information about the approaching crisis and its impacts generated anxiety and panic even among those without objective reasons to worry. The same group of respondents (women, young, and unemployed) explained that the permanent lack of money was complicating relations within families and was causing depression, stress, illness, and alcoholism. Sometimes, these strained relations within the family had led to divorce. Young participants in particular confessed that they were losing their self-confidence and were feeling marginalized and useless in society as they could not work.

Impacts on Men and Women

The research included specific questions related to gender differences in the impacts of the crisis. Although focus groups reported the vulnerabilities of specific subgroups, such as single mothers with young children, at a more general level they reported that there was no obvious difference with respect to the impacts of the crisis on women and men. As one of the participants mentioned: *"The crisis is relentless to all of us."* An exception to this general statement emerged as participants discussed the impacts of and responses to job loss.

Men are considered to be breadwinners of the family, and it is their income that defines the family's economic status. As a result, men are psychologically more vulnerable to job loss. The loss of self-esteem, the blow to their social status, and an increased dependency on their wives' incomes had, in some instances, led to alcoholism and depression among men.

Participants explained that men are concerned about their social status, and women are concerned about the well-being of their family and children. Women are seen as being more flexible and quick to adjust to new conditions, being ready to do any kind of work to feed their children. They are perceived as more willing to change their professional specialization and sector of employment and to look for jobs proactively. This flexibility in adjusting job expectations to changed economic circumstances was seen as a positive element of women's responses to the crisis, allowing them greater resilience to labor market shocks.

Respondents across the 30 FGDs explained that single mothers and families with preschool-aged or school-aged children had been struggling since the crisis because women who needed to work could not do so due to the lack of places in kindergartens. The lack of kindergarten places forces women to take care of the children at home, makes it hard for them to find a stable and well-paid job, and increases their financial hardships. One participant in a focus group in the West Kazakhstan oblast explained, "*We are on the waiting list for placement in a kindergarten while my child is ready to go to the preparatory grade in school. And we are still on the waiting list!*"

Coping Strategies

Respondents reported a multitude of strategies for coping with the crisis, ranging from eating less or cheaper food, to borrowing money, or growing food to sell. Their coping strategies can be broken down by the frequency of responses and the perceived usefulness of responses.

The primary coping strategy of employed and unemployed respondents, rural residents, families, and migrants across regions was to reduce their expenses; they simply do not have enough money for the consumption of goods (food and clothing). Participants reported buying less food or purchasing food in smaller, cheaper supermarkets, often reducing both quantity and quality of food consumption or buying products on credit. Participants also cut out nonessential expenses, such as new clothes or any luxury goods, and defaulted on payments of public utility fees. During an FGD in urban East Kazakhstan oblast, a participant described the shift in focus to essential items: "*I witness how it is difficult for my mother even if she never tells us that we do not have any money. Still she tries to feed us and she never buys anything for her own use."* And in Almaty oblast, a participant described how they economize on children's clothing: *"There is never enough money. We buy cheap shoes, yet they can wear out very soon. It affects children's health."* In addition, unemployed and rural respondents and families across regions reported that they stopped using modern communication technology, such as mobile phones and the Internet, and abandoned entertainment and recreational activities as household budgets became more constrained. Poorer households also economized by defaulting on loans and restricting unofficial payments. The latter was seen to have second-round effects as these unofficial payments are often necessary to receive fiercely competitive kindergarten places and new jobs.

Participants reported nonpayment of utility bills and education expenses. As utility expenses increased, poor people often had no option but to delay or default on the payment of their bills. Respondents mentioned that they and their neighbors save electricity, live in unheated houses, or use water from open wells, rivers, and lakes. But if electricity bills are not paid, the electricity is cut off, and some people said that they started illegally connecting to other electricity sources. This response raises the prospect of even greater hardship in the future and entails severe risks of getting into trouble with the authorities. Some senior citizens in Kyzyl Orda oblast described the situation in their neighborhood: *"Many people are being disconnected from the electricity sources due to unpaid bills and their inability to pay fines. . . . People that do not have much money are freezing during the winter period in their cold houses since they are saving coal."*

Some students and young people were required to contribute to the family income or earn their own income. The lack of money forced some students to transfer to home study to be able to work part time. In extreme cases, they had to leave high schools and universities and start working. Parents mentioned that their older children (above 15) were working in bazaars as loaders, cart keepers, or packers or were working to support other members of the family and performing household chores. Respondents were aware that this coping mechanism would have severe consequences for the level of education of poor people and would perpetuate poverty in the future.

Participants described the importance of an active life philosophy in coping with the impacts of the crisis. These participants demonstrated a positive attitude to handling economic problems by engaging in actions such as proactively searching for a new job, selling small services to the neighbors, growing vegetables and fruit, raising cattle, changing specializations to have better chances in the labor market, and trying to find jobs in other cities. Such responses were heard frequently and ranked as most effective in determining a household's capacity to weather hard economic times. As one unemployed worker in East Kazakhstan oblast stated, *"The crisis made people think, taught them to earn money, not to sit at home and wait for help. It is a lesson for people, an impulse for action."*

People with their own land either started or intensified their gardening and cultivation of domestic plots, and the numbers of people who grow vegetables and fruit, raise cattle, and sell agricultural products for cash had increased significantly, claimed respondents from rural areas. During an FGD in West Kazakhstan a participant mentioned: *"People in our village cultivate domestic plots, grow vegetables and fruits and sell goods in the markets in order to support themselves. We eat less meat and sell more in order to gain even a little profit."* Increased cultivation of land provided additional income and ensured their survival, but, participants explained, came at the cost of reducing the time available to seek paid work.

Some FGD participants who took a loan before the crisis were struggling with repayments due to loss of jobs. They reported selling cattle, houses, and cars or making major consumption cuts to repay the loans. Some people migrated to get away from credit agents. Others reported pawning assets or taking high interest rate loans from private lenders to repay bank loans and avoid the default on the mortgage and loss of property to banks. One villager in the East Kazakhstan oblast described his experience with small consumer credits: *"Our family's salary is not enough—even for food. All the money earned is spent for settling debts in the shops, because we mainly buy products on credit."*

Many of the FGD participants benefited from government support programs—child allowances, old age and disability pensions, housing allowances, and targeted social assistance (TSA) transfers, provided to low-income people and the registered unemployed. All of these programs existed before the onset of the global economic crisis; in fact, similar programs were in place during Soviet times, so interviewees did not view them as something special. Evaluation of the effectiveness of these programs is not the subject of this study, but the general impression from the FGDs was that these programs made a positive difference for their recipients and helped them meet the most basic needs. The amount of benefits provided and the coverage of some programs (for example, TSA) were, however, no longer adequate, forcing many respondents to seek assistance from informal sources. In addition, many of the FGD participants had memories of a much more generous social protection system that existed during Soviet times and were not particularly appreciative of the existing social assistance programs.

Most unemployed respondents reported that they had been forced to seek help through social networks—from relatives, friends, or neighbors—to cope with the intensified hardships of the crisis. Even if there was a programmatic response of the Kazakh government to alleviate negative effects of the financial crisis, it did not diminish the role of the community and these social networks. Borrowing money for consumption needs or asking for help from their relatives—especially in finding a job through informal networks—were widespread mechanisms. In contrast to past years, people stopped hoping for support from local government and the state. Poor people stated that they believe in depending and relying only on themselves, their relatives, and acquaintances. This attitude is shaped by the mentality of Kazakh people, among whom kinship ties are vital. If a person is put in a difficult situation, he asks his relatives for help. It was even said once during the FGDs that a *"poor person is the one who does not have any relatives."* The researchers reported that according to poor people, *"It is easier to find jobs using connections and contacts; it is easier to receive material support from one's relatives."*

Most participants suggested that the crisis actually deepened kinship ties and strengthened social networks and community cohesion as they often had to rely on support of their relatives. In the FGDs, immigrants especially bewailed not having any family ties in Kazakhstan. This augmented the adverse impact of the crisis for them, as one foreign-born Kazakh mentioned during an FGD in a village in Almaty oblast: *"We came from abroad. There is no work, no support and no relatives. Local people can feed themselves even if there is no job opportunity, because they have friends and relatives. As for us, foreign-born Kazakhs, we are exposed to crisis."* One focus group participant in Kyzyz-Ordinskaya region said: *"The problem of unemployment is especially harsh for those people, who do not have contacts or support from their relatives."*

The Employment and Retraining Strategy of the National Road Map Program

The government's programmatic response was aimed at mitigation of the negative impacts of the economic crisis and was introduced in spring 2009. We refer to this collection of activities as the Road Map program. The study gathered feedback on the first phase of the program's Employment and Retraining Strategy (employment strategy), which lasted from 2009 to 2010. This phase specifically aimed at transferring resources from the national budget to local authorities with the objective of temporarily alleviating the impacts of the crisis-related increased unemployment. With an allocation from the national budget of T 200 billion ($1.4 billion), the strategy had four main components that were coordinated and monitored by a specially created interagency commission. The research included participants in all of the following four components.

1. *Investment projects.* Local municipalities, which were selected based on the requirements and peculiarities of each region, were funded to implement investment projects. The aim of these projects was to create jobs by investing in local infrastructure projects, such as rehabilitation of roads, residential and municipal places, schools, hospitals, and social and cultural objects. This component received the largest share of the employment strategy funds. Based on prevailing international practice, wages for low-skilled workers were set slightly below the market rate to ensure self-targeting. This design made the program attractive for the poor.
2. *Social job assistance.* This assistance created jobs for socially vulnerable people and guaranteed employers funding for 50 percent of employees' salaries for up to six months. For the remaining half of the salaries, the employers were required to ensure reliable payment.
3. *Youth internships.* Through sponsored internships, this element of the employment strategy targeted young graduates of vocational schools, colleges, and universities with the aim of providing between three to six months of work experience.
4. *Vocational training and retraining.* This element of the program intended to provide training and retraining of unemployed people, with a view to supporting either the development of new skills that were more in demand by the labor market or by improving their skill level within their existing profession. The training offered vocational

education for welders, electricians, computer operators, accountants, cooks, and hairdressers. After participants completed their training, the national employment department was responsible for helping them find suitable jobs.[7]

Government reports state that from 2009 to 2010, the employment strategy of the Road Map program implemented almost 9,000 projects in which an estimated number of 392,000 workplaces were created. In addition, more than 109,000 "social jobs" in 16,500 enterprises were created, more than 90,000 young graduates received professional practical skills in internships, and 150,000 people acquired vocational training.[8] From 2009 to 2010, the Road Map program had a positive effect on the stabilization of the labor market through the provision of short-term employment.[9] The priorities established in the employment strategy were well-conceived in the sense that they sought to tackle labor market shocks—the primary impact of the crisis.

To some extent, the participants in the research confirm this positive assessment. All the respondents who were beneficiaries of the employment strategy activities noted that their participation brought *"some improvements in personal life and living standards."* An employer in western Kazakhstan concurs: *"The Road Map supports the local population. At least, one can see that something works for simple people; one can see that there are programs, some development, conducted by the Government. It feels so good that the state takes care of us! Although small amounts of money are distributed, it still feels good that some kind of attention is paid on behalf of state authorities."*

Nevertheless, the study also reveals some of the strategy's deficiencies. After their participation in the employment strategy's activities was concluded, every second research respondent experienced deterioration in their financial well-being. Less than 5 percent of study respondents received a regular job after their participation. And participants described problems with both scale and administration, such as difficulties in accessing the activities, corruption, a lack of transparency, and the insufficient outreach and generosity of benefits.

Many people in dire need to participate in the employment strategy's activities could not do so. The majority of respondents mentioned limitations of the employment strategy that made it impossible for vulnerable people to access the program. The most vulnerable groups were described as excluded because they could not register with the national Employment

Department. These groups included people younger than 18 years, people with poor health, people with disability, pregnant women, and the elderly. *"People with disability are refused to be given job placements, since they said jobs are only for healthy people,"* said a focus group participant from East Kazakhstan oblast. A focus group participant in the West Kazakhstan oblast observed, *"A woman, who had only one year until retirement age, was refused to be given a job in my presence."* Furthermore, rural area residents, who owned their own piece of land, could neither register nor participate.

Participants mentioned a lack of transparency, saying there was too little information available on the details of the strategy's activities: *"Often only a limited number of people knew about the launch of the activities. Distribution of information among target groups requires lots of time, which was not taken into consideration."* The lack of information was mentioned as a key reason why outreach to vulnerable groups was inadequate. Corruption and nepotism was described as hindering participation and was highly criticized by all respondents. Participants in all focus group discussions—predominantly in urban regions—talked, albeit cautiously, about cases of cronyism and corruption during the process of application for the employment strategy's activities. Focus group participants in all areas mentioned instances of informal selection. *"One needs connections, acquaintances, because Employment Office employees accept only their relatives and acquaintances,"* said a participant in Akmola oblast.

Other common complaints concerned the lack of long-term assistance to the poorest and insufficient outreach. The employment strategy was designed with a deliberate focus on providing short-term support to deal with a temporary situation. From a public policy perspective, it makes good sense to have a temporary solution to a temporary problem. Poor and vulnerable households, however, face long-term problems and, to some extent, judge the benefits of a short-term program against their needs to tackle long-standing poverty. The amount and duration of benefits fell short of expectations in terms of achieving sustainable long-term improvements in the livelihoods of the poorest households. Respondents across all regions pointed out that poor people's needs and demands were higher than benefits and vacant places available, and they stressed the inability of the strategy's activities to tackle their longer-term priorities. The funded activities were useful in providing short-term survival support to people who were in dire situations and willing to work for low salaries, but many of the participants had more ambitious priorities, namely finding a suitable long-term job that would provide a stable and secure income. Although the strategy's activities met the short-term expectations of 40 percent of beneficiaries, another 25 percent did not find their expectations met at all, largely because they hoped that the program would make lasting improvements in their livelihoods. One 45-year-old woman in East Kazakhstan oblast summarized this point: *"The Road Map will end and we will not have money again. We will experience material hardships, conflicts, scandals, and family issues will occur again due to a lack of money."* The research suggests that there is still considerable demand in Kazakhstan for long-term programs that can underpin livelihoods for poorer households.

Table 5.1 documents and compares issues raised for each component of the employment strategy, incorporating the views of both beneficiaries and nonbeneficiaries of the strategy's activities.

Conclusions and Implications for Policy

The present research interviewed groups that were expected to be particularly vulnerable to the impacts of the crisis. The results revealed that almost 50 percent of vulnerable respondents felt their livelihoods were weakened, leaving their households more vulnerable as the crisis unfolded. Descriptions across all groups and regions paint a picture of lingering hardship that intensified during the crisis, and most adverse consequences of the crisis were in the form of unemployment, which was associated with a dramatic fall in household income and potential food insecurity. The money earned was not enough, and respondents reported that low incomes often complicated relations within families and resulted in additional social and psychological stress.

The descriptions of coping strategies suggest that households often had to rely on mechanisms outside the formal assistance structures and, in some instances, deploy strategies that generated either further rounds of impacts or longer-term consequences. Reports that tertiary education was becoming less affordable indicate that the vulnerable people in Kazakhstan were investing in university education for their children before the crisis and that they continued to see it as an important priority even after the crisis hit. The regard for higher education was in sharp contrast to most of the other country case studies discussed in this book, where higher education was found to be beyond the reach of the poor. Tertiary education is an important instrument for promoting intergenerational socioeconomic

Table 5.1. Employment Strategy Activities

	Description and target participants	Disadvantages	Impacts on people
Investment projects	Job placements mainly for physical labor in infrastructure and construction projects. Men and skilled or unskilled blue-collar workers could take more advantage of these placements than women, college and university graduates, and white collar workers. Duration: 2–6 months.	Informal selection systems emerged, and potential employers favored their relatives and acquaintances. All construction works had to be finished by October, so that people had no work during the tougher winter period. Jobs were unattractive due to their short duration, hard labor conditions, and low salaries. The monthly payments of T 20,000[a] were inadequate.	Participants tended to evaluate the impact of the program based on whether they were able to secure a regular job. People who did not find another regular job felt disappointed. The overwhelming majority of participants reported that there were no sustainable improvements in financial well-being.
Social jobs	Advantages for unemployed people who were searching for temporary employment. These groups were able to earn money to feed their families. The Department of Labor, Employment and Social Protection of Population, guaranteed the timely disbursement of salaries. Employers benefited as half of their wage bill was taken over by social services. Duration: up to 6 months.	It was reported that some employers forced their employees to hand in the 50% salary of the Social Department in favor of the employers. So the workers only received 50% of the wage and the employers paid nothing. Local employment center staff confirmed that the activities for social job placements were launched in March and ended in September 2010 (no winter activities). The maximum monthly payments of T 30,000 (half from employer and half from the state) were inadequate.	Participants tended to evaluate the impact of the program based on whether they were able to secure a regular job after the social job ended. During placement, participants' psychological and financial well-being significantly improved, but the majority of participants did not secure permanent employment or experience a sustained improvement in living standards.

(continued next page)

159

Table 5.1. Employment Strategy Activities *(continued)*

	Description and target participants	Disadvantages	Impacts on people
Youth internships	Advantages for young people as the internships provided opportunities for communication, collaboration, and exchange. The young gained work experiences and had good chances to acquire a regular job after the internship. Advantages for employers as they received workers for free. Duration: 3–6 months.	Retraining centers and the local employment centers invited and favored their relatives and acquaintances. Local employment center staff confirmed that the activities for youth internships were launched in March and ended in September 2010 (no winter activities). The state payments of T 20,000 per month were inadequate.	Improved financial situation for families of participants on a broader scale and increased confidence for participating youth. Many participants could not find a job placement after the internship, so some of them worked in a social job. The internships provided additional experiences for participants; skills were developed, but the program did not provide permanent jobs.
Vocational training and retraining	Stipends for people who were willing to learn a new profession in high demand. Training centers improved their material and technical resources, such as equipment, educational training materials, computers, and office supplies. Duration: 3–6 months.	After training, just 40% found a job placement. Retraining and employment center staff favored their relatives and acquaintances. The training activities were launched in March and ended in August 2010 (no winter activities). The stipends of around T 7,000 per month were inadequate.	In a subjective assessment 87% of the respondents who benefited from the training said they could improve their living standards. But, according to researcher interviews, participants who did not find a regular job after the training reported that their main problem of unemployment remained the same.

Source: Employment and Retraining Strategy.
a. The average monthly salary throughout the country is between 50,000 and 80,000 tenge (T 80,000 = $550). Within the agricultural industry, the average salary rate is about T 35,000.

mobility and poverty reduction, so it is necessary to take actions to ensure that it remains affordable to the poor in Kazakhstan.

Many of the research respondents had participated in the activities of the Road Map program's employment strategy and had received short-term employment-based support, resulting in temporary relief. Even though some of the poor were disappointed with the temporary nature of the activities and with exclusion issues resulting from both formal and informal targeting criteria at the point of delivery, the design of the employment strategy activities may still have been the right one, given the context. Discussions suggest that more careful attention to timing and outreach might have enabled more people to take advantage of the employment strategy's opportunities. Attention to transparency in program operation and a broader, more accessible information strategy might have expanded outreach. There were issues regarding the low generosity of the scheme, although participants pointed out that this made the scheme more attractive to the very poorest and, therefore, could be viewed positively from a targeting perspective.

Foremost in the minds of research participants, however, was the longer-term challenge of developing sustainable livelihoods. There was little suggestion in the discussions and interviews that the effort and expenditures that were directed toward short-term assistance to employment and skill-building would bring any long-term benefits. These findings point to the need to ensure that temporary crisis response measures are followed up with longer-term poverty reduction measures. The latter could include, for example, child-care facilities to enable women to join the labor force and contribute to family incomes, establishment of subsidized credit facilities for university students, and improvement of the social assistance programs to help the most vulnerable These measures will support the "active life philosophy" emphasized by interviewees and contribute to the long-term economic development of the country.

Notes

1. Resolution of the Government of the Republic of Kazakhstan as of March 6, 2009, No. 264, about the measures to implement the address of the President of the country, titled: "Through the Crisis towards Renewal and Development," http://www.ipd.kz/images/stories/Downloads/arrangements2009.pdf.
2. Employment and Retraining Strategy, http://www.ipd.kz/images/stories/Downloads/arrangements2009.pdf.

3. Resolution No. 264.
4. Statistics Agency of Kazakhstan website: http://www.stat.kz/digital/stat_trud/Pages/default.aspx.
5. Road Map website: http://dorkarta.enbek.gov.kz/News/Details/24, statement by B. B. Nurymbetov, vice-minister of labor and social protection in the Republic of Kazakhstan.
6. Employment and Retraining Strategy.
7. Resolution No. 264.
8. Road Map website, http://dorkarta.enbek.gov.kz/.
9. Official statement by B. B. Nurymbetov, vice-minister of labor and social protection in the Republic of Kazakhstan, http://dorkarta.enbek.gov.kz/News/Details/24.

References

Bertelsmann Stiftung. 2010. BTI (Bertelsmann Transformation Index). *2010 Kazakhstan Country Report*. Guetersloh: Bertelsmann Stiftung.

World Bank. 2011a. *Kazakhstan—Partnership Program Snapshot*. Washington, DC: World Bank.

———. 2011b. *The Jobs Crisis: Household and Government Responses to the Great Recession in Eastern Europe and Central Asia*. Washington, DC: World Bank.

CHAPTER 6

Crises in Kenya: Living with Hunger in an Era of Economic and Political Shocks

Grace Lubaale and Naomi Hossain

Introduction: Living with Hunger in an Era of Crises

No country has been immune from the food, fuel, and financial crises, but the years 2008 through 2011 have been particularly turbulent and volatile for people in Kenya. As the accounts in this chapter document, these complex economic events interacted to result in extreme hardship for poor people, manifested most clearly in acute food insecurity and unambiguous signs of a society undergoing grave stress. For Kenya, the global economic downturn was prefaced and exacerbated by twin national crises of politics and food security. The global food, fuel, and financial crises struck during a protracted drought and in the aftermath of the mass political violence that followed the December 2007 election. Over the period of this research, the country experienced a political transition in which a new constitution enshrined economic and social rights, particularly the right to be free from hunger, and to have adequate food of acceptable quality (Article 43(1)(c)). Yet despite this new constitutional entitlement to protection from hunger, by 2011, the north of the country was being threatened with a famine believed to be the worst in the region for 60 years, and hunger among the urban poor took on a political dimension with public protests in major cities, especially Nairobi.

Based on research in 2009, 2010, and 2011, this chapter explores the impacts of and responses to these shocks on food security among people in two areas of the country: the informal settlement of Mukuru in Nairobi and communities in the Lango Baya coastal region, near Malindi.

The chapter illustrates some key themes in the analysis of vulnerability and resilience in relation to contemporary economic shocks. First, it highlights the complexity and multiple nature of the shocks that people in developing countries are exposed to, regardless of how integrated they may be into a global economy. Second, the findings about the serious nature of the social impacts demonstrate the value of this kind of participatory research in providing sensitive early warning signals. The accounts given here paint a vivid picture of communities under intolerable strains, signaling a situation of acute food insecurity. And third, the chapter highlights some of the gendered effects of these crises, notably in terms of who bears the burden of coping and how.

The chapter is organized as follows. The next section briefly outlines some of the wider economic and policy contexts against which the 2008–11 crises unfolded. It is followed by a description of the research sites and methodology used in the community monitoring work. The next section describes coping responses with a focus on strategies of livelihood diversification, adjustments to food consumption, the impacts on children and youths, the gendered dimensions, and effects on family life. This is followed by brief reviews of some of the responses to these crises, including a discussion of the social and political discontent that appears to have driven the official response. The conclusion touches on some of the enduring harms of these multiple economic shocks for poor people in Kenya, in particular the protracted period of food insecurity.

The Food, Fuel, and Financial Crises in the Kenyan Context

The Kenyan experience of the global economic crisis was complicated by twin national crises of politics and food security. The compound nature of the shocks experienced at this time makes it difficult to attribute experiences and responses to specific transmission channels. It is clear, however, that the combination of (1) postelection violence in early 2008, which led to loss of life, disrupted agricultural production, dislocated entire communities, and deterred tourists; (2) the financial crisis, which deterred investors, had negative impacts on exports and growth and increased the budget deficit, particularly in 2008 and 2009; (3) commodity price volatility; and (4) the prolonged drought, which affected agricultural exports and food security, are all likely to have had direct and indirect effects on Kenya's poor.

The Kenyan food crisis predated the 2008 global food and fuel price spike by several years: after five years of drought, the Kenyan government declared a national food security emergency in January 2009. Kenya appeared to have been hit particularly hard by the way the global food and fuel crisis exacerbated its domestic food crisis, but it seems to have recovered fairly early on from the effects of the financial crisis. The effects of the political crisis were visible in the gross domestic product (GDP) growth rate of 1.7 percent in 2008, after a high of 7.1 percent the previous year. By 2009, growth had picked up to 2.6 percent, and by 2010, it was up to 5.0 percent.[1] By early 2011, the state of the Kenyan economy was a cause for optimism, as 2009 and 2010 were marked by a considerable recovery on key indicators. Tourism had accounted for some 9 percent of Kenyan exports in 2004–07, but in the immediate aftermath of the postelection violence in 2008, the numbers of tourists dropped 34 percent, and earnings from tourism declined 20 percent (Mwega 2010). The volume of tourists from Europe and North America was expected to decline with the onset of the global financial crisis, but this sector actually had a slight recovery in 2009, suggesting that the violence rather than the financial crisis had caused the impact. In 2010, official estimates were that foreign exchange earnings from tourism had risen by 18 percent compared to 2009, and the numbers of international visitors had increased by 8 percent (KNBS 2011).

Tea, coffee, and horticultural exports fell during 2008–09. Yet improved weather conditions, government intervention to provide more subsidized agricultural inputs, and stronger prices for some agricultural exports meant the sector experienced impressive real growth of more than 6 percent in 2010 (KNBS 2011). Other impacts varied: remittances were down slightly in 2009 compared to 2008, but foreign aid increased substantially, presumably partly in response to the food security situation arising from the drought and the political upheaval of 2008 (Mwega 2009, 2010).

Although quantitative evidence of the poverty impacts of this series of complex shocks has yet to emerge, the impacts of commodity price volatility on the cost of living are known to cause direct hardship for poor households, particularly the majority who are not net food producers or who live in urban areas. As table 6.1 indicates, the 2008 food price spike was severe, with the cost of basic foods (which made up half of the consumer basket in 2008–09) increasing by more than one-third. The cost of living continued to rise the following year, but it was by a relatively minor 4 percent in total. The problem of inflation resurfaced in Kenya (as it did elsewhere in the

Table 6.1. Consumer Price Index, 2009–11

Category	Percentage change from previous year (weight in total)		
	Feb. 2009/ Feb. 2008	March 2010/ March 2009	March 2011/ March 2010
Food and nonalcoholic beverages	34.8 (50.50)	4.5 (36.04)	15.1 (36.04)
Housing, water, electricity, gas and other fuels[a]	6.1 (4.2)	5.3 (18.3)	6.5 (18.3)
All items	25.8 (100)	4.0 (100)	9.2 (100)

Source: Kenya National Bureau of Statistics, http://www.knbs.or.ke.
a. Fuel and power in 2009.

region and the wider world) in late 2010, with food price inflation reaching 15 percent in March 2011 (see table 6.1).

In anticipation of severe economic impacts from the global economic crisis, the government of Kenya put in place a stimulus package in the second half of 2009 and planned to increase social spending by 25 percent in 2010–11 (KNBS 2011). An initiative to distribute subsidized maize announced in the 2009–10 budget ultimately collapsed, but a national youth employment scheme, several cash transfer programs, and other initiatives have been rolled out since 2009 (Mwega 2010). A World Food Programme (WFP) food-for-work project was abandoned in 2009 because potential beneficiaries were too weak to do the manual labor required (WFP 2009; see also Hossain et al. 2009), but WFP programs and other nongovernmental activities contributed to a new policy emphasis on social protection provision.

We turn next to an exploration of what these complex shocks have meant in the lives of people living in poverty and vulnerability in two areas of Kenya. This discussion draws on evidence from three rounds of participatory learning and action research throughout the peak crisis period, in early 2009, 2010, and 2011. With its unique microlevel perspective on the shocks as they unfolded in people's lives, the research offers insights into their strategies and responses for coping. It also offers rare glimpses of the usually ignored social and well-being impacts of these crises and coping strategies, including how they affected men and women. The chapter draws on the longitudinal qualitative research in the two "listening posts," one in Nairobi, and the other in communities in the Lango Baya sublocation of the coastal Malindi district. It draws some preliminary conclusions about the pathways on which these shocks may have set people who were already living on low incomes or in poverty.

Research Context and Approach

The research was undertaken during February and March in 2009, 2010, and 2011. The locations were villages within the Mukuru urban settlement (population of more than half a million) about 3 kilometers from Nairobi's central business district, and in communities in the Lango Baya sublocation, about 50 kilometers from the coastal tourist resort of Malindi. Occupations in Mukuru are mainly in the informal sector, some serving the nearby industrial areas, and more concentrated in local petty trading activity. People in the Lango Baya area depend on subsistence farming, with some slight involvement in the tourism sector. In Lango Baya, the research team worked with ActionAid International Kenya, which has long-standing links in the area, including irrigation projects and other projects working with people living with HIV/AIDS.

Research participants in both the rural and urban communities were, by any standards, extremely vulnerable to economic downturn and food insecurity. The severity and extent of poverty in both areas before the onset of the 2008 food price spike or the global financial crisis emphasizes that these were communities with limited resources on which to draw to cope during the crises.

Although they shared high levels of poverty and deprivation, the two areas were distinctively different environments and societies. The communities in Lango Baya are made up of a large number of relatively settled subsistence farmers, chronically vulnerable to drought and protracted episodes of food insecurity. During the 2009–11 research period, food security conditions improved moderately for a while during 2010, but the period preceding and following were marked by severe drought. All the standard indicators of food security for this region indicated concerns about high levels of food security stress (KFSSG 2009a, 2009b, 2010; FEWSNET 2011).

Mukuru is in the poorest ward in the poorest constituency in Nairobi. In many respects it is characteristic of large slum settlements, with a relatively mobile population and high levels of social deprivation. Crime and rights abuses, family breakdown, and child-headed households are some of the social dimensions of deprivation in the area. A recent survey of Nairobi informal settlements helped to situate and enable a sense of the scale of the issues the qualitative research explored in more detail. The survey discovered that people in Nairobi's informal settlements depend on markets for around 90 percent of their food needs (Oxfam GB, Concern

Worldwide, and Care International 2009) and therefore are exposed particularly directly to food price inflation. The survey found that the cost of living had increased significantly in 2008, with price increases per item ranging from one-fifth to double their previous cost; at the same time, the incomes from the informal sector livelihoods on which people in those areas depend declined by between 20 percent and 25 percent (Oxfam GB, Concern Worldwide, and Care International 2009). Access to food had worsened significantly, and a range of "negative coping strategies" had been adopted, including an increase in high-risk livelihoods, such as sex work and criminal activities; reduced spending on items like water, soap, and toilets; withdrawal of children from school; greater reliance on credit; and households splitting up (Oxfam GB, Concern Worldwide, and Care International 2009).

The food security crisis—in effect now a chronic situation for the people in Lango Baya, Mukuru, and others throughout Kenya—has affected people very widely and inclusively. The effect of the crisis reflects both its extreme nature and the relative lack of advantaged occupation groups in these areas: there are no public sector employees and few formal sector workers of any kind in these locations. The main occupations include subsistence farming and traditional arts and crafts associated with the Malindi tourist trade in the rural areas and informal sector employment and self-employment in petty trade and vending, in personal services such as laundry, in transport work and portering, and in sex work in the urban areas. Both areas also have significant populations who are living with HIV/AIDS or households headed by women and children, including orphaned children.

Some of the interviewees and focus group participants were revisited over the three years, and others were met once or twice. The criterion for selecting research participants was that they were from low-income groups that were believed or known to be vulnerable to the global downturn, drought, or food and fuel price volatility. Focus groups were conducted among different occupation groups including farmers, tourism sector workers (artisans and resort employees originally from the Lango Baya area), traders, transport workers, and sex workers. Some focus groups were also conducted with social categories such as youth, village elders, local leaders, people living with HIV/AIDS, and schoolchildren. In each site, on each research visit, up to eight focus groups were conducted, with participant numbers ranging from 6 to 15. Working with partner organizations, the researchers also conducted interviews with individuals from particular groups, such as food traders, tourism sector workers in Lango Baya, child and youth household heads, children in vulnerable situations, and female heads of households.

The research used a range of qualitative and participatory tools to enable people to explain their experiences and strategies for coping. The tools included food basket exercises and food or diet diaries, matrix scoring and matrix ranking exercises, time-use exercises, and institutional and welfare mapping activities. Case study interviews were conducted using a semistructured checklist format. Some additional community-level information and perspectives were gained through contact and interviews with key local informants and through gathering relevant secondary data. The research results need to be interpreted within their clear limitations, including that the findings are evidently not representative in any sense and can give no sense of the scale or distribution of these impacts or coping responses across the population of Kenya. What they do enable is a more modest set of qualitative insights into the dynamics and processes of coping, and they have been analyzed for their insights into these processes. Similarly, although the design of the research means it can offer no evidence of the magnitude or severity of the economic impacts (for example, in terms of income poverty, consumption, or nutritional levels), the data it does provide concerning the severity of the social impacts offer a sense of the magnitude of the effects, although against the alternative metric of the impacts on well-being and social relations.

Coping with Crises

The Nature of the Shock

The experiences of the crises as reported by people in the Lango Baya and Mukuru communities were closely focused on the effects of higher food prices and the effects of the food price spikes of 2008 (still being felt in 2009) and 2011. During our first research visit, in early 2009, it was plain that people in both locations were reeling from the effects of the food price spike, which had come on top of the prolonged drought and in contexts that featured chronic poverty even during periods of national economic growth (Hossain et al. 2009). At that time, people in Mukuru reported that the price of maize (the staple food) had trebled between February 2007 and February 2009, and paraffin (the main fuel for cooking and light) and rents had doubled or almost doubled. Mukuru residents noted that prices of all goods and services had risen since 2007, but nominal wages were stagnant and in some cases even declined. Jobs were not secure, and any efforts to organize workers were met with instant dismissal. The local construction industry, a source of casual employment for many of the young men in the area, had also taken a hit in the downturn. As one young male research participant explained:

> *"There are no jobs, even the normal construction jobs are not available, if you search for one, the person in charge looks at you with a sarcastic eye and if you are not from his ethnic background then you are told to come back tomorrow."*
>
> Young man in Mukuru, February 2009

The situation in the Lango Baya sites was somewhat different, but there too, food prices were a preoccupation. Those employed directly in tourism or in sectors associated with tourism in nearby Malindi had also suffered from unemployment associated with both the declining economy and postelection violence. For poor people in this area, the cost of food items like maize, beans, and rice was unpredictable but generally increasing. As one woman described the situation in 2009:

> *"These days it has become very difficult. Even though we are alive, our health is deteriorating. I used to have three meals each day, but now I hardly manage a meal each day. When I am unable to get food, I just sleep, with hope that tomorrow will be better. A bag of maize meal at 1,100 shillings is too expensive for me to buy. I need at least 5 bags for a month. At that rate, I need about 5,000 shillings to buy that bag of maize meal for a month. Yet I also need other items as I cannot live on maize alone. You see, I can hardly afford a meal each day."*
>
> Woman near Malindi, February 2009

Although most of the local people depend on subsistence farming, they still rely heavily on purchasing food and other items needed for their livelihood. Agricultural input costs were a concern, but farmers of maize, beans, and livestock in the Lango Baya community did not mention high fertilizer prices, because the high cost meant they were unaccustomed to using it. Before 2007, farmers claimed that outputs had been sufficient to feed families and sell some surplus. But since 2007, poor rains had meant poor harvests. Livestock prices had declined as a result of the lack of pasture resulting from the drought: cows that sold for 9,000 Kenya shillings (K Sh) in 2007 were selling for K Sh 7,000 in 2009, and goat prices had dropped from K Sh 1,000 in 2007 to K Sh 800 in 2009. An ActionAid irrigation project involving provision of two pumps to draw water from the nearby river was helping some, but only those who could afford the fuel to operate the pumps. Even these farmers reported facing uncertainty as a result of crop theft:

> "I have been growing maize, beans, and other crops through irrigation in the hope of harvesting enough to feed my family and to sell. Thus, I have been sacrificing a lot in terms of minimizing expenditure in order to buy fuel only to find my crop stolen from the shamba (field). This kind of theft was unheard of in the period before 2007. It has been brought about by lack of food since those that steal do it to feed themselves and their families and not for commercial purposes."
> Farmer in Lango Baya area, 2009

In the Lango Baya area, food shortages as well as high prices had become a concern in 2009. In early 2010, with food prices stable and signs of wider economic recovery, there were no signs that the situation had worsened, but equally few indications that people were feeling better off than a year previously. Women in Mukuru noted that the prices of staples had declined slightly in 2010 compared to 2009, but that prices of other items (kerosene, water, sugar, and cooking fat) had recently risen, and wages had not, leaving purchasing power static. By contrast, in Lango Baya, poor rains in 2009 had kept food prices high into early 2010. Farmers again reported irrigation constraints as a major obstacle to increased production, also noting that pest infestation and localized flooding had negatively affected cultivation in 2009. In both locations, fuel had become unaffordable after recent rises in kerosene and charcoal. Individual experiences of inflation are reflected in national consumer price inflation indices (table 6.1). Some consumer prices dropped in 2009 compared to 2008, but they remained high and volatile. Our assessment of the situation in 2010 was that the effects of the food price spike and economic downturn had been cumulative, wearing down people's resilience and resources for coping, even if they had not been hit by a fresh round of shocks (Hossain et al. 2010).

It was clear that volatile food and fuel prices pervaded everyday life in the two locations. Even better-off people in Mukuru reported feeling the effects as shopkeepers, creditors, landlords, and as victims of rising crime; some said they had sold land or dipped into savings to keep businesses afloat. The effects on the lives of the poor were more direct and more severe. Many were getting by with a combination of ingenuity, social support, and extraordinary effort. Yet the research identified increasing concerns that livelihood diversification was coming to mean illegal, environmentally damaging, or antisocial activity, as the opportunities for more productive economic activity were exhausted. More people seemed to be reaching the limits of their capacities to cope at home, and there were widespread reports, and some documented instances, of parents, particularly men, abandoning their families.

Livelihood Diversification

In both Mukuru and Lango Baya, people tried to diversify their livelihoods in the face of persistent food insecurity. In Mukuru, joblessness was a major concern, consistent with survey findings that income from casual waged labor, the main income source for around half of poor urban households, had declined by 28 percent over 2008.[2] Many adult men reported searching routinely and fruitlessly for casual work. Some had moved in with women food vendors (a group experiencing relative food security) or taken to drink, abandoning family responsibilities in their frustration. There were instances of enterprising, positive adaptations: women moving rapidly into prepared food sales, popular because of high fuel costs; and children earning pocket money playing organized football matches. Some of the reported strategies, however, had the potential for negative effects on those adopting them or on the wider society (table 6.2).

By 2011, the limits to diversification within the informal sector appeared to have been reached, with workers in this sector widely complaining of low earnings and high competition. As one Mukuru woman living with HIV/AIDS put it:

> "Sometimes you can go for two weeks without selling even one item or you sell one or two, yet you are supposed to buy food too. So, this forces you to look for other casual jobs and this is too hard for us."
>
> Woman in Mukuru, 2011

Urban informal sector workers also commented on the negative impacts of the authorities on their efforts to diversify. Women in Mukuru who had diversified into informal laundry work reported that women running small businesses were harassed by city council *askaris* or city council security personnel, and that led to loss of earnings out of fear of being jailed. They said that the city council should "promote the small enterprise businesses instead of demolishing stalls." Carthandlers or porters had similar problems with

Table 6.2. Livelihood Diversification Strategies Reported in Mukuru in 2010

Type of diversification, by whom	Likely impact, on whom
Traders and retailers buying smaller units to avoid theft, selling smaller units and cutting margins to maximize sales, selling lower quality products, providing credit, acquiring new credit, using witchcraft to compete with rival traders	Positive for community, local market if increases affordability, but negative for competitors if earnings are driven down. Potential debt problems for the poor; witchcraft negatively affects social cohesion.
Women providing local laundry and domestic cleaning services, retailing water, setting up new grocery and prepared food enterprises	Additional pressures on women's time, physical burdens, and domestic care work. Adverse effects for women's health, care of children, older people, the sick.
Teachers investing in several businesses to ensure cash flow, joining rotating savings and credit associations (ROSCAs)	Likely to affect commitment and time spent on teaching, and therefore the quality of education.
Children and youth gathering waste for sale (*kuchemba*), running errands for traders, babysitting, construction labor, sex work, begging, gambling	Some work positive for learning and earning experiences. School dropout likely with paid work. Waste recycling hazardous, and sex work risks exposure to violence, pregnancy, and STDs.
Various groups involved in theft, mugging, pickpocketing	Dangerous and illegal, risks exposure to criminal justice system, contributes to declining social cohesion.

Source: Focus group discussion in Mukuru, 2010; see Hossain et al. 2010.

the *askaris*, and *touts* (transport workers) in Mukuru also complained of harassment by traffic police.

Adjustments to Food Consumption

The single best indicator of how well households are doing is how well they are eating. In these communities, how well people were eating closely mirrored the fluctuations in global food prices. In 2009, people were struggling to eat enough, and it was common to hear of households subsisting on a single meal a day. In 2010, the situation had moderately improved over the previous year for many—but not all—in Mukuru. Schoolchildren reported that their households had two meals a day, compared to only one in 2009. But in Lango Baya, most people were still reporting eating one meal daily, of *ugali* (porridge) and vegetables. People living with HIV/AIDS explained that they ate twice daily, but needed to eat more for their antiretroviral (ARV) drugs to work. Across households, children were reported to be fed first, and adults shared the remaining food, without preference being given to men. The main coping strategy was to cut quantities. But in general, before reducing total amounts of food, people would cut down on more expensive items such as cooking oil, spices, onions, and so on.

That few people in either area spoke much of cutting down on meat, poultry, or fish during this period is an indication of how poor they were to begin with: such protein-rich items would have been a rare luxury before the food crisis. By 2011, food prices had risen again, and most meals consisted of *ugali* and a small amount of vegetables or beans. Even these items were often in inadequate quantities or served only once a day in many households. Table 6.3 summarizes the range of reported household responses with respect to provisioning.

The high cost of fuel also affected how and what people ate. Several people noted that it was cheaper to buy ready-made meals like *githeri* (corn and beans) than to buy or source fuel and cook food with it. One woman explained that she was reserving kerosene for lighting and cooking with charcoal which she combined with *changa change* (balls of charcoal dust that could be acquired free from local charcoal sellers). Other Mukuru households used *muraa* or sawdust for cooking, but she

Table 6.3. Food-Related Adjustments Reported in 2009, 2010, and 2011

Quantity	Quality and preference	Social dimensions	Outcomes
Skipped meals Eating once a day Fewer meals Smaller meals Making "light" *ugali* (*bokoboko*) to stretch ingredients further Replacing meals with tea	Lack of diversity (*ugali* and vegetables) Eating nonpreferred foods Cooking without oil or spices Gathering wild vegetables Buying cheap food from roadside vendors Eating *ugali* mixed with soup or salty water	Children eat first, adults share leftovers Shopping in smaller quantities Borrowing, buying on credit Visiting other houses at mealtimes in the hope of a free meal (*kudoea*) Adults eat at night only Absent men do not get fed, but drunk men sometimes eat the leftovers intended for children	Children more regular at school where meals are provided Hunger as "normal" More sickness Antiretroviral medications do not work properly Conflict over gender roles Family breakdown: men move in with women food traders, women look for better-off husbands Children unable to perform in school Additional time and effort for women in procuring affordable food, and gathering fuel and wild foods

Source: Focus group discussions in Lango Baya and Mukuru in 2009, 2010, and 2011.

said this was dangerous and unhealthy, causing chest complications and skin infections. Elsewhere in Mukuru, a group of transport workers said that they had started to burn plastics for cooking fuel.

Children and Youth

People in surveyed communities generally emphasized their desire to invest in children's education, but the costs of schooling could be prohibitive. School feeding programs, where available, were consistently highlighted as an important source of support for family coping strategies during this period. Despite disliking the standard fare of *mburuga* (boiled wheat with yellow beans), children in Mukuru said "we never miss school because we are given free food." As the economic conditions worsened, however, school lunch programs were terminated in several local schools, with negative impacts for children's learning achievements and school attendance:

> *"Education has suffered a lot because children can no longer eat at school. The school feeding program stopped and as a result many children stopped going to school. Those who go sleep a lot because of hunger, and cannot continue with school for long. But the school feeding program has been revived somewhat and children have started going back to school."*
>
> Primary schoolteacher, in Mukuru, 2011

School feeding programs were reinstated in some areas in 2010 and 2011 after some were shut down in 2009.

Children were found to be undertaking a wide range of work, but this did not necessarily entail dropping out of school. Children in Mukuru were collecting and selling firewood and scrap metal, running small errands for shops and food kiosks, doing laundry, portering, or acting as cleaners and pay-collectors for privately owned pay toilets. It is likely that the scavenging activities reflect the recovery of the recycled waste trade with the global economic recovery. Children also confided that some (mainly boys) were also engaged in picking pockets (*kupiga ngeta*), targeting rich people and drunks in Mukuru.

One man gave a sense of the desperation young people in particular were facing in Lango Baya:

> *"In my view, when we talk about how the youth have been affected by these crises, I would say they have been badly hit. The prices of commodities have increased, unemployment is severe. Because of the desperation, people are willing to do literally everything! Some of the things people do, you really would not like to know, but it is dehumanizing. In some cases,*

the youth have resorted to drinking illicit brew as means of addressing the high levels of stress. In Lango Baya, drunk people are commonplace, but that is the explanation."

Man in Lango Baya, 2011

The view that high food prices and increasing unemployment were leading to increased levels of youth crime, including the creation of criminal gangs, was expressed in both areas, and examples of such groups and their activities were given.

The worst reports of how children were coping were heard in 2009, when mentions of increasing criminal activity and sex work among children and youth became common. A Mukuru head teacher told the following story of criminalization among schoolchildren:

"A copper bell belonging to our school was stolen by one of the students and sold to a scrap metal dealer at an industrial area at a cost of K Sh 20. The bell was very valuable to the school since it was bought when the school was first opened. We pursued the issue with the chief and after investigations, we learnt that the boy had sold it to a middleman who then sold it off to the dealer. By the time we got to the dealer, the bell had already been smelted. I received threats from the middleman that I would be raped should I pursue the issue further."

Head teacher, Mukuru, 2009

Children in Nairobi were also reported to be carrying criminals' guns for a fee of K Sh 25. Teachers spoke about instances when children were robbing each other of food in primary schools.

Most respondents thought that the numbers of girls and young women entering into sex work had increased; these concerns were aired in both Mukuru and Lango Baya. In Mukuru, there were also reports of men and boys selling sex to other men. Girls and young women in Mukuru said that under the pressure of food insecurity, mothers sometimes encouraged their daughters to sell sex, using the expression *"there is no need to sleep hungry when you are sitting on food/a shop"*—in other words, when you can sell sex. Some younger respondents knew of girls who had dropped out of school to marry or work in the sex trade. One woman in Mukuru explained that the competition from young sex workers increased in 2010 and 2011:

"Some time back, one could hustle and get a hundred shillings from a client but these days you can only get maybe twenty shillings because of the economy and the fact that these days there are other beautiful ladies

who do not have children like us and hence they snatch customers from us . . . the competition is very severe."

Woman in Mukuru, 2011

Gender and Family Life

As women are typically in charge of feeding families, rising food prices have direct and immediate impacts on women's primary roles in the home. Yet because many of the impacts on women take place within the unpaid care economy, these effects tend to be absorbed invisibly (at least to the outside world) as harder work, longer working hours, and more stress.

Women reported raised levels of stress, particularly around the difficult choices and sacrifices involved in feeding children. Women household heads in Mukuru said that they could not afford to give their children fruit, despite its importance for their health, because, for example, a mango costs K Sh 25 ($0.30), for which they could buy a whole lunch. Laundrywomen in Mukuru admitted that they rarely ate lunch, as that was a time when the children were at school (where they were given meals), and they rarely ate unless they were feeding the children. Some Mukuru women involved in occasional sex work were finding it particularly difficult to cope with high food prices, and one woman explained: "*As we have children, we would rather go without but provide for our children.*"

The burdens of women's care work were exacerbated in situations where men had in effect abandoned their domestic responsibilities:

"*In these crises, women and children suffer most. It is not unusual to find, like my neighbour here whose husband ran away a long time ago. He claimed he was seeking employment in town, but never returned from town when he found employment. He never sent any support home. However, when the job ended, he came back here briefly, noticed life was miserable and he left never to be seen again.*"

Woman in Lango Baya, 2009

Another said:

"*Is it possible . . . that families have broken up because of food? Of course, there are many, many who abandon their homes, leaving the wife and children without anything. The wife is subjected to lots of indignities because she must provide something for the children.*"

Woman in Lango Baya, 2009

During the first round of research, reports were mainly of men leaving to set up homes with other women, particularly food traders. Later rounds of research found that the fluidity of marital relations worked both ways: women also said that a survival strategy involved marrying better-off men when times were hard, only to leave them when circumstances changed:

> *"When you have failed to get money at all, you look for a boyfriend to marry you, you won't fail to get one, and when you are financially stable, you leave them."*
>
> Woman in Mukuru, 2010

Reports of domestic tensions and violence in the home appeared to fluctuate with food prices. Women in Mukuru said that alcoholism among men caused family breakdown and other problems. In 2009, a man in Mukuru said, *"A man in hunger cannot afford leisure. Even if one drinks beer, it is not for leisure as before, but just to kill the stress."*

Some focus group participants said that the lethal local brew "kill-me-quick" was replacing the beer that people used to drink for leisure. A woman in Mukuru complained that men *"come home drunk and even feed on the leftovers for our children."* But it was by no means only men's drinking that was a concern; rather, respondents also described ill-treatment of children by mothers under conditions of stress and alcoholism.

Responses to the Crises: Sources of Support and Political Perspectives

Informal and Customary Sources of Social Protection

Many people relied on informal sources of help and credit to get by on a day-to-day basis. One Lango Baya farmers' group distributed their produce for free when the hotel market shrank in 2008. In Mukuru, interviewees noted that whenever people lacked meals or money to buy food, they would visit or send children to friends and neighbors in the hope of sharing their meals. Sometimes this strategy failed, as their friends and neighbors also lacked food. This strategy was understood to be most common among youth and unmarried men, and is known as *kudoea* or "taking advantage." Shop or vendor credit was another important way of getting by.

The widely held view was that community-level assistance had declined in both locations. People were increasingly "selfish," focused on their own business and families. It was clear that people could be reluctant to ask for help, as there was a stigma attached. In Lango Baya, a woman living with HIV/AIDS said, *"They—other households—look down on you as if they do not need you. We only depend on God; He is the one keeping us alive."*

A women's group in Lango Baya explained that helping people attracted others looking for help, and people soon learned it was best to deny help to anyone. In Mukuru, people now shut their doors at mealtimes to discourage visitors hoping for a free meal. In Lango Baya, traders were resorting to witchcraft in the fierce competition for customers. The concern here is that such perceptions indicate that, collectively, people have reached the outer limits of their capacities to cope and support each other during the crisis.

Access to customary sources of support sometimes also gave rise to tension between social groups, most notably in Mukuru, and mainly in 2009, when the crisis seemed to have been at its worst. The most tangible signs of growing tensions emerged in relation to majority Christian views that Muslims only looked after their own.

The exclusion of people of other faiths from the support provided by Muslims seemed to generate animosity and intense hostility. Some people argued that when there is support from the church or government there is no discrimination, yet Muslims were seen to be encouraging discrimination, and possibly using food to convert desperate residents to the Islamic faith. Also in Nairobi, there were stories of young boys being sold to Asian traders for sex in exchange for food; such reports highlight how deprivation has heightened awareness of socioeconomic difference along religious or ethnic-cultural lines, creating or exacerbating social tensions.

Experiences of Formal Social Protection

In line with the official policy of increasing social protection in 2010, over the three years of the research, a wider range of sources of official support and nongovernmental organization (NGO) assistance became available in the two communities. School feeding programs were widely popular, as they provided a reliable food source and were aligned with households' own strategies and ambitions for their families. The school feeding programs were important sources of support for families with schoolchildren, but infants and preschool children could benefit only if parents brought them to the school at mealtimes. This practice was not strictly within the rules, but it was reported to be commonly the case among poorer households. In contrast, the food-for-work program was widely criticized in Lango Baya, despite providing a significant source of food to poorer households.

Complaints included that many needy people were excluded by the overly narrow beneficiary selection criteria; the work was excessive, particularly for undernourished people; and the benefits were meager. The positive experience of school feeding programs contrasted with this negative assessment of the food-for-work program. It is worth noting that the WFP abandoned its food-for-work scheme in July 2009, with the minister for Special Programmes stating it was "wrong to subject those facing famine to digging trenches and making dams on empty stomachs" (WFP 2009).

Despite the existence of more sources of support at the end of the research period than at its start, concerns remained about how such support was designed and the transparency with which the programs were implemented. One concern was the unpredictability of the support. Women in Mukuru who had been members of the new *kazi kwa vijana* (work for youth) Kenyan Youth Employment project found that their incomes from this project were erratic. A woman focus group participant said:

> Sometimes in the kazi kwa vijana *you do not know how much you will be paid. Sometimes you get paid K Sh 3,000 [$35.71] at the end of the month, and at other times, the payment rises to K Sh 5,000 [$59.52], though in the contract we signed for pay of K Sh 5,500 [$65.48].*
>
> Woman in Mukuru, 2011

There were also concerns about the poor quality of relief food. A group of Lango Baya women living with HIV/AIDS complained that officially distributed relief food included "*beans that won't cook*" and "*maize with a strong smell of pesticide that affects their health negatively*"; they also noted that they were not provided any cooking fat.

Credit needs emerged as a prominent theme among the slightly better-off in both locations. Traders, retailers, farmers, and aspiring entrepreneurs all gave examples of credit constraints limiting their activities. These findings highlight areas that microcredit has to date failed to reach.

Popular Pressure for Responses to the Crisis

Over the three years of the research, the official social protection response appeared to strengthen and widen, so that there were many more programs or sources of support to point to in 2011 compared to 2009. But the 2011 research round also uncovered a strong mood of popular discontent about the economic situation and the political response to it. This frame of mind was particularly marked among urban people, especially among young men (see Hossain and Green 2011).

Despite the government's evident efforts to provide greater social protections, the research uncovered a sense of a lack of government responsiveness. In Mukuru, porters said that government officials were ignorant of the problems of their community, and women thought the government was distracted by less important issues and wasted money on activities that did not benefit the people. As one woman living with HIV/AIDS explained it:

> *"Instead of the leaders helping us by reducing food prices, they spend money going to tell people that Ocampo* [the International Criminal Court prosecutor] *should not come* [to pursue inquiries against those responsible for the 2008 election violence]."

A Lango Baya woman thought that the government was aware of the food crisis through its local representatives, but that "bad politics and corruption" meant it failed to address the problem. Mukuru people said that their political leaders were only, if ever, accessible just before elections. During times of food insecurity, they were said to distribute relief food along tribal lines or to those closest to the chief. One child asked: *"Is there a councilor representing us? Because I have never seen him."*

> *"The other day the government was saying that the hunger problem does not exist. Yet people in Turkana are succumbing to it. Are they* [the government representatives] *really aware?"*
>
> Construction worker, Mukuru, 2011

The idea that the government was not accountable for action on hunger emerged in several different forms. The constitutional reforms that established the right to food in law and the responsibility of the government to act to provide it have clearly stimulated popular interest in holding their government to account for failures to act. One woman living with HIV/AIDS in Mukuru remarked that the new constitution *"does not care for the needs of the poor,"* but several others commented that the new constitution gave teeth to their demands for food aid. One woman noted:

> *"In the new constitution, we have the right to be provided food by the government. So when we lack food, we camp in the chief office until we are given relief food."*[3]

For the moment, however, the right to food remains a legal right more than an actual right. After a prolonged period of crisis, the dominant perspective on the food security situation to emerge from these research sites was frustration with the current political system. As one Mukuru transport worker argued vehemently:

> *"The leadership should change completely and especially to one leader instead of both premier and president. This government is so corrupt, how come in* [President Daniel Arap] *Moi's era food accessibility was so good unlike today, even though there was no devolvement of funds? Maybe it is time we went the way of Egypt. Kenya should not import anything, its exchange is high, it has got all the natural resources it needs but still we suffer! Leadership is bad! We need a leadership change!"*
>
> Transport worker, Mukuru

Conclusions: The Enduring Harms of a Protracted Food Crisis

The multiple crises of 2008–11 affected poor people in the two research communities most directly through the impacts on food security and the strategies they had to adopt to cope with them. The crises interacted in the lives of the people in these communities through the compounding effects of unemployment, inflation, and political change. The levels of social and political discontent examined in the previous section may help to explain the scaling up of official efforts to protect people from these shocks. The social protection interventions introduced in 2010, however, may be too late to protect many people in Lango Baya and Mukuru from the harmful and enduring effects that result from the protracted, widespread, acute food crisis experienced in these locations.

The multiple crises described in this chapter had three lasting effects on people's lives in the two communities. The first was social fragmentation. In both Mukuru and Lango Baya, household-level tensions played out in conflict over gender roles and household disintegration, and other signs of tensions appeared between social groups. That many people reported a decline in informal community support also bears out the impression that one of the lasting impacts of the crisis may be a decline in social cohesion.

The second impact is the rise in illegal and risky behavior. The research uncovered some concerns about rising crime, in particular sex work, as responses to the economic downturn and inflation. These behaviors were prominent in the Mukuru slums. The effects of rising crime are likely to contribute to the decline in social cohesion, but they also involve more risky livelihoods. In Lango Baya, there were concerns that desperation and the casualization of sex work were contributing to rising HIV/AIDS infection rates. Policing levels had increased in the slum community, but the evidence does not show improved security for the people there.

Third, indications of environmental depletion and a deterioration of the local environment were noted at both sites. Recent fuel price hikes had encouraged charcoal burning and tree cutting. In Lango Baya, virtually all households cook with charcoal produced from burning trees taken from the area's much-depleted forest cover. In Mukuru, almost all households also use charcoal for cooking.

The findings of the research also suggest that protracted crises undermine the authority of the government. Protests and unruly forms of political challenge to the government in early 2011 suggest that the views gathered in our 2011 research may well be more widely held. It is to be hoped that such pressures on the government, particularly in the context of a new constitutional right to food, may encourage a faster and more timely response to future episodes of economic crisis in the lives of poor people in Kenya.

Notes

1. From African Economic Outlook, http://www.africaneconomicoutlook.org /en/countries/east-africa/kenya/, based on International Monetary Fund and government of Kenya data.
2. This estimate of job losses refers to Nairobi slums, including Mukuru. KFSSG (Kenya Food Security Steering Group) 2009a.
3. The 2010 constitution enshrines "the right to be free from hunger, and to have adequate food of acceptable quality." It also provides for enacting and guaranteeing the right. Text of the Kenya Constitution: http://www.fao.org /righttofood/news42_en.htm.

References

FEWSNET (Famine Early Warning Systems Network). 2011. "Kenya Food Security Outlook: October 2010 through March 2011." http://www.reliefweb.int.

Hossain, N., R. Eyben, R. Fillaili, G. Lubaale, J. Moncrieffe, M. Mulumbi, and M. M. Rashid. 2009. *Accounts of Crisis: Poor People's Experiences of the Food, Fuel and Financial Crises in Five Countries*. Brighton, U.K: Institute of Development Studies.

Hossain, N., R. Fillaili, G. Lubaale, M. Mulumbi, M. Rashid, and M. Tadros. 2010. *Social Impacts of Crisis: Findings from Community-Level Research in Five Developing Countries.* Brighton, U.K: Institute of Development Studies.

Hossain, N., and D. Green. 2011. *Living on a Spike: How Is the 2011 Food Price Spike Affecting Poor People?* Oxford: Oxfam GB and Institute of Development Studies.

KFSSG (Kenya Food Security Steering Group). 2009a. "The 2008/'09 Short-Rains Season Assessment Report." Nairobi: Kenya Food Security Steering Group: Office of the President (Ministry of State for Special Programmes); Ministries of the Development of Northern Kenya and other Arid Lands; Agriculture, Livestock Development, Fisheries Development, Water and Irrigation, Public Health and Sanitation, Medical Services, Education; ALRMP; WFP/VAM; FEWSNET; UNICEF; FAO, Oxfam GB; UNDP.

———. 2009b. "Malindi Long Rains Assessment Report, 13th–17th July 2009." http://www.kenyafoodsecurity.org/.

———. 2010. "Kenya Food Security Outlook Jan–Jun 2010." http://www.kenya food security.org/.

KNBS (Kenya National Bureau of Statistics). 2011. "Kenya Economic Survey 2011: Highlights." Kenya National Bureau of Statistics, Nairobi.

Mwega, F. M. 2009. "Global Financial Crisis Discussion Series Paper 7: Kenya." Overseas Development Institute, London.

———. 2010. "Global Financial Crisis Discussion Series Paper 17: Kenya Phase 2." Overseas Development Institute, London.

Oxfam GB, Concern Worldwide, and Care International. 2009. "The Nairobi Informal Settlements: An Emerging Food Security Emergency within Extreme Chronic Poverty: A Compilation and Synthesis of Key Food Security, Livelihood, Nutrition and Public Health Data." Oxfam GB, Concern Worldwise, and Care International, Nairobi.

WFP (World Food Programme). 2009. "Kenya Puts Off Food for Work Plan." World Food Programme news release, July 20.

CHAPTER 7

Coping with the Global Economic Crisis in Mongolia: Findings from Focus Group Discussions

Anna Reva, Rasmus Heltberg, Altantsetseg Sodnomtseren, and Sarantuya Jigjiddorj

Introduction

Mongolia was hit hard by the global economic recession, notably the fall in commodity prices. Gross domestic product (GDP) contracted by 1.6 percent in 2009 after growth of 8.9 percent in 2008 (World Bank 2010). The country is narrowly specialized in production of a few primary goods with minerals making up 70 percent of total exports (UNDP n.d.). Since mid-2008, the prices of main export goods, including copper, zinc, crude petroleum, combed goat-down, and cashmere, dropped by close to or more than 50 percent, although prices of coal and gold held strong. Furthermore, construction activity fell sharply in 2009 as both the public and private sectors reduced investments and bank loans became less accessible. Foreign direct investment inflows into the mining and construction sectors were also reduced as global investment flows declined (ADB 2010).

These developments had negative impacts on welfare, and some groups of the population were particularly affected. The World Bank and the Asian Development Bank (ADB) initiated qualitative data collection to identify the impacts of the crisis as seen by individuals and households, examine the coping mechanisms, and analyze the effectiveness of the government's responses as perceived by respondents. To assess the evolution of crisis impacts and coping strategies, four consecutive rounds of research took place in May–June 2009, August–September 2009, January–February 2010, and November 2010–January 2011.

The research was conducted in urban and rural areas of Mongolia and involved interviews and focus group discussions (FGDs) with about 500 people (over the four rounds of data collection) belonging to groups identified as particularly exposed to the impacts of the crisis.[1] These groups included: (1) herders that may have suffered from the drop in cashmere and wool prices; (2) formal and informal miners whose employment status and income may have been affected by reduced global demand for commodities; (3) workers of the nontradable sectors such as construction and services whose employment and income may have suffered from the general economic slowdown; (4) recent migrants to Ulaanbaatar who are working in the informal sector or who experience high levels of employment insecurity; (5) young people (recent university graduates and workers) who may have faced increased difficulty in finding or keeping their jobs; and (6) the self-employed working in rural areas who may have suffered from reduced demand for their services or products and a fall in incomes.

The first three rounds of research showed that households across Mongolia were under serious economic stress, with the poor most strongly affected. The fourth round recorded broad-based recovery and improvement of living conditions for all surveyed groups. Labor market shocks—rising unemployment, reduced salaries, and diminished profits of small businesses—and price shocks, such as falling prices for cashmere and livestock products and rising prices for imported food and consumer goods, were the key transmission channels. The economic hardship also had social impacts, including increases in alcohol abuse and crime. Interviewees in Mongolia commonly mentioned reduced consumption, increased reliance on credit, distress livestock sales, and diversification of income sources among their coping responses. Government assistance, albeit small, was an important source of support to poor households during the crisis and following the harsh conditions of the winter *dzud* of 2010.

The rest of the chapter is organized as follows: the first section describes the key transmission channels and social impacts of the crisis; the next section discusses the coping strategies. The third section focuses on the sources of support, and the fourth offers concluding observations and implications for policy making.

Transmission Channels and Social Impacts

The primary impacts of the crisis were observed through labor market effects and price shocks, both of which affected the poor disproportionately. The economic downturn also had social impacts—changed gender relations and increased alcohol abuse and crime.

Labor Market Effects

The economic crisis had a major impact on the labor market, with rising unemployment, reduced salaries, and intensified competition for scarcer jobs. Increased difficulty in finding employment was reported by recent university graduates, urban migrants, low-skilled people, and those working in the informal sector. The bargaining power of employers increased, and a number of interviewees reported wage cuts and abusive practices by employers, including requests to work longer hours for the same salary, paying below the agreed amount, or hiring workers on a probationary period and firing them after one or two months without paying the salary. Discrimination in hiring decisions based on age, gender, and appearance (for women) was also common. Employers often gave preference to workers under the age of 30; furthermore, some organizations preferred hiring men for fear of incurring losses because women are entitled to a one-year maternity leave. Recent migrants to Ulaanbaatar were most affected by reduced employment opportunities due to low skills and lack of connections, which were increasingly important in a job search. They also had low awareness of workers' rights and were particularly vulnerable to employers' abuse.

Shrinking employment opportunities in the formal sector contributed to increased competition for informal sector jobs and a decline in incomes of informal sector workers. For example, the number of people engaged in illegal gold mining increased dramatically between May 2009 and February 2010 despite the health risks and the hard physical labor associated with this activity. The increased number of miners reduced individual chances of finding rich sites and correspondingly reduced miners' incomes. Workers engaged in small-scale tourism activities reported fewer clients than in the precrisis year, yet the number of service providers went up. Similarly, many small businesses, particularly those engaged in trade and service provision, reported that sales went down by half in comparison to the precrisis year.

"Last May, the sales income was much higher than it is now. Our sales used to be around Tog 120,000 a day, and we made approximately Tog 3,000,000 of sales per month. The sales decreased sharply, and now we hardly make Tog 30,000–40,000 of sales per day. Sometimes we do not sell any garments."

A 38-year-old female garment retailer, May–June 2009

Two factors contributed to decline of profits of the small businesses: reduced domestic demand for products and services and depreciation of the Mongolian currency, which raised the price of imported goods. Declining access to affordable loans was a widespread concern of entrepreneurs and a limiting factor in diversification of business activity and growth of small enterprises. The interviewees claimed that improved access to credit, reduced tax burden, simplified procedures for obtaining licenses, and skill-building programs are some of the steps the government could take to help them withstand the crisis and facilitate business growth.

Impact of Economic Recovery. The last round of this qualitative research (November 2010–January 2011) recorded the impact of the economic recovery and significant improvements in the labor market. The availability of jobs in the formal and informal sectors increased; the salaries of miners and civil servants were raised by 30 percent, which resulted in increased household spending and better sales for market traders and small business owners. Although recent migrants to Ulaanbaatar also benefited from improved job availability, they continued to face problems associated with breach of contracts by employers, low pay, and poor working conditions. The perceived instance of employers' abuse was so high that some migrants reported distrust in job advertisements posted by local governments and preference toward casual self-employment such as wood chopping or coal reloading. The income of such activities was reportedly enough to cover basic food costs.

Price Shocks

The fall of price for cashmere in the spring of 2009 had a major impact on herders' livelihoods. Many of them had taken loans in the expectation of a rising cashmere price. When this did not happen, herders, particularly those with a small number of animals, engaged in distress sales of meat, leading to an oversupply of meat and thus lower prices. The impact of the reduced prices for livestock products was exacerbated by the rising prices of imported food (sugar, flour, rice).

In addition, transport costs increased and were cited as a constraint for access to markets, mobility, and job search. In rural areas, rising transportation costs deepened herders' dependence on middlemen forcing them to sell livestock at lower prices.

> "This summer very few middlemen came to buy sheep and goats. I could not sell even a single sheep. Those who have money can transport animals and sell their animals. For others like me it is impossible. Our province has one meat processing company. But it offers lower prices than middlemen do. Therefore, we have no other way than to sell to the middlemen. The middlemen have a lot of bargaining power."

> Herder from Battsengel soum, Arhangai aimag,
> August–September 2009

Farmers living in remote locations complained that no middlemen came to buy sheep and goat skins in 2009, so they had to throw them away. Some of the interviewed low-income urban residents indicated that transport costs from the outskirts of Ulaanbaatar where they lived to more central locations where they worked were so high that they gave up their jobs in favor of growing vegetables and other subsistence activities.

Interviewees also complained that school-related expenses, such as the cost of uniforms, textbooks, and other supplies, had increased steeply, which could potentially be attributed to reduced government spending on education due to decreased revenues. University tuition fees went up as well. The rising costs of education were of particular concern to low-income families and households with many children.

Impact of Economic Recovery. The economic recovery was accompanied by a continued rise in consumer prices. Data for December 2010 showed a rise in inflation to 14 percent year-on-year following a 12 percent year-on-year increase in the previous month (World Bank 2010). Prices for domestic meat and dairy products increased sharply following the devastation of the livestock sector by the dzud of 2010. Prices for cashmere and animal skins also went up, reportedly due to increased demand from Chinese buyers. Higher prices for livestock products improved the livelihoods of herders. Although inflation was a source of concern for many interviewees, their spending improved due to higher incomes and the government's social transfers. Expenses on education became less burdensome due to higher government spending on schools, provision of free textbooks, and the newly introduced subsidy to offset part of the university tuition costs.

Social Impacts

Lack of employment opportunities and reduced incomes had significant social impacts. The role of women in income generation increased, as the earnings of men were no longer sufficient to cover the households' living expenses. Deteriorating living standards have contributed to the increase of alcohol abuse and crime and led to family tensions, which sometimes resulted in domestic violence.

Changes in Gender Relations. Growing economic hardship made women shift from unpaid domestic labor to income-generating activities. Many women reported engaging in small business activities such as running food stores, cafes, and motorbike parts stores as well as spinning wool, producing souvenirs, or making shoes. Increased earning power led to improved self-esteem and a larger role of women in household decision making and social life at large. The interviewed men said that women were consulted more often in the case of livestock sales or major household purchases. In rural areas, microcredit in combination with training on nonpastoral livelihoods was a major driving force for women's entrepreneurial activities. Some urban women reported that training activities organized by local government helped them start their small businesses.

Women were also praised for their ability to manage household budgets, which helped protect basic food consumption and education expenditures. Many women reported buying food in bulk at wholesale prices, sewing new clothes from older garments, and collecting dung for heating and cooking. Yet, the working women often suffered from the disproportionate burden of their responsibilities as caretakers.

Increased Apathy, Alcohol Abuse, and Crime. Reduced incomes, deteriorating standards of living, and unemployment led to apathy and depression, particularly among young people. It also reportedly increased alcohol consumption and crime in urban and rural areas. The situation did not improve following economic recovery of 2010–11. Urban residents complained that it was no longer safe to go out after dark. Theft and pickpocketing also became common.

> *"In the black market when working day ends, people all get drunk. They sell something and drink the money. Homeless people come to collect leftover food and steal things."*
>
> Candy and fruit trader from Narantuul market,
> August–September 2009

In rural areas, animal theft increased significantly, particularly in locations close to major roads and towns. The poor were more likely to have their animals stolen. They lacked hired help and often left the animals unattended. The poor also did not possess motorbikes to chase the thieves or cell phones to inform the police.

> *"I had very nice cows. Last year the cows were stolen. My wife was herding the animals and she came in to have some tea. We saw the animals near our ger. It became dark and one car passed through our ger. That evening we could not find our cows."*
>
> Herder from Bayandelger soum, Tuv aimag,
> August–September 2009

Rise in Domestic Violence. Unemployment among men and alcohol abuse were seen as the reason for increase in domestic violence, which was more common in urban areas. Focus group participants explained that rural areas still had herding jobs, which kept men busy throughout the year:

> *"Presence of domestic violence is often observed among our* khoroo (microdistrict of Ulaanbaatar) *citizens. Sometimes we find women having black eyes. I observe that unemployed men usually spend their time drinking alcohol and playing games. When they are at home, drunk men often get into conflict with family members and start fighting. It is very depressing for women, children, and older family members. Households who suffer from a drinking family member do not call police. They feel that after a few cases they would be sentenced by court. In this case, the family members will be responsible for paying an attorney fee, therefore they don't call police and attend women's center."*
>
> Social worker of 25th khoroo, Songino Khairkhan district,
> Ulaanbaatar, November 2010–January 2011

Impact of Economic Recovery. The economic growth did not have much impact on the social changes brought about by the crisis. Women continued to engage in income-generating activities and reportedly gained a higher status in family and society. Despite improved labor market conditions, crime rates did not go down, according to interviewees. It was not possible to judge whether the frequency of domestic violence was reduced, as this issue is viewed as private and not discussed in much detail with strangers.

Table 7.1 presents a summary of major crisis-related impacts at different times.

Table 7.1. Summary of Major Impacts during the Four Rounds of Research

1st round: May–June 2009	2nd round: August–September 2009	3rd round: January–February 2010	4th round: November 2009–January 2011
Wool and cashmere prices decreased sharply, but meat prices were stable.	Meat prices collapsed because too many herders attempted to sell meat to compensate for losses of income from cashmere.	Meat prices reduced further in early winter as a lot of herders attempted to sell larger than usual amount of meat in anticipation of the *dzud*.	Prices of food and consumer goods increased sharply.
Prices rose for imported food (flour, rice, sugar).	Prices for imported food stabilized but herders had to sell more livestock products to afford the usual food basket due to reduced meat prices and currency depreciation.	Increase in education-related costs remained an issue of concern.	Formal and informal sector jobs showed increased availability.
Increase in education-related expenditures caused an additional stress for households.	Increase in the costs of education continued to burden households.	Herders recorded massive losses of livestock due to *dzud*.	Salaries of civil servants and employees of state-owned enterprises increased by 30%.
Job availability, working hours, and salaries were reduced in the formal sector; bonuses were canceled for workers.	Bank loans became less available in rural and urban areas; the maximum loan amount for herders went down from Tog 5 million before the crisis to Tog 500,000 in fall 2009.	Herders showed increased interest in nonpastoral activities.	Sales and profits of small business improved.
There was reduced availability and increased competition for informal sector jobs.	Formal sector workers continued working part time with reduced salaries; formal sector jobs were still shrinking.	Rural urban migration increased due to devastation of traditional herder livelihoods.	Herders benefited from higher prices for meat, cashmere, and animal skins.
There were reduced sales and profits for small businesses.	Seasonal jobs in rural and urban locations did not increase in the summer time.	Access to bank loans remained constrained for herders due to reduced value of collateral (livestock) and continued restrictions on the maximum loan amount.	Herders continued to show interest and engaged in nonpastoral activities.
Crime and alcohol abuse increased in rural and urban areas.	Small businesses continued experiencing slower sales turnover and reduced profits.	Interviewees complained of deteriorating health conditions due to reduced consumption of nutritious food.	Access to bank loans improved; the maximum loan amount: for herders was restored to the precrisis level (Tog 5 million); employees with stable incomes (e.g., formal miners) could take loans with lower interest and extended duration; the poor with no collateral still could not access loans.
	Increase in crime and alcohol abuse remained an issue of concern for respondents.	Despite the recovery of the national economy, low-skilled jobs continued shrinking. The salary of formal miners increased due to higher prices and seasonal demand for coal.	Interviewees were able to spend more on nutrition and health services.
		Increase in crime and alcohol abuse remained an issue of concern for respondents.	Education costs were no longer a cause of stress; the government introduced a university-tuition subsidy.
			Increase in crime remained an issue of concern.

Source: Interviews with FGD participants.

Coping Strategies

Respondents of all income levels felt the impacts of the global economic crisis through declining employment opportunities and incomes and the rising prices for imported food. Reduced consumption, increased reliance on credit, distress livestock sales in rural areas, and diversification of income sources were the most common coping strategies. Rural-to-urban migration continued to rise despite job reduction in Ulaanbaatar.

Reduced Consumption

Reduced consumption was the most common coping response, observed in all focus group discussions. For the wealthy population groups, reduced consumption meant spending less on durable goods, luxury goods, and entertainment, but for the poor it meant saving on the quality and quantity of food. For example, informal gold miners and some low-income urban residents said that with rising food prices and declining earnings, they could afford only one warm meal per day. Rural households reported saving on vegetables and sweets.

> "With decreased income, we have to cut consumption. If we finish food, for example, sugar, we do not buy more immediately. We wait until next month. We do not buy clothes anymore; we will only buy for children going to school and will not buy for those who stay at home. I sew clothes for younger children from old clothes of elder ones. We don't buy vegetables and eat only flour, rice, and meat. We pick up wild onions. We do not buy any other things."

Herder from Bayandelger soum, Tuv aimag,
August–September 2009

Diversification of Income Sources

Many participants of focus group discussions reported that relying on one source of income was no longer sufficient to meet consumption needs (for subsistence farmers) or to stay in business. Diversification of livelihoods and business activities emerged as a common coping strategy in urban and rural locations. Entrepreneurs and small businesses reported expanding the range of products or services they offered.

> "We used to renovate a two-bedroom apartment for Tog 1,200,000; now it costs Tog 700,000. So, we decided to diversify our business and started producing windows."

A 54-year-old female interior designer/renovator, Ulaanbaatar,
May–June 2009

A number of herder households became interested in settled or semisettled farming and in adding value to livestock products through small-scale processing, such as producing dried milk, spinning wool, and the like. Growing vegetables primarily for household consumption was one of the most popular activities. Donor-funded projects that provided support in building greenhouses and growing vegetables were greatly appreciated by the beneficiaries, and there was substantial interest in replicating and scaling up of these initiatives. Some rural households also tried to engage in nonagricultural activities like making shoes, catering, and providing tourism services. Access to credit and technical assistance was often cited as an important factor in helping farmers diversify their livelihoods.

> "We borrowed Tog 300,000 and spin wool. We buy a kilo of wool for Tog 4,000 and make 3 packs of wool needle. We sell one pack of wool needle for Tog 3,000. With new jobs, both of us [husband and wife] are working. My husband does spinning and I do it as well. It is not common that men do this kind of job at home."
>
> Couple from Bogd soum, Bayanhongor aimag,
> August–September 2009

Rural entrepreneurs faced a number of challenges in operating their businesses. The major constraints on business development identified in the focus group discussions were the following: (1) limited access to markets (due to high transport-related expenditures), (2) insufficient access to credit, and (3) inadequate skills. Entrepreneurs operating in rural areas faced limited local demand for their products and often had to sell their produce to middlemen at wholesale prices. Those who could afford transportation costs could sell their products at *aimag* (provincial) centers or in Ulaanbaatar at much better prices. Access to credit was cited as a major problem in both urban and rural locations. Small-scale microcredit initiatives were effective in helping entrepreneurs start their businesses but were not always sufficient for their expansion. The interviewees also commonly cited lack of skills, including sewing and production of dairy products and sweets, as a limiting factor in business start-up and development.

The interest in diversification in rural areas was stronger in the last two rounds of this research (during 2010–11). This could be attributed to the effects of economic crisis and the recent dzud, which resulted in a large number of animal deaths and impoverished many households whose livelihoods were dependent entirely on livestock.

Illegal Gold Mining

Declining income-generating opportunities in urban areas and falling prices for livestock contributed to the increase in the number of illegal gold miners. In the summertime, women and children also participated in gold mining despite the numerous risks associated with this activity. Some people engaged in gold mining on a temporary basis to cover seasonal expenditures (mainly the cost of education), to compensate for losses of livestock, or to accumulate some savings and start a small business. Yet for the impoverished rural households, gold mining became a major income-generating activity.

> "You cannot imagine that many people, including women, are involved in mining just to support their lives. Many of them let their children drop out of schools and colleges because of financial difficulty. Some students have to break their studies."

> Shop owner, Bayanteel soum, Uvukrhangai aimag,
> May–June 2009

Miners expose themselves and their children to significant health risks. Most do not wear protective clothing and do not follow any safety rules. There are no health clinics at mining sites, and miners have to go to *soum* (district) centers if they get injured. Their access to health services is restricted, however, because they do not pay for health insurance. Miners operate illegally and are not registered at local government bodies; therefore, they usually do not have access to any social services.

With the growth of the national economy in 2010–11, informal mining became much less popular. Nevertheless, it is still practiced by the poorest households, particularly those close to the mining sites. Informal miners are in need of public support. Many of them would like to obtain some skills and credit to shift to other occupations or start their own businesses.

Livestock Sales in Rural Areas

Mongolian herders were severely impacted by declining world cashmere prices. All herders suffered from this external shock, but the poor were disproportionately affected. To compensate for the decreased income from cashmere, they engaged in distress sale of meat. As a result, meat prices fell and the poor had to sell a large number of animals to finance basic consumption. They were left with reduced herds—their major asset.

The situation was further compounded by livestock losses due to the dzud. The losses were higher among the poor as they could not afford the costs of animal fodder. The short-term coping strategies of poor herder households will have lasting impacts on their livelihoods. They were not able to fully benefit from the increased prices for cashmere and livestock in 2010–11, and it will take years to rebuild the herds.

The wealthier herder households—those with 500 or more animals—were more resilient. They could wait until cashmere prices recovered because they could draw on their savings and other sources of income. They had a better sense of price movements, could afford transportation costs to urban locations instead of relying on the middlemen, and could sell livestock products at better prices. They also had better access to credit. Overall, wealthier households seemed to seek longer-term coping strategies such as increasing the number of livestock and enhancing animal productivity, improving the quality of fodder, and adding value to their products.

The resilience of herder households to commodity price movements was strongly correlated with the number of livestock they possessed, proximity to markets, and diversification of income sources. Households with fewer than 100 animals were considered very poor and most vulnerable to any shocks (price fluctuations, disasters, theft, and so forth). These households were not hired by companies or wealthier farmers to herd their livestock as they would not be able to pay for any lost animals. They also faced difficulties in obtaining bank loans because they did not have sufficient collateral. Households with more than 500 animals were considered more resilient to various shocks than farmers with smaller herds. Distance to markets was another important factor in determining vulnerability as prices for livestock products were much higher in Ulaanbaatar than in local markets. Very few herders could afford the costs of transportation and had to sell their products at much lower prices to middlemen. One opportunity for income diversification was the rise of tourism, which made residents in areas adjacent to tourist camps less dependent on agriculture.

Protecting Children's Education

People at all levels of income tried to protect education expenditures and keep their children at school. Low-income families had to sell more livestock or take loans from the banks to cover the increasing costs of schooling (uniforms and educational supplies). Children from rural households were helping their parents cover education-related expenditures by engaging in herding animals, preparing fodder, offering horse and camel-riding services to tourists, and engaging in other activities. University students and children from low-income families were assisting their parents at illegal gold sites. Some students from poor families had to terminate their university studies or take a temporary leave of absence as their parents could no longer afford rising tuition costs. Wealthier students who had completed their course of studies but were unable to find jobs decided to continue their education until the job market improved.

Increased Rural-Urban Migration

Despite job reduction in Ulaanbaatar, rural-to-urban migration was increasing. People came to Ulaanbaatar in search of better employment opportunities and health and education services. They faced enormous difficulties with obtaining land and residential registration as well as in finding jobs due to lack of skills. Long-term unemployment was widespread among migrants. In May–June 2009, when the first focus group discussion took place, two-thirds of interviewed migrant households did not have any family members with a wage job and were engaged in informal activities like gardening, fence guarding, or shoemaking. Migrants did not have sufficient collateral to take loans, which precluded them from starting or expanding business activities. The interviewed migrants were not motivated to return to rural areas due to the costs associated with resettlement, repurchase of livestock, and creation of summer and winter camps in new lands.

Although the migrants' livelihoods improved with the recovery of the Mongolian economy during the fourth round of research, lack of skills and social networks, constrained access to credit, and life in unorganized settlements with poor access to water and other essential infrastructure continued to disadvantage them.

Coping Strategies of Different Population Groups

There was a noticeable difference in the severity of impacts and the types of coping strategies used by different people. The poor—urban migrants to Ulaanbaatar, herders with fewer than 100 animals, and illegal gold miners—were most strongly affected. They were also limited in their coping responses due to lack of skills and a low asset base, which made them ineligible for bank loans. The most common coping strategies of these groups were the following: drastic reduction in consumption, including limiting the quantity and quality of food; selling assets; working longer hours; and diversifying sources of income if such opportunity became available. The poor had relatively few possibilities for income diversification, with illegal gold digging being the most common activity.

Wealthier population groups, such as formal miners, small business owners, or herders with a large number of animals, had a wider range of coping strategies, including borrowing from banks, adding value to their products, for example, by spinning wool, or expanding the range of products and business services offered.

Impact of Economic Recovery. Significant improvements in livelihoods of all income groups were observed during the fourth round of research, November 2010–January 2011. Positive changes included increased job availability; higher salaries of civil servants and employees of state-owned companies, which were raised by 30 percent; and higher government spending on education, which alleviated the burden of school-related expenditures. Herders benefited from the increased prices for meat and livestock products, and most of them were able to repay bank loans. Many rural people who were postponing medical expenditures during the crisis were now able to take better care of their health.

Although all income groups benefited from economic growth to some extent, the improvements were rather uneven. The wealthier herder households could buy durable goods, invest in real estate in a soum center or Ulaanbaatar, and make productive investments in their businesses or livestock breeding. Poor herders, who were disproportionately affected by the crisis and the dzud, could improve nutrition and buy some clothes, but they could not afford to improve *ger* covers, leaving them vulnerable to winter cold, or to make investments that would lift them out of poverty. Formal miners could afford to buy electrical appliances and real estate; they could also have access to bank loans on privileged conditions such as lower interest rates and extended duration. Informal sector workers, for example, recent migrants to Ulaanbaatar, were able to earn just enough to cover food expenses but could not afford productive investments. The number of people engaged in illegal gold mining decreased with improved availability of jobs in services and agriculture, but informal mining remained a major source of income for the impoverished rural households, particularly those living close to gold mining sites. Many of these miners no longer own any livestock and have few livelihood options.

Sources of Support

Households across Mongolia most commonly relied on the government's social protection, loans from banks and microfinance institutions, and support from family and community members. Some interviewees also benefited from the assistance of donor organizations and nongovernmental organizations (NGOs).

Government's Assistance

The free school education policy and the government's social transfers played a major role in helping the poor weather the negative impacts of the global financial crisis. Free school education, meals for primary school students, and free child-care services helped protect children's education during the crisis. Many low-income interviewees reported that their fixed income consisted mainly of social welfare payments including pension, child benefits (during 2009), allowance for poor households, and disability allowance. The child benefit program, which provided regular monthly and quarterly payments, was of great importance to rural and urban households, especially during times of reduced incomes. According to interviewees, the child benefit program was often the only source of cash for poor households. Furthermore, child benefit documents were often used in food stores as collateral to obtain food on credit.

> *"Not all people realize how beneficial child benefit money is. It really contributes a lot to low-income families. It helps us when we do not have money."*
>
> Informal miner couple, Bayanteel soum, Uvurkhangai aimag,
> May–June 2009

> *"Child support money was a major income source for poor and very poor households. Moreover, the child support money documents were used as a collateral in the shop to get some daily food. Unfortunately, the support stopped; livelihood will worsen more."*
>
> Participants, Dundgovi aimag,
> January–February 2010

The government terminated the child benefit program in the end of 2009 because of fiscal constraints. Instead of the program, a one-time payment of Tog 70,000 as part of the so-called mineral resource sharing money was distributed by the newly created Human Development Fund. According to interviewees, the money was quickly spent for Tsagaan Sar

(Mongolian New Year), and the poor were left with no predictable source of cash income for months to come.

Following economic recovery, the government renewed cash transfers, and starting from August 2010, Tog 10,000 a month (around $8) have been distributed to every citizen of Mongolia. Poor households appreciated such assistance and reported that it helped them cover food consumption, but the amount was too small to lift them out of poverty or make major changes in their lives. The wealthier households were skeptical about the benefits of universal cash transfers; instead, they believed the government should invest the resources in job creation, infrastructure, and support services for business development. Some also thought that cash transfers should be targeted and provided only to the vulnerable, such as single mothers or the elderly.

Another source of cash assistance was the Food Card Program (supported by the ADB), which provided Tog 14,000 per month to 25,000 poor individuals from November 2009 to August 2010 and helped cover basic food consumption. The program was well targeted and appreciated by recipients.

The government also initiated several programs for herders to help them cope with a drop in the global cashmere prices and later with the dzud. In May 2009, quality restrictions on cashmere were lifted, the export tax was abolished, and the number of ports authorized for cashmere exports was raised from 3 to 20. These measures did facilitate a rise in cashmere prices in August 2009, but most poor households had already sold their cashmere and did not benefit from these policies. Government initiatives for alleviation of dzud impacts were appreciated by FGD participants and reached many poor households. Support programs included provision of Tog 300,000 to households that lost most of their animals (through the Restock with Livestock Program), distribution of free or subsidized animal feed to herders in severely affected areas, and other in-kind assistance. After the dzud, local governments also became very active in educating herders about improved pasture management, care for weak animals, and disaster management.

Loans from Banks and Microfinance Institutions

Borrowing from banks and microfinance institutions was one of the strategies that helped households cope with price shocks, reduced incomes, and rising education expenditures and helped to restore their livelihoods after dzuds. Interviewees, however, complained about high interest rates charged by banks in addition to reduced loan amounts and a shorter duration of the loan period in comparison to the precrisis years. Furthermore, the poorest households—herders with fewer than 100 animals, informal gold miners—did not have access to credit and had to sell things in pawn shops or borrow from shops and relatives. Support from microfinance institutions, such as the Rural Women's Organization, was useful in helping recipients launch new businesses, but the assistance was not always sufficient to ensure their growth.

> "I lost most of the animals because of dzud. Our family was left with only 40 animals. So, I borrowed money from the women's organization twice, at six-month intervals. At maximum, I borrowed Tog 300,000. I initially bought 15 baby goats. Now, I have 121 goats. Thanks to the women's microcredit program, I now have about 150 animals. I pay the loan interest using my pension in the winter time. I can make some money during cashmere period. So, the life is not so bad."

> Woman from Bogd soum, Bayankhongor aimag,
> January–February 2010

In Mongolia, most FGD participants said they managed to repay their loans to banks and microfinance institutions after the economic recovery of 2010. There were no reports of loss of land, houses, or other essential assets due to inability to pay off the debts. Poor households that had not repaid the loans at the time of the FGDs were able to extend the loan period.

Assistance from Donors and NGOs

Some households benefited from the assistance of donors and NGOs that operated in Mongolia even before the crisis. Donor support involved small and medium enterprise development projects, enhancements of rural infrastructure, animal husbandry improvement, and dzud assistance. NGO support commonly focused on promotion of nonpastoral activities: growing vegetables, sewing, and baking. Interviewees expressed their appreciation for such projects.

> "Luxemburg foundation helped us to grow vegetables. Ten households were involved in the projects as a community group. I feel happy to work in a group. We started last year planting 1.5 hectares of land and started to benefit for own consumption. We would like to learn more and wish to grow more vegetables."

> Man, Govi-Ugtaal soum, Dundgovi aimag,
> January–February 2010

Family and Community Support

Family ties and community support were vital for coping with the crisis, particularly for poor families. Low-income urban migrants reported receiving food products from family members in the countryside. Similarly, wealthier urban residents sent remittances to their relatives in rural areas. Informal gold miners who worked in teams said they shared food, which cost them less. Social networks were also essential for finding jobs in urban locations.

> "I have eight children and five of them work in Ulaanbaatar. When I face a shortage of money, I call my children. Sometimes, I send meat and dairy products to them. Recently my daughter came on vacation and paid my debt of Tog 500,000."

> Female herder from Nariinteel soum, Uvurhangai aimag,
> August–September 2009

> "I found a good job because of my relatives. I am working in this company since June and I like my job."

> Thirty-nine-year-old female, 20th khoroo, Bayanzurkh district,
> January–February 2010

Most poor families did not have savings and could not access bank loans as they lacked collateral. They reported borrowing from friends and relatives or local stores in emergency situations. In case of severe illness or death of a family member, the community collected money and gave it to the affected household.

> "People borrow goods and food. Some people borrow money to go home or if somebody passes away. They pay back when they earn money. Their payment period is getting longer. Some people disappear without paying for what they borrowed."

> Shop owner at the gold mining site, Bayanteel soum,
> Uvurkhangai aimag, May–June 2009

Impact of Economic Recovery. Improved fiscal revenues enabled the government to increase pensions by 30 percent, introduce monthly cash transfers, increase spending on school education, and introduce a subsidy to offset university tuition fees. These measures were appreciated by low-income households. Economic recovery also improved access to credit, although individuals without collateral remained ineligible for loans.

Conclusions and Implications for Policy

The qualitative research undertaken in Mongolia showed that households were severely affected by the global economic crisis. Labor market impacts observed through layoffs, reduced availability of jobs in formal and informal sectors, reduced salaries, and price shocks (reduced prices for cashmere and higher prices for food and transportation) were the key transmission channels. The effects of the crisis were compounded by the winter dzud of 2010. Households responded by cutting consumption, diversifying sources of income, borrowing from formal and informal sources, and, in rural areas, by distress sales of livestock to finance basic consumption. The government's social assistance, although small, not always regular, and in some instances not targeted to the poor, was nevertheless appreciated by low-income FGD participants and helped them weather the crisis.

Although all income groups suffered from the effects of the global economic downturn, recent migrants to Ulaanbaatar, informal gold miners (for whom gold digging is the major source of income), and herders with fewer than 100 animals were most severely affected. These groups of people suffer from chronic poverty and are vulnerable to any shocks. They are least likely to benefit from economic recovery and require targeted assistance. The economic crisis also exposed the vulnerability of herders with up to 500 animals for whom livestock breeding is the only source of income. This group was not insecure before the global economic downturn, but the compound effects of collapse in cashmere prices and the dzud showed the risks of dependence on one primary commodity.

The broad-based growth in 2010–11, accompanied by increased job availability in formal and informal sectors, higher prices for livestock products, and increased social transfers, improved the livelihoods of all income groups, but these improvements were rather uneven. The wealthier households reported buying durable goods and real estate and making productive investments in their businesses or livestock breeding. The poorest population groups could improve nutrition and buy some clothes but could not afford the purchase of durable goods and investments that would lift them out of poverty.

The global economic crisis revealed several structural and social vulnerabilities in Mongolia. Among these vulnerabilities are a narrow production base, which makes the country very sensitive to commodity fluctuations and disasters; the lack of effective supply chains for meat and low value added for livestock products; and the vulnerability of the chronic poor and certain weaknesses of the social safety nets. Furthermore, rising crime and violence can have high costs for individuals, businesses, and communities. Addressing these issues can help make Mongolia's population more resilient to future shocks. The following implications for policy reforms emerged from this research.

Diversify Economic Activity

Mongolia's heavy dependence on exports of a few primary goods—gold, copper, and cashmere—has made the economy vulnerable to global fluctuations in commodity prices. The livelihoods of herders are totally dependent on prices for livestock products. Many of the interviewed rural households reported that they would like to diversify their income sources through vegetable growing and nonfarm economic activities. Skill-building programs, better access to credit, and lower cost of capital were commonly cited among the desired support initiatives. Further development of the service sector, particularly tourism, also holds promise for growth.

Develop Supply Chains for Meat and Increase Domestic Value Added for Livestock Products

Increasing producer prices of livestock products through enhancement of herders' access to markets (both domestic and international) and the development of value chains for cashmere, wool, and meat products have the potential to soften the negative impacts of economic crisis and to improve herders' livelihoods. Local markets for meat get easily saturated, resulting in a drastic decline of meat prices, as demonstrated during the economic crisis. The situation is similar during dzuds when many herders try to sell a larger than usual number of animals, but may also happen in good years due to improvements in livestock productivity.

Farmers commonly mentioned dependence on middlemen and the high costs of bringing meat to urban centers. Improvement of domestic supply chains for meat and development of export outlets, particularly to China and Russia, can smooth the impact of economic shocks and adverse weather and raise herders' incomes. Development of meat exports will require improved adherence to sanitary standards as well as progress on trade negotiations (Green Gold Pasture Ecosystem Management Program and Mongolian Society for Range Management 2009). Similarly, measures to enhance the quality of cashmere and wool products, strengthen the processing industry, and develop direct links between herders and processors can help increase herders' incomes and generate additional employment opportunities.

Improve Safety Nets

The crisis has shown the importance of predictable, regular, and sustainable social assistance programs for the poor. The child benefit program was greatly appreciated by interviewees due to the regularity of its transfers, but it was terminated at the time when it was most needed. The FGD participants were not sure whether the universal cash transfers introduced in August 2010 were the beginning of a continuous transfer program or were a temporary intervention to share the "mineral resource wealth" in a year of economic growth. It would be beneficial to limit the transfers only to poor households and increase the generosity of benefits. Regularity and sustainability of social assistance programs will be vital for helping the poor cope with future shocks, accumulate assets, and move out of poverty.

Certain vulnerable groups—illegal gold miners, herders with fewer than 100 animals, and recent migrants to Ulaanbaatar—require particular attention. These groups suffer from a low asset base, lack of skills, and limited access to bank loans. These constraints make them particularly vulnerable to any shocks and prevent them from taking advantage of economic opportunities in good years. Additionally, urban migrants suffer from problems with finding land, obtaining registration, and accessing information about jobs. Addressing the needs of these groups will be important for the alleviation of chronic poverty.

Prevent Crime and Domestic Violence

Increasing crime rates were of major concern for both rural and urban residents. Well-known approaches to crime prevention include increasing the frequency of police patrols in crime-ridden areas; creating neighborhood watch programs with the engagement of local community; and establishing social programs that target at-risk youth through sports activities, skills development, internships, and the like. It is equally important to prevent domestic violence and provide adequate support for its victims. Potential measures can include raising public awareness about domestic violence, educating young people that domestic violence is never an acceptable behavior, teaching health and social workers how to identify the signs of domestic violence and help the affected individuals, and establishing hotlines and support centers for victims.

Note

1. The researchers attempted to visit the same households in each round, but it was not possible (herders were moving to summer or winter camps; small market traders could not always be found in the same place, and so on), so no more than 20 percent of respondents participated in all four rounds of data collection. The researchers did, however, interview people belonging to the same occupations—herders, miners, and so forth—throughout the four rounds.

References

ADB (Asian Development Bank). 2010. *Asian Development Outlook 2010*. Ulaanbaatar: ADB.

Green Gold Pasture Ecosystem Management Program and Mongolian Society for Range Management. "2009 Draft Livelihood Study of Herders in Mongolia." Swiss Agency for Development and Cooperation, Bema.

UNDP (United Nations Development Programme). undated. http://www.undp.org/asia/pdf/financial_crisis/Mongolia.pdf.

World Bank. 2010. *Mongolia Monthly Economic Update: January 2010*. World Bank, Washington, DC. http://web.worldbank.org/WBSITE/EXTERNAL/COUNTRIES/EASTASIAPACIFICEXT/MONGOLIAEXTN/0,,contentMDK:22817117~menuPK:327714~pagePK:2865066~piPK:2865079~theSiteP K:327708,00.html.

CHAPTER 8

Perceptions of the Economic Crisis and Poverty in Senegal: A Quantitative and Qualitative Analysis

Abdou Salam Fall, Lea Salmon, and Quentin Wodon

This chapter provides an assessment of the impact of the global food, fuel, and financial crisis on household well-being in Senegal. The assessment is based on a quantitative analysis of available household survey data and qualitative focus groups and individual interviews implemented in selected locations.

Before the recent crisis, Senegal was to a large extent considered one of several African success stories in terms of economic growth and poverty reduction (Azam et al. 2007). Most of Senegal's development indicators showed progress (table 8.1). According to estimates based on nationally representative household surveys, the share of the population in poverty decreased from 67.9 percent at the national level in 1994–95, to 54.0 percent in 2001, and to 50.8 percent in 2005–06 (Ndoye et al. 2009). Due to high population growth (2.6 percent in 2009), the number of the poor continued to increase. Poverty reduction in rural areas was weaker than in urban areas as some of the poorest did not benefit from the sustained period of economic growth that followed the devaluation of the CFA franc (CFAF) in 1994. Still, overall, it was clear that substantial progress was being achieved.

Since the last household survey was implemented in 2005–06, however, it appears that the situation has deteriorated. Reliable household survey data to assess changes in poverty after 2005–06 are not available, but a number of indicators suggest negative effects on the sources of livelihoods and on the cost of living as growth slowed down and exogenous shocks took their toll.

Table 8.1. Senegal: Development Indicators, 2000–09

Population (in millions)	9.9	(2000)	12.5	(2009)
Population growth (annual %)	2.6	(2000)	2.6	(2009)
Population ages 0–14 (% of total)	45.5	(2000)	43.6	(2009)
Life expectancy at birth (years)	54.1	(2000)	55.6	(2008)
Percentage of population living below the national poverty line	57.1	(2001)	50.8	(2005)
Adult literacy rate (%)	39.2	(2002)	41.9	(2006)
Percentage of male and female pupils completing grade 5	72.3	(2000)	70.9	(2007)
Under 5 mortality rate per 1,000 live births	119.5	(2000)	92.8	(2009)
Maternal mortality ratio (per 100,000 births)	560.0	(2000)	410.0	(2008)

Source: World Bank 2010.

On the productive side, from the CFAF devaluation in 1994 to 2001, average GDP (gross domestic product) growth in Senegal was around 5.0 percent a year, well above the average of 3.2 percent in Sub-Saharan Africa. As a consequence, poverty rates fell significantly, and GDP per capita went from $526 in 1994 to $626 in 2001 (World Bank 2003). During the period of sustained growth between 2002 and 2005, GDP growth reached 4.7 percent, which allowed poverty rates to decline further, down to 50.8 percent. In part because of weather shocks, including drought, economic growth in 2006 reached only 2.3 percent, which was below the rate of population growth and thus indicated a reduction in real per capita GDP. The GDP growth rate in 2007 rebounded to 4.8 percent but fell back again to 2.7 percent in 2008–09, despite better agricultural output. Growth was expected to rebound and reach 4 percent in 2010 (IMF 2010). But overall, the post-2005 growth performance (3.4 percent between 2006 and 2010) has been well below the projections adopted in the second Poverty Reduction Strategy for the period 2006–10, which called for a medium-term growth rate of 5 percent per year (see Azam et al. 2007, and Ndoye et al. 2009, for a discussion of growth patterns and poverty trends in Senegal; see also République du Sénégal 2006, 2008).

In 2008, households were confronted with a rapid increase in food and fuel prices (Boccanfuso and Savard 2008). In the first three months of 2008, the price of rice in Senegal increased by 30 percent. Given that a substantial share of basic staple foods is imported (this is the case for rice, a commodity for which local production remains limited), the increase in food and fuel prices is likely to have led to a substantial reduction in the purchasing power of the population, especially the poor. Budget deficits and weak targeting systems of social programs prevented the government from allocating substantial additional funds to safety net programs that could have helped to alleviate the situation for the poor. One could therefore expect that the welfare and living conditions of vulnerable populations may have deteriorated significantly in Senegal over the past few years.

The objective of this chapter is to assess the likely impact of the economic crisis on the poor and to analyze what strategies the population used to cope with the crisis. The assessment is derived by combining simulations based on data from the country's latest nationally representative household survey for 2005–06 with results from qualitative work using focus groups carried out at two times in 2010. Three main conclusions can be drawn from the quantitative analysis. First, before the crisis, Senegal had experienced an impressive reduction in poverty, and this remains true whether one uses objective consumption-based measures of poverty or subjective assessments by households. Second, despite such progress, many households still felt that they were not able to satisfy many of their basic needs. Third, simulations suggest that the increase in food and fuel prices during the crisis may have had a substantial adverse impact on poverty. Qualitative data from focus groups and individual interviews confirm that living conditions of much of the population have become more difficult. Many interviewees spoke about a lack of gainful employment as well as threats to their traditional livelihoods. Rising costs for basic necessities, higher levels of indebtedness, and limited access to credit also contribute to a deterioration of standards of living. Households have limited means to cope with the crisis apart from increasing working hours, especially for women, and adjusting their consumption patterns toward lower-cost, lower-quality food. Evidence suggests that the crisis increased tensions within some communities and put stress on traditional mechanisms of solidarity between households. The overall picture is of a society that has made substantial gains over the past two decades but remains highly vulnerable to both external and internal shocks.

Following this introduction, the chapter consists of four sections. The next section describes the methodology used for data collection and analysis, relying both on the 2005–06 survey and the focus groups implemented in specific areas of the country likely to have been affected by the crisis. The following section provides a summary of quantitative results regarding trends in poverty before the crisis, as well as the potential impact of some aspects of the crisis, with a focus on the impact of higher food prices. The third section discusses the results of the qualitative work, with a focus on specific groups of affected workers, both in terms of the shocks incurred and coping strategies used. The final section offers conclusions.

Data and Methodology

Household survey data to assess the impact of the crisis in Senegal are limited. Measures of poverty are based on national surveys that are implemented every five years on average. In between surveys, it is typically necessary to rely on simulation techniques to assess the likely impact of various shocks. The quantitative analysis presented in this chapter relies on three subsequent household surveys implemented by *Agence Nationale de la Statistique et de la Démographie* (ANSD) (National Agency for Statistics and Demography): the ESAM I, ESAM II, and ESPS surveys. ESAM stands for *Enquête sénégalaise auprès des ménages* (Senegalese Household Survey), with data collection for the two surveys dating back to 1994–95 and 2001–02. The ESPS (*Enquête de suivi dela pauvreté au Sénégal* [Follow-up Poverty Survey in Senegal]) is a survey with a shorter questionnaire that was implemented in 2005–06 but has the advantage of a larger sample size. A new survey, not yet available, was under implementation in 2011. Although the three available surveys have important differences, they are sufficiently comparable to establish a reliable poverty trend for the country over the period, as discussed in the section on quantitative analysis.

Because no subsequent surveys with consumption data were implemented after the ESPS to assess the impact of the crisis as it unfolded, the ESPS survey provides the only available data to conduct simulations (as opposed to ex-post estimations) on the likely impact of the crisis. The section on quantitative analysis focuses on the impact of the increase in food prices on poverty. In addition, the survey can also be used to analyze the perceptions of the population about what it means to be poor, their ability to satisfy basic needs, and trends in poverty over time in the country. Thus, although the 2005–06 survey cannot be used to measure the impact of the crisis ex-post, it nevertheless provides valuable information that can be compared to results from the qualitative work implemented in 2010.

The qualitative data collection was implemented in two waves using focus group techniques (Fall, Rokhaya, and Tidiane 2010). It aimed at gaining a better understanding of the crisis and how it affected the life of the population, as well as the changes it brought about and the coping mechanisms that it generated. A total of 265 people participated in the focus group discussions (FGDs), with an average of 9 individuals per group. Participants came from various sectors of the economy: the primary sector (rice growers, farmers, livestock growers, fishermen, and so forth); the secondary sector (industrial workers); and the tertiary sector (service providers). Four researchers worked in the field to collect the data, with 9 FGDs taking place in the capital and 21 in the other regions of the country. Besides the broader Dakar area, the field work took place in the South (Casamance); Center (Diourbel Suneor, Fatick, Kaffrine, Kaolack, Mbour, Thiès, and Touba); East (Kédougou, Kolda-Faramba, and Tamba); and North (Ndombo Allarba, Matam, Mbodiène, and Saint Louis). In addition, individual interviews were conducted with 137 people who had already participated in focus groups. The interviews concentrated primarily on the topics of vulnerability, how individuals viewed themselves on a welfare scale, how recent changes affected them, and to what extent they were able to rely on aid from others and from social capital to cope with the crisis.

The choice of participants in the FGDs was based on a selection of areas where the vulnerability of the population to the crisis was deemed substantial and on different occupations that could have been affected. An examination of the existing literature made it possible to map the groups based on their vulnerability relative to the various regions of Senegal. Some FGDs focused on poor householders such as farmers, while others dealt with better-off segments of the population, such as jewelers or small informal businessmen, to assess to what extent these groups also were affected by the crisis.

Although the FGDs cannot claim to provide a representative sample of the population as a whole, they provide rich complementary data. Such data can lead to a better understanding of the various ways households have been affected by the crisis and coped with it than can the household survey-based simulations of the likely impact of some aspects of the crisis at the national level.

Quantitative Analysis

Trends in Objective and Subjective Poverty before the Crisis

Unlike the Central African Republic, which has experienced a modest growth of 2.5 percent a year since the end of conflict in 2003 and was therefore unable to make any significant progress against poverty, Senegal had benefited from a sustained period of economic growth until 2005.[1] This period of growth helped reduce the headcount of poverty to 50.8 percent in 2005, with a sharper decrease in urban than in rural areas. Trends in higher order poverty measures such as the poverty gap (the product of the headcount and the distance separating the poor from the poverty line as a proportion of that line), and the squared poverty gap (which takes into account for the poor the square of the distance from the poverty line as a proportion of that line) suggest similar positive results. At the same time, there are indications that the severity of poverty, as measured through the squared poverty gap, may have increased in rural areas between 2001–02 and 2005–06, so that not all households benefited to the same extent from the postdevaluation period of expansion (table 8.2).

The decrease in objective measures of poverty based on consumption data was confirmed through subjective data on the perceptions of households regarding both the levels of poverty and the changes in poverty over time (table 8.3). Indeed, the ESPS questionnaire includes a module that deals with the perceptions of poverty among households, and these perceptions can be compared to similar questions in the ESAM II survey. Table 8.3 shows that the share of the population that considered itself poor decreased from about 67 percent in 2001–02 to about 51 percent in 2005–06, a level similar to the objective measures of poverty based on consumption. The geography of the decrease in subjective perceptions of

Table 8.2. Trends in Poverty Measures in Senegal, 1994–95, 2001–02, 2005–06 (%)

	National	Dakar	Other urban	Rural
		1994–95		
Headcount of poverty	67.9	56.4	70.7	71.0
Poverty gap	23.6	17.7	24.4	25.3
Squared poverty gap	10.6	7.4	10.8	11.7
		2001–02		
Headcount of poverty	57.1	42.0	50.1	65.2
Poverty gap	18.3	12.0	16.1	21.4
Squared poverty gap	7.9	4.7	6.9	9.4
		2005–06		
Headcount of poverty	50.8	32.5	38.8	61.9
Poverty gap	16.4	8.3	10.8	21.5
Squared poverty gap	7.5	3.0	4.5	10.2

Source: Ndoye et al. 2009.

Note: Headcount of poverty refers to the share of the population that is poor according to measures of consumption per equivalent adult and a poverty line based on the cost of basic food and nonfood needs.

Table 8.3. Trends in Subjective Well-Being in Senegal, 2001–02, 2005–06 (%)

	Subjective well-being	2001–02	2005–06	Difference
National	Very rich	0.27	0.93	0.66
	Somewhat rich	2.81	4.62	1.81
	Average	29.94	43.12	13.18
	Somewhat poor	43.79	34.73	−9.06
	Very poor	23.19	16.61	−6.58
Dakar	Very rich	0.16	0.47	0.31
	Somewhat rich	5.11	2.42	−2.69
	Average	49.41	55.58	6.17
	Somewhat poor	31.95	35.16	3.21
	Very poor	13.36	6.37	−6.99
Other cities	Very rich	0.49	1.27	0.78
	Somewhat rich	4.52	4.63	0.11
	Average	36.78	52.13	15.35
	Somewhat poor	38.21	32.04	−6.17
	Very poor	20.01	9.93	−10.08
Rural	Very rich	0.23	1.02	0.79
	Somewhat rich	1.34	5.53	4.19
	Average	20.01	35.25	15.24
	Somewhat poor	50.31	35.35	−14.96
	Very poor	28.11	22.84	−5.27

Source: Authors, using ESAM II 2001–02 and ESPS 2005–06 data.

poverty differed from that of objective measures, but the overall trend nationally was similar.

Figure 8.1 provides additional data regarding the perceptions of households about their ability to meet various needs, again with a comparison between 2001–02 and 2005–06. Most of the population feels that it is not able to meet many of its needs: for food, housing, clothing, health care, and education. In addition, the share of the population declaring nonsatisfaction of basic needs is higher than the share of the population that perceived itself as being in poverty. Even in 2005–06, more than two-thirds of households report that they cannot meet their health care needs, and the proportion is similar for education (accounting for the fact that some parents do not have school-age children). A large majority also feels that their incomes are not sufficient to meet their needs. At the same time, the data show a decrease over time, albeit limited, in the proportion of the population that declares being able to meet its basic needs between 2001–02 and 2005–06. To give just two examples: the share of the population declaring not having enough income to meet its needs declines by seven percentage points between the two survey years at the national level, and the share of the population declaring not being able

Figure 8.1. Trends in Levels of Satisfaction for Basic Needs in Senegal, 2001–02, 2005–06 (%)

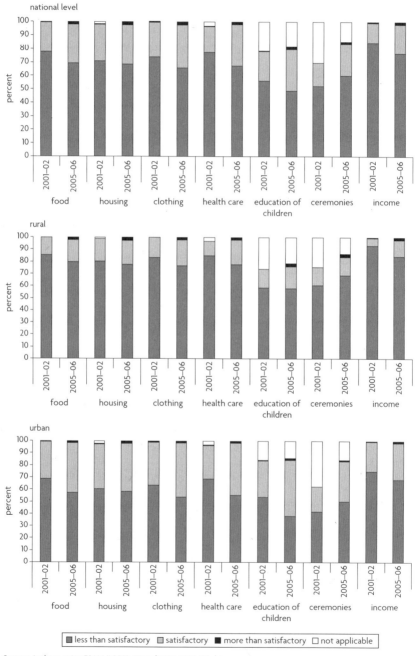

Source: Authors, using ESAM II 2001–02 and ESPS 2005–06 data.

to satisfy its food needs declines by nine percentage points. These data suggest improvement over time.

Potential Impact of the Crisis

Economic growth was reduced in 2006 and subsequent years. When combined with the sharp increase in food and fuel prices that was affecting the population as of 2008, the slower growth suggests that some of the gains in poverty reduction that were achieved in previous years may have been reversed. Here, we focus on estimating the likely impact of one of the shocks to which households were exposed: the increase in the prices of imported foods.

To assess the likely impact of the increase in food prices on poverty, we use a number of simplifying assumptions. First, we assume that the cost of an increase in food or fuel prices for a household translates into an equivalent reduction of its consumption in real terms. We do not take into account the price elasticity of demand that may lead to substitution effects and thereby help offset part of the negative effect of higher prices for certain items. In addition, due to limitations in the ESPS data, which do not provide detailed information on the production by households of food items that are likely to have been affected by the increase in world food prices, we assume no potential positive impacts of the increase in world prices for basic staples on the side of producers. Therefore, we look only at the potential negative impact on consumers of the increase in food prices. In some countries, this limitation might generate a serious bias in the estimates, but in Senegal, imported foods tend to be those items, such as rice, that the population does not produce for sale locally. Thus, the overestimation of the impact of increases in food prices due to not taking into account potential positive effects on producers may not be too large.

We do, however, take into account information on food that households produce for their own consumption. This information is available in the survey, but not the simulations because changes in prices do not affect households when food is autoconsumed. Poverty measures obtained after the increase in prices are then compared to baseline poverty measures at the time of the survey to assess impacts. We do not take into account the potential spillover effects of the increase in food or fuel prices through the economy as a whole (a rise in fuel prices may lead to higher food prices through higher transportation costs, for example, but such multiplier effects are ignored here for simplicity).

Consumer price inflation data from ANSD suggest that the price of some imported food items increased substantially, especially in early 2008. Between January and March 2008, the price of rice increased by 30 percent, and the price of milk increased by 8 percent. In addition, some of those products represent a substantial share of the total consumption of households, especially among the poor. For the poorest quintile, rice, vegetable oils, and sugar together account for 20 percent of total consumption of households, and the increase in their prices would have a large effect on poverty.

Table 8.4 provides estimates of the impact on the headcount index of poverty, the poverty gap, and the squared poverty gap of various levels of increase in selected food prices. If the price of five products (rice, vegetable oil, sugar, wheat and millet, and milk and dairy products) were to increase by 30 percent, the share of the population in poverty would increase by six percentage points, which is significant. This dramatic change did not actually take place, because prices did not increase that much or permanently. In addition, households shifted to the consumption of other foods (as noted in the section on qualitative analysis), which should have helped to reduce somewhat the impact on poverty. Nevertheless, the increase in food prices is likely to have led to a substantial increase in the share of the population in poverty, and the proportional impact on the poverty gap and squared poverty gap versus baseline values is likely to have been even larger. In other words, the impact of the increase in food prices could well have wiped out (temporarily) much of the gains in poverty reduction achieved between 2001–02 and 2005–06. Also, especially for higher order measures of poverty, such as the poverty gap and the squared poverty gap, the impact is likely to have been larger in rural areas and cities outside of Dakar.

Qualitative Analysis

Lack of Employment and Threats to Livelihoods

The evidence from the quantitative analysis presented in the previous section suggests that although substantial poverty reduction was achieved from 1994 to 2005 in Senegal, the rate of poverty reduction slowed down toward the end of this period, especially in rural areas. Moreover, the slowdown in economic growth and the increase in food and fuel prices was expected to have a significant negative impact on households after 2006. In addition,

**Table 8.4. Potential Impact of an Increase in Food Prices
on Poverty in Senegal, 2005–06**

	Base	5%	10%	15%	20%	25%	30%
Rice							
National	50.8	51.0	51.2	51.6	52.2	52.5	52.7
Dakar	32.5	32.7	32.9	33.0	33.5	33.8	33.8
Other cities	38.8	39.1	39.4	39.6	40.2	40.7	41.1
Rural	61.9	62.2	62.4	62.9	63.5	63.8	64.1
Vegetable oil							
National	50.8	50.9	51.1	51.2	51.4	51.6	51.8
Dakar	32.5	32.7	32.8	33.0	33.1	33.3	33.3
Other cities	38.8	38.9	39.0	39.2	39.3	39.5	39.7
Rural	61.9	62.1	62.2	62.4	62.5	62.9	63.1
Sugar							
National	50.8	50.9	50.9	51.0	51.2	51.4	51.4
Dakar	32.5	32.5	32.7	32.7	32.8	33.1	33.1
Other cities	38.8	38.8	38.9	39.1	39.2	39.5	39.5
Rural	61.9	62.1	62.1	62.2	62.4	62.5	62.6
Wheat and millet							
National	50.8	50.9	51.1	51.3	51.3	51.5	51.6
Dakar	32.5	32.7	32.8	33.2	33.4	33.4	33.4
Other cities	38.8	38.9	39.1	39.3	39.4	39.9	40.1
Rural	61.9	62.1	62.2	62.3	62.4	62.5	62.6
Milk and dairy products							
National	50.8	50.8	50.9	51.0	51.0	51.1	51.2
Dakar	32.5	32.5	32.7	32.7	32.8	33.1	33.3
Other cities	38.8	38.8	39.0	39.1	39.1	39.2	39.3
Rural	61.9	61.9	62.1	62.1	62.1	62.1	62.2
All five food products							
National	50.8	51.5	52.6	53.5	54.5	55.9	56.8
Dakar	32.5	33.3	34.2	34.8	36.1	37.4	38.3
Other cities	38.8	39.6	41.1	42.1	43.1	43.9	45.0
Rural	61.9	62.6	63.7	64.6	65.6	67.1	68.0

Source: Authors' estimations using ESPS 2005–06 data.

some households that used to benefit from remittances from abroad (7 in 10 Senegalese households have family members who live abroad) may have been affected by a reduction in remittances due to the crisis.

The qualitative data from the FGDs confirm that the impact of the crisis on Senegal's population has been significant from price shocks and a slowdown in economic activity for some of the groups and geographic areas surveyed. Activities once considered not rewarding are now being sought after. The lack of opportunities for employment has triggered a scramble for the available, mostly unskilled jobs. The slowdown in economic activity and employment opportunities was felt especially in the suburbs of Dakar, where people were having trouble meeting basic needs. As a young woman residing in Parcelles Assainies put it: *"It's true, people are hungry! In my household for example, I am the only one that works. How can we live properly? 'Menulis nekk'* (It is impossible). *We have problems all the time. 'Lepa trade'* (Everything is hard). *In a large family of 15, only one person works and supports the others."*

To cope with the lack of gainful employment, individuals tend to take on any opportunity that might present itself, even if it brings in very low earnings. As a young man explained: *"If I see someone selling fabrics and I'm sure I can have something in the transaction, I go for it."* Apparently, some public servants even took early retirement packages so they could meet their daily expenses and pursue private sector job opportunities at the same time. But for the majority of the older generation, retirement is experienced as a loss of resources, especially for spouses of retirees who are often forced to seek additional income for the household. The presence of tables and food served outside the doors of homes or in small public markets located close to the house is partly explained by these unending quests for small additional resources. The economic downturn is also visible when cheaper materials are substituted for the more expensive, such as recycled boxes for cooking instead of wood.

Many participants in the FGDs have been going through long periods of "unpaid jobs" or unemployment, and, for those who have kept their job, income streams have weakened. According to a restaurant owner: *"For more than ten days we do not work. The merchandise hasn't been sold. We'll have to wait until it is sold to start over. And all this is because of the crisis. Before, we worked morning and evening. We had no time, but now you can spend days and days doing nothing. It's very hard; all we could do before, we are no longer able to do it; so those problems are accelerating."* Lack of earnings also forces some to work longer hours, as is the case for this elderly person: *"My children help me, no one else helps me. At my age I should only rest, but it's quite the contrary."* Individuals involved in various trades and small businesses, including the apparel industry (sewing), also mention a downturn, due to difficulties in imports and distribution channels. The consequence of such difficulties is symbolized by the phrase *"poss yi da gno reuss"* (the pockets are empty). *"The business no longer works as before. When it worked well, we were paid in the evening and we came home happy."* These difficulties lead to delays in payment of worker wages by small entrepreneurs and cause a spillover of the crisis into the informal economy. As observed in other countries, the increasing competition for sales because of the reduction in demand is apparent in Senegal.

Apart from the downturn, structural issues remain. Shopkeepers are concerned with issues such as the decline in imports of containers and the increasing competition from Chinese merchants who sell cheaper but lower-quality products. Shopkeepers have to compete with local street vendors who do not have the same overhead costs; for example, as part of the informal economy, they do not pay taxes. Shopkeepers also feel that the government does not sufficiently protect nationals against foreign competition: *"Before, I was importing six containers of raw materials for shoes, but over the last two years I could not even import a single container per year because of competition. In Senegal, consumers do not buy quality; everything that interests them is low price. The Chinese sell shoes at very low prices but of poor quality, but these sell out quickly and easily. People prefer to buy Chinese shoes at CFAF 1,000—even if they get broken on the first day."* Traders do not necessarily associate their current difficulties with the crisis but rather to the poor organization of the sector. According to traders, the government is responsible in part for these difficulties because of *"the ease of establishment for foreigners"* and *"retailers out of control."*

The urban transport sector has been affected by the rising price of fuel, with consequences for the sector's workers. A bus driver aged 50 at the garage of Lat Dior (Dakar) spoke with great bitterness about the impact of the crisis on him: *"Work is hard on us. People do not respect us and business no longer works as before; we can only accept this since our families rely on us. In 2007, I earned CFAF 10,000, and I had money to send to my parents. But this is no longer the case now. The economic crisis has affected all sectors here in Senegal and especially those who operate in the transport sector."*

The weakness of economic activity translates not only into a lack of sales, but also into difficulties in recovering payments from customers. Close relationships and trust established over many years between sellers and buyers allow for spreading out repayments of buyers' debts. This practice facilitates sales when customers do not have high purchasing power. But at some point, it leads to perverse effects and difficulties in collecting debts or an inability to file a lawsuit because of a family relationship between buyers and sellers. Traders have difficulties reconstituting their stocks because they are not paid on time: *"We are also hindered by credits that are not fully repaid. Recently, we sent products worth 4 million francs to customers in France. They gave us an advance of 1 million francs, but so far they have not paid the balance. The balance is a loss for us. We have a lot of problems, because in that case I just mentioned, if we were given our money, we would have bought our raw materials at the right time."*

Other sectors, such as clothing, have similar difficulties. Spreading out payment terms often turns into nonpayment. A tailor explained how customers use tricks to obtain services without having to pay, especially when they are part of the family or close friends: *"Some twenty people owe me CFAF 2,000 to CFAF 4,000. They often come here, place orders, and give you an advance. Others tell you to do the job and they'll pay you back when they'll pick up the fabric. But then they come here to lament, saying they have no money. These are the kind of things that make our job very difficult, and we have to put up with it because they are often relatives, neighbors, people you really know—so you cannot deny certain things."*

Rising Costs, Indebtedness, and Limited Access to Credit

As already mentioned, the price of some basic food items, such as rice, had increased sharply as of 2008 and was a constraint often mentioned by participants in the FGDs. In the catering sector, rising costs have led to an increase of sales prices, which in turn causes solvency problems for customers who are no longer able to afford goods. Rising costs also affected the fisheries sector: *"At the time, things were not so complicated, the gas and also the canoes did not cost that much. . . . Outboard motors that used to cost CFAF 250,000 now cost CFAF 1,100,000."*

Jewelers complained about higher purchase prices that they cannot control because they must import raw materials. Although the production and trade of jewelry was once a booming business, the market became paralyzed by raw material shortages. As one of the jewelers interviewed said: *"We can currently only afford to buy old jewelry from women, we do not have that material in Senegal."*

Nor is the transport sector spared. The following excerpt from an interview with a bus driver shows how the combination of several adverse factors considerably weakens the craft carriers: *"We work on the basis of a not fixed rate and it depends on how much every day customers are able to pay. If users were paying normal fees . . . , we would not be at this point.*

The price of fuel has increased, spare parts are expensive too. . . . Then we're harassed down daily by men in uniform who may want bribes. And if you are short on your payments, it's deducted from your paycheck. This means that sometimes you find yourself with crumbs."

Economic difficulties have apparently led to a reduction in savings, higher indebtedness, and the transfer of assets, contributing to higher vulnerability among households. Discussions with a group of jewelers suggest that their savings were sharply reduced because of lower profits: *"I was part of a tontine [an informal group saving mechanism], where I contributed 5,000 francs per day, but I stopped doing it. So did a lot of people because the business does not work anymore. Our situation is becoming daily more precarious."* Low savings have an impact on the ability to obtain loans and mutual assistance mechanisms, and on a household's ability to face unexpected expenses, for example, for health care. A fisherman, aged 55, explained that while his business gave him financial security in the past and provided care to his children, his situation is less steady now: *"I am a fisherman. I used to make savings and this helped me to build my house, care for my children if they fell ill, or help people in case of need. But that no longer exists; this is history now. My savings also enabled me to have other properties and acquire other canoes. Previously, the tontine allowed me to save. But now, people no longer have enough for their daily spending, so they no longer have the possibility to organize the tontine. What I have is not even enough."*

Although many FGD participants need credit for productive activities, they expressed their dissatisfaction with the lack of access to funding sources. First, the banks impose constraints. The jewelers were very explicit, as one said: *"For my business to run properly, I need 5 kg of gold per year, yet the kilogram of gold cost 16 to 17 million francs. I can only afford this sum with a bank loan. But the banks require sound guarantees and charge higher rates."* Similar problems are encountered in other sectors, including fisheries, where the means of production and maintenance require investments that fishermen can no longer afford in the current sluggish market: *"If I could have 300,000 francs per month, it could really help me to resolve certain situations. In the past, I could easily have that amount because things were going well. But now, my situation is difficult because I have only one engine. So my boat cannot operate at 100 percent."*

Small traders also tend to lack access to credit: *"As far as credit is concerned, only the major carriers have access. We do not have an underwriter, and banks do not help us."* Faced with high credit risk and a slowdown in economic activity, banks are restricting lending to the most creditworthy customers only. Some operators might be able to access credit but fear that they may not be able to pay back the loans and so prefer not to take risks as retailers.

To overcome limited access to bank credit, initiatives such as cooperative arrangements among professional groups are being set up. Most of these arrangements, however, are hampered by the effects of the crisis on the revenues of contributors. In the Sandaga market, a large cooperative fund operated on its own equity, but because the members could not make regular payments, it closed up: *"Before, that is to say 10 years ago, we had a cooperative fund operating. But with the crisis, people could not pay. Hence, the fund failed. We have no help from the government. If there was no crisis, we would have our own funds, but now we are no more able to have them."*

Coping Mechanisms

Adjustments in Consumption: Reducing the Quality and Quantity of Food. It is clear from the FGDs and the individual interviews that the crisis has changed food consumption habits. Indeed, some rural households, especially farmers, have managed to maintain their food consumption because often they can rely on their own production. The impact has been severe in urban areas, where households have been exposed to soaring prices for basic commodities, such as rice, that are usually imported. To deal with inflation, they have been forced to revise their food purchases downward: *"We have changed our daily lives; we don't eat anymore what we used to eat. I am happy with whatever comes. There was a time when I could spend daily CFAF 10,000 and have chicken and meat. We ate good fish but now I try to spend CFAF 5,000 and accept everything that I get. I have no choice. Fortunately, our families understand and adapt to the situation as it affects the entire family."*

Adults are the first to cut their food consumption: *"We prefer to feed the children and stay like that. As for me, in the morning I'm going to sell my wares. Sometimes it works; sometimes it does not. All day I do not eat. But I do everything for my children to eat."* But children are also affected: *"There are problems of malnutrition, and I think it's unfortunate for our children. When we were kids, the food was good and food was available. We ate well."* The situation is particularly difficult in women-headed households.

Some households choose a diet of lower quality, less rich in protein, while others reduce their purchases: *"I'm at the bottom of the scale; I give each day CFAF 3,000 to my wife to cover our expenses. If I stay two days without work, we do not eat at all. I have no savings. I am in this situation since last year."* Even if they continue to prepare dishes judged rich, such as *thiébou dien* (the Senegalese national dish), it will be done with less oil or fish. The consumption of meat is almost excluded or eaten only during ceremonies. Urban households in poverty often have just one meal a day, and one observes a return to grains such as millet that are not imported and therefore are more affordable. In some instances, households reported selling assets and productive equipment to finance food consumption. One fisherman *"sold several times canoes and outboard motors to get money to cook at home. Now the emphasis is on* "lekku baadolo' (junk food)."

Food rations are being cut to ensure minimum consumption in the household: *"Before the crisis, I could buy 10 loaves of bread per day for breakfast. Now we can only share five loaves of bread."* The common practice of reserving leftovers for indigent people is disappearing, even in relatively affluent classes: *"Before we were preparing enough, but now we don't have this option anymore; it's the same situation for everybody. All that we could do before, we cannot do it now."* If dinner is still served, it is made of local ingredients, such as basic millet porridge and couscous: *"For dinner we only eat couscous-based* mbuum (green leaf) *or* fondé (porridge). *We no longer think about meat. We cannot afford it anyway. I eat it only occasionally and in small amounts."* But, for the poor, the preparation of these foods is still made difficult by increasing prices of some ingredients such as sugar and milk.

The consumption of fish is shifting to previously neglected species from other more noble species. This is the case of *yaboye* (mackerel with a lot of bones), which used to be seen as the "poor people's fish" but is now increasingly consumed by more affluent households. As a jeweler explained: *"I can say that in recent years, I cannot eat good fish but the yaboye."*

A progressive elimination of imported dairy products and coffee seems common in poorer areas, as explained by a restaurant owner: *"Before, you could buy milk and butter, but now it is no longer the case. We weren't used to consume the Touba coffee for breakfast, but since the crisis people drink it a lot, also children."* Indeed, the consumption of Touba coffee, a traditional and less expensive drink of the Mourides (a Sufi Muslim brotherhood influential in Senegal), has become a sort of social phenomenon with vendors distributing it at every street corner.

Still another strategy used by households to cope with higher food prices is to share meals. It is common for neighboring households with kinship ties to combine resources and make a meal to feed everyone. On the outskirts of Dakar, this practice is still common as a mechanism of solidarity around the basic core of a family, which gets together for lunch, the main meal. This practice has become a key means of securing food for some low-income households.

Cutting Education, Health, and Energy Expenditures. Evidence shows that some households have pulled children out of school due to the crisis: *"My children have dropped out of school because of strains in life; I don't have the opportunity to pay for their studies."* A fisherman who is a polygamist explained: *"I took two of my children off school. The oldest is 16; he is upholsterer and the other at 14 is a fisherman. By leaving school, I asked them how they can contribute to help their mother, who is my first wife. It makes my job easier, because I can only take care of the second wife."* Other households pull their children out of private school and enroll them in public schools that are more affordable.

Decreasing and unstable incomes reduced households' ability to cover the health care needs of family members. A businessman explained that *"the business no longer works, hence, income is limited. I have a child, who studies at Al Azhar* [Islamic Institute]. *He has problems with vision, but I am not able to bring him to the hospital knowing that prescriptions are expensive. He suffers, but I cannot help him. Sometimes he cannot even learn the lessons. Now everybody is sick; we cannot guarantee adequate health care to our family or give them a good education, and it has been like that for two years."* The poor seem to accept the lack of access to health care, and they are resigned to many being sick and without treatment.

To be able to maintain basic food consumption, households were also saving on gas and electricity. An interviewed retiree explained: *"My power has been off for seven months. The bill is CFAF 50,000. I light a candle at night, and I admit that this situation is very difficult. I cannot pay this bill yet. Other expenditures are more important, and I prefer to live without electricity rather than running out of food."* Another FGD participant said: *"My wife is saving on butane gas. We no longer prepare the dinner at home. My wife cooks four times a week 'nari cin'* (rice with sauce) *in order to save the sauce for the evening. That way we prepare only the* 'ñankatang' *or simply buy bread to accompany it with the remaining dressing. This allows us to avoid using the gas twice a day.*"

Increased Labor Force Participation by Women, Youth, and Children. For women, deployment of new productive activities outside the home has emerged as an important endeavor, including the creation of economic interest groups (EIG), which help pool resources from participants. One woman recounts her journey as follows: "*I got the idea to create a group. Since I worked for Oxfam, it allowed me to be a member of several associations. All the time I was with women; their courage impressed me every day. And then I told myself that I will create an EIG. At first I put together several women; we contributed CFAF 500 each at the end of each week. Currently, we have CFAF 75,000.*" While men may provide for most basic needs within the household, women need to work to pay for any extras: "*I prefer to work because life is hard and my husband cannot meet all my needs. I have my tontine, and sometimes I need to buy clothes and jewelry for events. Our husbands assure daily expenses, but we must work to ensure our personal needs.*"

The entry of women into the productive sphere gives them sway in the management of the household economy. As one participant said: "*Some* [women] *are replacing men, who are showing less ingenuity in a precarious environment.*" The crisis therefore requires households to diversify their sources of income, but it may also strengthen the independence of women, often with the support of husbands: "*Oh yes, my wife often leads some business. You know, women are very brave and mine does not hesitate to deal with difficult situations. You see, I am not alone, and I thank God because things could be worse.*" (For how changes in income sources may affect intrahousehold decision making and allocation patterns in Senegal, see Bussolo, De Hoyos, and Wodon 2009; more generally on gender and poverty in Senegal, see Koopman 2009.)

It is not uncommon for women to take over sole responsibility for finding the resources needed to prepare meals: "*The work does not work anymore. Look, it's up to me to prepare the meal tomorrow. I hope that by tomorrow I'll come through.*" In households of pensioners, the role of women is especially important: "*Currently, all mothers are in the same situation; we are living through difficult times. My husband is retired; my children do not work; I'm the one who manages all the problems. I pay the electricity, water, and care for the other spending. It's hard for a woman, but I don't have a choice. I work a lot so my children can eat.*" The same holds for widows: "*I represent the man and the woman; I'm the head of the household. The children cannot find work; my husband passed away. I pay for water, electricity, and daily expenses. 'Xam nga or if Metina Jigéen'* (you know it's hard for a woman)."

The collective involvement of family members is another way for households to cope with the crisis. Families are forced to be more enterprising, and each family member contributes or participates in daily expenses. As explained by a young head of household: "*In my family, I think everybody tries to do something to earn money, and even my sisters can do housekeeping jobs to take care of themselves. If anyone has something, it may work because you will not have to help a particular person.*" An older retailer suggested that in times of crisis each household member must contribute to earn the respect of others: "*When I see that some members of my family spend all their time sleeping, I tell them to go and do something. There are jobs that some young people do not want to do; they prefer to wait to see better options, but they have to work.*" This all-out collective involvement is not always positive, however, as it may lead to a reduction in schooling for children, especially for girls.

Diversification of Economic Activities. Multiactivity, or the combination of several jobs, is another coping strategy used by households. Some people have two or three jobs, especially young people who undertake several activities simultaneously in petty trade, the resale of secondhand goods, construction, or the area of sports and culture: "*I have a cousin, who calls me frequently in his projects, and I worked with him often but not every day. Sometimes I buy secondhand mobile phones and sell them to friends, and I get my profits. I am also a breeder (laughter) because I have 5 sheep at the moment. In 2007, I sold a sheep for CFAF 130,000 and one week after the tabaski* (Islamic celebration of the sacrifice), *I sold another for CFAF 180,000.*" Such gains are, however, often marginal and occasional and do not enable workers to emerge from their precariousness permanently.

Impacts of the Crisis on Communities: Weakening of Traditional Safety Nets

The extended family has long been the core of traditional support mechanisms, but this solidarity is now endangered because of exposure to multiple vulnerabilities: "*The crisis is there; it took years to manifest by unsatisfied needs, increased problems of life, and the high food prices. Currently I have a hard time to meet my family needs. And that's why my two other women have filed for divorce. Before, I was managing my family as it should be. Women and children had all at their disposal. But then I had problems; the work was not sufficient anymore to manage household expenses; it's a problem. I stayed for months without work last year."*

The crisis also weakens some traditional safety nets on which less well-off family members used to rely. Hence, taking care of relatives' children, a practice that used to be common in Senegal, is becoming more difficult. For example, jewelers used to be regarded as notables in their community because of their economic power, but they can no longer fulfill that role. One of them confided this clearly: *"Now I no longer accept that close relatives give me their children because I can no longer afford to maintain them. We completely changed our way of life because life is hard now; we eat what we have—otherwise we're not going to come through. I am a father and I have a lot of expenses and thus I have to manage things for me to come through. I have no support; my children are too young; they go to school, and I also take care of my brothers. . . . In addition, when my father was alive, there were many people from our village who lived with us, but after the death of my father they returned to the village."* The hosting of visiting relatives from the regions is less automatic than it used to be in some ethnic groups. Families used to accommodate in Dakar anyone from their region of origin, but the crisis has weakened bonds with communities of origin. This erosion of traditional safety nets could have negative effects for long-term social capital.

Lack of Government Support, Crime, and Corruption

A number of structural conditions make life even more difficult in times of crisis. Poor access to basic services was noted among the groups surveyed in the outskirts of Dakar. A district like Medina Gounass is regularly flooded during the rainy season: *"We have troubles in Gounass, and it gets worse during the rainy season. As access becomes a problem, the water keeps us from our activities. And worse, our children often fall ill because of mosquitoes. The government should review the sanitation of the area. Sewage spills into the streets, and roads are not well suited in most major arteries of Dakar. I can fix my car right now and just make a round trip there and break my car again."* Other issues have been raised in relation to the lighting of streets, road paving, sanitation, and the availability of schools and health care facilities at affordable prices. The issue of poor access is but one aspect of a broader crisis of confidence in public services: *"There is no health post in Medina Gounass. Only Guédiawaye and Gouye Fatou Maiga have a health post. The management of patients at King Baudouin is bad. The nurses do not respect you. Beyond noon, you're forced to buy a ticket at CFAF 1,000 to enter. Prescriptions are also too expensive."*

In outlying areas like Pikine and Guédiawaye, residents establish a link between youth unemployment and insecurity. The qualitative data suggest that insecurity has increased considerably among the groups surveyed, especially in urban areas. For them, job creation should be the priority of the state: *"Young people do nothing, and there are often some cases of thefts and assaults. We must strengthen the security of people and improve lighting. Young people are desperate, and they expect the government to have a job for them. We are living in total insecurity. The state should install street lights, but this is not the case. Added to this, young people should have more things to do and not spend their time attacking honest citizens."*

Corruption, harassment by traffic police, and business regulations imposed by local authorities were mentioned by some informal sector workers as factors that impeded their ability to do business and to cope with worsening economic conditions. Police officers reportedly engaged in racketeering to extort money from retailers. The extent of these practices was variable, but in a sector such as transport, it seemed to have emerged as a major indirect effect of the crisis, leading to discontent among drivers: *"Police tire us, they live on us. I know a police officer who works at the police headquarters. He wakes up every day at 5 am to dispute the road with drivers. Before arriving at his workplace, he stops all bus drivers and each driver must give him at least CFAF 1,000. He does the same thing going home from work. I would like to expose this policeman on the radio even if I could be jailed."* Another driver explained: *"Our major problem remains the police. There is corruption. I am discouraged because of the* yelp [the police who harass]. *Every day you give the police CFAF 8,000. If you take this amount from your salary, you have nothing. We want to work but they rip us off. We always get up at 5 am to 6 am but the police are already on site. Especially at Liberté Score."* Unregistered and unlawful street vendors are also vulnerable to the requests by the police: *"For us vendors, those who worry us the most are the officers and agents of the City Council with their unending taxes. If there is no celebration, we pay CFAF 200 a day, but during festivals, we pay CFAF 4,000 to CFAF 5,000. If it were not them, things would work for us, we get along fine, and we organize ourselves so that there is no problem."*

Corruption in the judiciary was another problem mentioned in FGDs. As part of a judicial proceeding, a tenant exposed a proven case of corruption from a lawyer: *"I was paying CFAF 35,000 for my rental, but the owner decides one day to increase this to CFAF 150,000 without telling me; I got a lawyer believing I would win the trial because I was in my rights, but to my surprise, I realized that he had bought the judge and I lost the case. In this case, how can you help yourself?"*

Conclusion

This chapter has aimed to provide an assessment of the impact of the food, fuel, and financial crisis on household well-being in Senegal, using the quantitative analysis of available household survey data and qualitative focus groups and individual interviews. Because the latest survey with data on consumption available in Senegal dates back to 2005–06, the qualitative work that was conducted in 2010 provides a unique window into the impact of the crisis that could not be obtained through existing survey data.

Three main conclusions can be drawn from the quantitative analysis. First, before the crisis, Senegal had experienced an impressive reduction in poverty. The proportion of the population in poverty was reduced from 67.9 percent at the national level in 1994–95 to 50.8 percent in 2005–06. Subjective assessments by households on their own welfare confirm an improvement over time. The second finding from the quantitative analysis, however, is that despite such progress, many households (more than two-thirds) still feel they were not able to satisfy basic needs in areas such as food consumption, health care, education, housing, and clothing. An even larger share of the population states that it does not have enough income to meet its needs. Finally, a third finding from the quantitative analysis is that the increase in food and fuel prices during the recent crisis is likely to have had a large negative impact on poverty, in part because imports of food items and fuels represent a significant share of the total consumption of households, especially for the very poor. The negative impact of rising prices, the reduction in economic growth, and higher unemployment or underemployment since 2006 suggest that poverty may have worsened substantially.

Qualitative data from focus groups and individual interviews confirm that the situation of much of the population has become more difficult. Many people talked about a lack of gainful employment as well as threats to their traditional livelihoods. This situation applies not only to poor farmers and fishermen, but also to better-off groups such as small businessmen and jewelers. Rising costs for basic necessities due to the increase in food and fuel prices and losses of employment have led to higher levels of indebtedness. Limited access to credit implies that many households and small entrepreneurs have limited means to cope with the crisis; they lack the ability to smooth consumption patterns or keep their business activity going. Strategies used by households to cope with the crisis include working longer hours through second and third jobs, or entering the labor market, which is the case especially for women. Most households declare that they have also adjusted their consumption patterns by, for example, shifting to lower-cost, lower-quality foods. Evidence shows that the crisis may have increased tensions within some communities because of the rise in petty crime. The crisis has also put stress on traditional mechanisms of solidarity between households that used to protect some of the most vulnerable.

The picture that emerges from the study is that of a society that has made substantial gains since the 1990s but remains highly vulnerable to shocks. Although the sample in the qualitative work does not permit robust generalizations, some of the more detailed results from the focus groups suggest a tentative classification of households into four groups according to their degree of vulnerability. At the bottom are households in extreme poverty, such as some of the households that were displaced by the conflict in Casamance in southern Senegal. Those households require special assistance to be able to cope with the additional negative effects of the crisis. Next are groups caught in a downward spiral: they may not have been poor initially, but they have been affected by the crisis. These groups would include transportation sector businesspeople, craftsmen, retirees, cotton factory workers, and flood victims without access to basic social services. Still another group has shown a greater ability to resist the crisis through institutional support and their own internal resources. This group would include farmers supported by NGOs; female processors of local products, grain, and fish; factory workers enjoying basic social protection; and jewelers. Last are the most resilient groups. Among them are the landmine victims in the South who have carried out activities in agriculture and services that improved their living conditions between the two rounds of the qualitative survey. Others in this group are the families of migrants who have invested in agriculture and trade by taking advantage of good rainfall and the resulting harvests and trade. In some areas, resilience that grew on the basis of collective entrepreneurship appears to have helped change constraints into opportunities through the development of local resources and promising production and service niches. One direction for further research could be to better understand how such collective action at the local level is instrumental in improving resilience.

Notes

The chapter was prepared with support from the Trust Fund for Environmentally and Socially Sustainable Development housed at the World Bank and funded by the governments of Norway and Finland. Comments from Rasmus Heltberg are gratefully acknowledged. The opinions and analysis presented are those of the authors only and need not reflect those of the World Bank, its executive directors, or the countries they represent. Assistance for survey data analysis from Clarence Tsimpo is gratefully acknowledged, as is qualitative data collection in the field by a team from the Université Cheikh Antia Diop led by Abdou Fall.

Poverty measures in the Central African Republic and Senegal are not strictly comparable. Especially in the case of Senegal, in comparison to other countries in West and Central Africa, poverty measures appear high given the level of economic development in the country; and this is due to methodological choices in the measurement of poverty in that country.

References

Azam, J. P., M. Dia, C. Tsimpo, and Q. Wodon. 2007. "Has Growth in Senegal after the 1994 Devaluation Been Pro-Poor?" In *Growth and Poverty Reduction: Case Studies from West Africa,* ed. Q. Wodon. World Bank Working Paper 79, World Bank, Washington, DC.

Boccanfuso, D., and L. Savard. 2008. "The Food Crisis and Its Impacts on Poverty in Senegal and Mali: Crossed Destinies." Working Paper 08-20, University of Sherbrooke, Quebec.

Bussolo, M., R. De Hoyos, and Q. Wodon. 2009. "Higher Prices of Export Crops, Intrahousehold Inequality, and Human Capital Accumulation in Senegal." In

Gender Aspects of the Trade and Poverty Nexus: A Macro-Micro Approach, ed. M. Bussolo and R. E. De Hoyos, 165–84. Washington, DC: World Bank and Palgrave Macmillan.

Fall A. S., C. Rokhaya, and N. Tidiane. 2010. *Rapid Assessment of the Impact of the Economic Crisis on Senegalese Households*. Round 1, September. Dakar: LARTES-IFAN.

IMF (International Monetary Fund). 2010. "Senegal: Sixth Review under the Policy Support Instrument, Request for a Three-Year Policy Support Instrument and Cancellation of Current Policy Support Instrument." Staff Report 10/362, International Monetary Fund, Washington, DC.

Koopman, J. 2009. "Globalization, Gender, and Poverty in the Senegal River Valley." *Feminist Economist* 15 (3): 253–85.

Ndoye, D., F. Adoho, P. Backiny-Yetna, M. Fall, P. T. Ndiane, and Q. Wodon. 2009. "Tendance et profil de la pauvreté au Sénégal de 1994 à 2006." *Perspective Afrique* 4 (1–3): Article 8.

République du Sénégal. 2006. *Document Stratégique de Réduction de la Pauvreté-2, 2006–2010* (Strategic Document for the Reduction of Poverty). Dakar: République du Sénégal.

———. 2008. *Food Security Assessment in Senegal*. Dakar.

Tembo, R. M. 2009. *The Impact of the Financial and Economic Crisis on African Economies: The Case of Senegal—The Response of UNDP*. Dakar: United Nations Development Programme.

World Bank. 2003. *Senegal: Country Economic Memorandum*. Washington, DC: World Bank.

———. 2010. *World Development Indicators*. Washington, DC: World Bank.

CHAPTER 9

Economic and Political Crises in Thailand: Social Impacts and Government Responses

Veronica Mendizabal, Supang Chantavanich, Samarn Laodumrongchai, Mya Than, Artit Wong-a-thitikul, Warathida Chaiyapa, Cheewin Ariyasuntorn, and Pamornrat Tansanguanwong

Introduction

Thailand's economy is characterized by a significant outward orientation, with exports accounting for well over half of its gross domestic product (GDP). The global financial crisis of 2008–09, therefore, had a significant impact on economic sectors sensitive to external demand, particularly manufacturing, and only a limited direct impact on Thailand's strong financial system. When the global financial crisis hit the economies of Thailand's main trading partners, the European Union, Japan, and the United States, demand for Thai manufacturing exports plunged, contracting by 8.9 percent in the fourth quarter of 2008 and a further 16.0 percent by the first quarter of 2009 (World Bank 2009b). Thailand's main exports severely affected by the crisis were primarily electrical appliances and electronics, followed by autos and auto parts. Textiles and garments, as well as furniture, leatherwear, and other labor intensive-industries were also hit; from a macroeconomic perspective, however, these industries are a small share of exports experiencing a declining trend and progressively moving to lower-wage locations such as Cambodia and Vietnam.

A second round of effects from the global financial crisis included the dampening of consumer confidence and the reduction of domestic demand. The closure of the international airport in Bangkok during the last quarter of 2008 in the context of the Thai political crisis (box 9.1) posed additional challenges to the economy because of the severe impact on the tourism sector. The resulting contraction of tourism-related activities, which lasted for months, had a strong and negative impact on a large number of lower-income households dependent on the sector for their livelihoods (table 9.1). Agricultural prices remained low during most of 2009, rebounding by the last quarter of the year. By then, the crisis had all but dissipated thanks to the recovery of exports and later tourism. The Thai economy grew by 7.8 percent in 2010, up from minus 2.2 percent in 2009 (IMF 2010).

To better understand the severity of impacts and the differentiated effects of the crises on vulnerable workers, the Asian Research Centre for Migration (ARCM) from Chulalongkorn University in Bangkok and

---

BOX 9.1

Thailand's Political Crisis

The 2008–10 political crisis had its roots in the unresolved crisis of 2005–06 when a coup deposed the elected prime minister, Thaksin Shinawatra, among allegations of corruption. Thaksin, who remained popular among the rural poor, went into exile. His party, the People Power Party (PPP), won the general elections for a third consecutive time in 2007, reigniting the protests of the opposition united under the People's Alliance for Democracy (PAD) also known as the "yellow shirts." A lengthy period of PAD protests culminated in November 2008 with the occupation of Bangkok's International Airport and its closure for eight days. Negotiations for a solution to the conflict ended in the rule of the constitutional court dissolving the PPP on charges of electoral fraud (vote buying). By December 2008, in what may be considered a PAD victory, a coalition government was formed headed by Abhisit Vejjajiva. New protests were organized in April 2009, this time led by the National United Front of Democracy against Dictatorship (UDD), known as "red shirts" and supportive of former prime minister Thaksin. Protests resulted in a state of emergency but were contained, only to resurface stronger and more violently a year later in March 2010.

Source: Authors.

Table 9.1. Key Indicators

Key Indicators	
Population	67.0 million
Life expectancy	69 years
Urban population	33.0%
Human Development Index rank of 182	87
GDP per capital	$7,394
Poverty*	11.5%
Unemployment 2009	1.5%

Sources: UNDP 2009; World Bank 2009a; World Bank 2010a.

* Percentage of population living on less than $2 a day.

the World Bank conducted a series of rapid assessments involving repetitive rounds of qualitative research, returning to the same communities between 2009 and 2010. A total of 180 people participated in the study in four provinces. Researchers interviewed workers from the formal and informal sectors, cross-border migrants, rural households, and representatives of small and medium enterprises.

After this brief introduction, the next section provides more details on the methodology, characteristics of the sample, and the sites where the study was carried out. The third section provides an overview of the changes affecting the people in the sample in terms of labor market shocks, their impact on employment and income, the division of labor within the household, shifts in migration patterns, and remittances and general quality of life. The fourth section summarizes the coping strategies used by the various groups and the role of informal safety nets and social solidarity in times of crisis. The fifth section describes the government response and initial perceptions on its effectiveness in buffering crisis-related social impacts and is followed by concluding remarks.

Methodology and Sample

Two rounds of qualitative field research were conducted between March 2009 and January 2010. The sample consisted of 180 people through 23 focus group discussions (FGDs) and 33 in-depth interviews (IDIs) in four provinces of Thailand. In Bangkok, FGDs were held with informal workers in the five largest city slums[1] and included garbage collectors, home-based workers (self-employed and contract workers), souvenir manufacturers, port workers, motorbike taxi drivers, and street vendors. In Nakhon Ratchasima province in the northeast of the country, one of the regions with the highest poverty rate, and where agriculture is the dominant economic activity, the focus was on the impacts of the crisis on remittance-recipient rural households and included households with and without land. This distinction was considered important to understand land and agriculture as safety nets. In the coastal area of Samut Sakhon province, FGDs were organized with employed and unemployed Thai workers, legal and illegal Burmese migrant workers, and owners of small and medium enterprises (SME). Ayutthaya province was selected for its importance as a center for automobile and electronics manufacturing, and the sample in this province focused on factory workers in export-oriented sectors from assembly line to managers. Domestic migrant workers make up 70 percent of Ayutthaya's population. In-depth interviews were carried out in all sites with a variety of informants including business representatives; national, provincial, and municipal officials; journalists; police officers; chamber of commerce and trade union representatives; and staff from nongovernmental organizations (NGOs)and charitable institutions.

Transmission Channels: From Macro Shocks to Impacts on People and Communities

When first interviewed in March 2009, company representatives from the auto industry, textiles, information technology (IT), and electronics indicated that the reduction in external demand for their products, coupled with a credit crunch, forced many of them to scale down production and to cut back labor inputs in the form of reduced working hours, no overtime, extended holidays, and in the worst cases, layoffs. A year later, by the first quarter of 2010, the situation had improved in most of the export-oriented manufacturing sectors with some larger companies experiencing renewed external demand for their products. The auto industry, for example, mirrored corporate responses at the global level, and although a few companies stopped production early in 2009, others remained competitive by meeting changing consumer preferences. By 2010, the automakers who had adapted their production were leading the recovery of the sector with small and fuel-efficient cars. The rate of recovery for smaller enterprises was, on the other hand, much slower, and many of the small and medium businesses in the sample continued to have limited access to bank loans and were struggling to survive. The following section recounts the impacts of these macro-level changes on formal and informal workers, rural households, and migrant workers.

Effects on Factory Workers

Between the last two quarters of 2008 and most of 2009, factory workers experienced growing underemployment and unemployment. According to the Thai Department of Labor Protection and Social Welfare, more than 100,000 people were laid off between December 2008 and January 2009. Estimates suggest that between September 2008 and March 2009, the underemployment rate rose to 1.9 percent from 1.1 percent during the same period a year earlier, with approximately half a million people working less than 20 hours per week during the third quarter of 2008, although they were willing to work more (World Bank 2009b). Voluntary resignations also increased during this period as fewer working hours and bonus cuts resulted in sharp reductions in income. There were accounts of female and male workers who left their jobs because without overtime, commissions, or bonuses, they could not cover the transport expenses to get to work or the basic costs of living in urban or industrial areas. Those resigning were unable to claim unemployment benefits, adding to the tension between staying in jobs that had stopped being profitable or quitting and having no safety net to fall back on. The workers who stayed in their jobs tried to make up for the reduction in income by finding additional work, which in most cases was short term, irregular, low skilled, and low paid.

Findings suggest that female workers were particularly affected by their position in the labor market. Female workers are overwhelmingly represented in sectors that were affected by the crisis, such as export manufacturing and services (Paitoonpong and Akkarakul 2009), and constitute the large majority of unskilled and lower-paid workers, for example, those on assembly lines. Company managers interviewed indicated that without having explicit gender considerations, when forced to cut staff, their main concern was maintaining skilled workers and letting the unskilled go first, which affected women disproportionately.[2] Workers also indicated that employers were adopting various strategies to avoid paying severance and unemployment benefits, such as hiring people on probation and firing them just before the end of their probation period, or registering laid-off workers as voluntary resignations, which resulted in smaller compensation. In some companies, the latter practice reportedly affected women more than men.

Demand for labor increased rapidly in late 2009 as the economy recovered. Yet, contrary to what would have been expected, few workers were applying for these jobs, and manufacturing firms reported a shortage of as many as 100,000 workers in February 2010. In Ayutthaya province, the Employment Department indicated that around 20 percent of the workers who had been laid off had taken advantage of the government support programs to access seed funding for microenterprises and training programs and were not interested in returning to their factories. Other interviews suggested that many workers who had returned to their rural communities intended to remain there for the entire harvest season, as agricultural prices rebounded in late 2009, raising farm incomes and wages. The reluctance of workers to return to their factories resulted in a tight labor market, and companies were expecting tough wage negotiations as, according to the interviews, the massive layoffs had led to greater awareness of labor rights by workers, and labor shortages were strengthening their position. Some companies, particularly in the IT sector, were trying to attract new recruits by offering higher wages, bonuses, and improved benefits. By February 2010, the workers who had remained in their jobs indicated that with the economy improving and fewer workers to accomplish production targets, working hours had increased excessively and workers at all levels were experiencing high levels of stress.

Impacts on the Rural Poor

In 2009, more than 66 percent of the Thai population was living in rural areas, with 11.0 percent of the people categorized as poor compared with 3.3 percent in urban areas. The study focused on rural households with various degrees of dependency on remittances from family members. The common composition of families in the sample was that grandparents took care of small children while the economically active population migrated to urban centers or abroad, mainly to Israel, Qatar, or Taiwan, China. During the first round of assessment in March 2009, all of the respondents in rural areas indicated that their remittances had fallen and become irregular.

The study suggests important variations in the degree of resilience to declining remittances between households with land and the landless. Rural households without land were strongly impacted by the reduction in remittances, a situation further aggravated by lack of savings and limited access to credit, including from schemes established to help the poor. People in these households tried various strategies to cope. Some relied on village authorities to help them find day jobs, some sold assets, and a few sent their children to work part time. Some also searched for work in neighboring farms, mostly without success given their age and the preference of employers for younger workers. In addition, people mentioned that an increase in the use of mechanized agriculture in the past years had reduced the overall availability of jobs in this sector. By January 2010, and despite macroeconomic data indicating that the economy had stabilized, rural households without land were still experiencing high levels of hardship.

Unlike the landless in the sample, people with land indicated being better able to maintain their usual levels of food consumption, as they could rely on their own rice and vegetable production, fish from their ponds, and wild foods. In addition, credit from village funds or the Bank for Agriculture Cooperatives remained available to them because they could use their land as collateral. During the peak of the crisis (last quarter of 2008 and the first half of 2009), land provided a safety net for these households and allowed them to incorporate laid-off family members returning from the cities into agricultural work, at least initially.[3] It is plausible that the difficulties faced by poor landless households in obtaining farm work were in part related to an oversupply of farm labor resulting from factory workers returning to rural areas. The crucial role of land in times of crisis was already observed during the Asian Crisis in 1997 when large numbers of laid-off workers returned to their rural villages and were able to sustain themselves and their families through agriculture and foods from the commons (Corner 2010).

Impacts on Workers in the Informal Sector

The size of the informal work sector in Thailand is significant. More than 23 million people, representing 62.7 percent of the national workforce, earn their living as informal workers, compared with 37.3 percent in the formal economy. Informal workers do not enjoy a minimum wage or unemployment benefits. Generally, these workers receive low pay, work under poor conditions, work with hazardous substances without adequate protection and information on safety standards (for example, producers of imitation gold ornaments, garbage collectors), have limited access to capital, and are excluded from protection under labor laws (Tulaphan 2008). The number of informal workers engaged in agriculture reaches over 60 percent, with another 32 percent working in cities as contract workers or self-employed for manufacturing and service industries (NSO 2007, 2008).

Urban informal workers were affected by the crisis in multiple ways. Workers in tourism-related sectors were hit by the double whammy

of the global economic crisis and the Thai political conflict, and contract home-based workers producing for global value chains (such as
garments and imitation jewelry) were among those hardest hit by a
contraction in outsourced orders from factories. Women were particularly affected as they represent the majority of these workers.[4] Declines
in domestic demand and consumption affected the self-employed (taxi
drivers, street vendors, and garbage collectors) who saw demand for
their goods and services plunge. Prior to the crisis in 2008, these workers
were earning between 80 and 700 Thai baht (B) ($2.66–$23.33) daily,
but their incomes started to fall during the last quarter of 2008. The data
in table 9.2 were collected during the first two rounds of monitoring
and compares precrisis salaries in early 2008 with two crisis months in
late 2008 and early 2009.

**Table 9.2. Daily Wages of Informal Workers of HomeNet,
Klong Toey Slum, Bangkok, 2008 and 2009**

Area of work	Daily rate in Thai baht			
	January 2008	November 2008	January 2009	
Handicraft and food-processing workers	100–150	80–100	80–100	No wage difference indicated between male and female workers. Wage difference for level of skill.
Producers of imitation gold ornaments	100	60	60	No wage difference indicated between male and female workers. High skills required to perform this work.
Home workers (seamstresses)	80–100	50–100	50–100	No wage difference between male and female workers. Workers required to buy their own inputs. Decrease in sales indicated. Workers forced by the situation to get additional jobs to cover their personal expenditures.
Skilled construction workers	300	—	100–200	Fewer jobs available resulted in workers searching for jobs outside Bangkok.
Porters	600–700	200–300	200–300	The reduction in daily income reflected both less pay per unit of work and a fall in demand resulting in fewer units of work.
Seamstresses	100+	—	50	Reductions in price per unit.
Laundry workers	15–20/kilo	—	10	Irregular work and wage per unit.

Source: Adapted from Chantavanich et al. 2009.

Note: — = not available.

Unemployment and underemployment during the crisis period pushed large numbers of formal workers to seek alternative sources of income, which resulted in growing competition for informal jobs. The decrease in orders and oversupply of workers pushed the price per unit of work down. Home-based seamstresses explained that they had been producing jeans for B 12 ($0.40) a piece until mid-2008 when middlemen claimed that fuel and transport costs had gone up and reduced the price per unit to B 9 ($0.30); by early 2009, the price per unit had fallen to B 4 ($0.13). In 2008, these women had been producing 500 pairs of jeans per month and could earn B 6,000 ($200). The same production in 2009 was yielding B 2,000 ($67). Their income had been slashed to a third of what they had previously earned.

Lower incomes throughout the year caused severe liquidity shortfalls that were compounded by higher food prices in early 2010. Although eligible to register as self-employed, none of the workers in the sample had joined the social security fund. Because of their irregular income, they had feared being unable to pay the monthly premium of B 280, so when the crisis hit, none of them could benefit from the six-month unemployment compensation. The situation turned precarious for many of the informal workers in the sample, as described by a female home-based worker in the Klong Toey slum in March 2009: *"In the evening, it is already 7 pm. But we don't know yet where to find food to eat tonight."* She had no savings and no money for rent, so she and the granddaughter she takes care of were forced to stay with an acquaintance hoping for the situation to improve.

By January 2010, participants in the sample had depleted any savings they had, and a large majority increased their debt with relatives or informal moneylenders, in some cases to unsustainable levels. There were reports of people who were living in fear of losing, or who had already lost, their land and property because they could not pay off the loans. Despite increasing competition, however, a few of the interviewees indicated borrowing to start microenterprises in the food and service sectors, such as opening food stalls or becoming motorbike taxi drivers. Unfortunately, these investments were not always successful, and people ended up with more debt. An interviewee from Klong Toey slum took a loan of B 5,000 to start a new business. Six months later she had debt of B 60,000. She was frustrated and could not explain how it happened: *"If we stay where we are, we know how much debt we have; when we tried to earn more and struggled to work, we ended up having more debt than before."*

The communities in the sample also experienced various forms of social impact. In the slums, people indicated that drug consumption, mainly amphetamines and glue, which are cheaper to use and easier to sell than other drugs, had become widespread among the youth and that dealers were using children as young as 10 to sell drugs. Out of nine females participating in a group discussion, six had husbands in jail charged with drug-related crimes or illegal gambling. Interviews with the police confirmed that the rate of petty crime and theft had increased, as had the number of underground lotteries and illegal gambling operations, suggesting that chronic economic and social problems deepened during the crisis. When visited a year later in 2010, the participants expressed desperation as the situation was not improving. Instead, it seemed to be getting worse, with food and fuel prices on the rise.

Effects on Cross-border Migrant Workers

Cross-border migrants are among the most vulnerable populations in Thailand. There were 500,000 registered migrant workers from Cambodia, Laos, and Myanmar in 2007.[5] Estimates of migrants that include illegals run as high as 3 million. Demand for migrants in low-paid industry jobs not favored by local workers, such as food processing, peeling shrimp, construction, fishing, domestic work, agriculture, and garments, is high. These workers are cheaper than domestic workers, have no right to a minimum wage or to collective bargaining, and most of them cannot get registered with the social security fund. In the past years, reports of serious human rights violations have emerged, describing widespread police and employee abuse toward migrants, including exploitation, extortion, and restriction of movement.[6]

The crises increased the vulnerability of migrants via reductions in income and strained relationships with Thai workers who saw them as competition. Migrants reported an increase in violence toward them caused by job scarcity and competition for jobs, and they were concerned about their safety. The crisis also increased the political use of immigration as an issue, as the government tried to respond to growing domestic unemployment and discontent. In this sense, one of the earlier government announcements regarding migrant workers in 2009 was the freeze of new work permits, the nonrenewal of 500,000 work permits for registered migrants, and the deportation of undocumented migrants on grounds of protecting the jobs of domestic workers. Another measure introduced in late 2009 was "nationality verification." To be registered and allowed a temporary stay in Thailand, migrants had to obtain identity documents issued by their home countries. Workers from Myanmar, particularly those from minority groups, feared returning to their country to obtain identity papers. Moreover, registering would not change the migrants' status, and they would still be ineligible to access labor benefits such as accident compensation.

Others faced the practical issue of paying for the registration and verification process, which had a cost of B 3,800 (about $126). The complexity of the registration process gave rise to a market of brokers helping migrants with paperwork and charging them between B 8,000 and B 12,000 ($265–400). According to people interviewed, the usual daily wage for migrant workers is around B 300 ($10). Approximately 200 Burmese workers left the province of Samutsakorn in November 2009 when the national verification entered into effect. Their departures created concern in the industries highly dependent on migrant labor. When manufacturing companies experienced renewed demand in 2010 and suddenly encountered labor shortages in the domestic market, these companies started lobbying provincial authorities for increasing the number of migrants and for allowing them to work in skilled-level positions. Samutsakorn province, where fish processing is the main industry, agreed to both requests, but Ayutthaya province remained firmly opposed to migrants filling gaps for skilled work.

Main Coping Responses and Second-Round Impacts

Faced with multiple and simultaneous challenges resulting from the economic crisis, people tried their best to cope, using a range of strategies, in some cases extreme and with potential long-term consequences for their well-being. Table 9.3 summarizes the coping mechanisms.

Reduction in Overall Consumption

All of the people in the sample reduced their consumption of nonessentials and the quality of food and nonfood products consumed, switching from cooking oil to pig fat, buying eggs and mackerel instead of pork and less or lower quality alcohol and cigarettes. Some of the people interviewed were also relying more on ready-made food, which they recognized has lower nutritional value but is also cheaper than cooking from fresh ingredients. Migrants were trying to reduce their expenses by living in groups

Table 9.3. Main Coping Strategies Used by the Groups in the Sample during Q1 2009 and Q1 2010

Strategies	Formal workers		Informal workers		Migrants	Rural households	
	Male	Female	Male	Female		With land	Without land
Reducing amount of food	—	—	X	X	—	—	X
Reducing quality of food	X	X	X	X	X	X	X
Acquiring informal loans	—	—	X	X	X	—	X
Shifting sector of work	X	X	X	X	—	—	—
Children dropping out of school to work	—	—	X	X	—	—	X
Joining producer network			X	X	—	—	—
Getting additional jobs	X	X	X	X	—	—	X

Source: Authors, based on interviews and FGD responses.

and sharing costs on accommodation and food. All participants were also reducing the frequency of visits to relatives in other provinces as a way of saving on transport costs.

During 2009, the urban poor and the landless had also resorted to the drastic strategy of reducing the amounts of food consumed, reducing their meals from three to two times a day by having breakfast later in the day and dinner earlier. Some parents in the slums explained that they were no longer able to provide their children with money for lunch at school, and had reduced lunch allowances from B 30 to B 20 or even B 15. Some people were under such severe economic difficulties that they had to rely on food donations from monks to feed their families or were sending their children to work in temples to get free food. Reducing food consumption to cope with declining resources was mentioned in March 2009, and the strategy was still in use a year later in February 2010. This finding is at odds with macroeconomic data for the last quarter of 2009 and early 2010, which indicate strong economy recovery. It is possible that the extent of damage on the resource base of the most vulnerable in the sample, caused by a combination of lost income (remittances, low demand for their services or products), depleted savings and assets, and high debt resulted in longer-lasting effects and weakened their capacity for recovery (see Dercon and Saphiro 2007 for the effects of shocks on the poor and poverty mobility).

Accessing Informal Loans

Borrowing to cover liquidity shortfalls was a key coping mechanism for all respondents. Most of the informal workers interviewed in the slums, landless in rural areas, and cross-border migrants had increased their debt commitments during 2009 by purchasing food on credit, borrowing from relatives and friends, accessing village funds, or getting informal loans from moneylenders. Borrowing from banks was impossible for informal workers and for the landless because of the many requirements, including proof of employment and collateral. Loans from friends and family were for the most part interest free but also small and short term (2–3 months). Loans from moneylenders could be accessed quickly and had longer repayment periods, but also high interest rates, reaching in some cases as much as 20 percent per month.

Many borrowers ended up in serious difficulties trying to pay back their debt. There were instances of both Thai and migrant families unable to pay back their debts and fleeing their homes, further exacerbating their vulnerability. A disturbing finding was that drug dealers were becoming informal moneylenders and were forcing their highly indebted borrowers to sell drugs to repay the debts, a situation that resulted in many of these borrowers running away to other provinces to avoid being abused. This finding is possibly related to the sharp increase in drug dealing reported in the slums during the crisis period.

Shifting Sectors

Factory workers used the strategy of shifting sectors with a good degree of success. In view of the reduction in income in manufacturing, workers moved to agriculture and back to manufacturing when external demand stabilized, creating a situation in which the low unemployment rate of around 1.5 percent remained relatively unchanged throughout the crisis.[7] In spite of the important reductions in income by moving from manufacturing, a high-income sector, to low-income agriculture, there were overall gains in using this strategy. Participants indicated that staying in the city underemployed or unemployed would have been impossible given the high costs of living, which could be covered only with overtime and extra bonuses. Severance payments and unemployment insurance, which is set at 50 percent of the last salary received, could cover only basic expenses and was provided for a set period of six months.

Informal workers, on the other hand, did not turn to rural areas in search of agricultural work. Workers in the sample explained that they had established themselves in the cities long ago and over time had lost their links with extended families in the countryside. These workers preferred to search for additional work in areas just outside their communities.

Additional Jobs and More Family Members Working

Multiple-worker households became the norm in urban areas, and both males and females were trying to find additional work. Men looked for jobs that could generate higher income even if that entailed a longer commute. Men were willing to migrate away from home to do jobs in construction or motorbike taxi driving. Female workers indicated preference for additional jobs that would allow them to work from home and take care of their children, although home-based work, such as online sales, had been declining steadily since the crisis started. To maximize the ability of family members to access paid jobs outside the home, older siblings or grandparents were recruited to take care of the younger children and do the housework.

Initial fears of widespread school dropouts expressed by participants in early 2009 did not materialize, but there were indications throughout 2009 that children in slums were working. The Mercy Center, an established charitable institution in Bangkok, indicated that as many as 20 percent of the children had left the Mercy Center school in the Klong Toey slum to help their families earn some money by becoming street vendors of lottery tickets and flower garlands. NGO workers were concerned about the associated risks and heightened vulnerability of children working on the streets, and staff at a port hospital in Bangkok indicated that the rate of underage pregnancies rose in 2009. People in the slums indicated that more young teens, both male and female, were involved in drug dealing and sex work to earn money.

Joining Producer Networks

Some homeworkers in the slums joined producer networks that helped them to link subcontractors and to share orders among network members. The strategy had only limited success as homeworkers described instances in which subcontractors had disappeared without paying for the products delivered, examples that further highlight the vulnerability of informal home-based workers. A member of HomeNet, the Foundation for Labor and Employment Promotion, explained:

"We are not regular workers. What we are doing has a risk. Payment is not guaranteed when we submit our work. But we have no other choices. We usually take jobs for 3–5 days then deliver 100–200 pairs of trousers to the network. At present I can gain 4 baht for a pair of jeans. The network deducted 0.50 baht and gave me 3.50 baht. The deduction is to cover transportation and electricity [for the electric sewing machine].*"*

Informal Safety Nets

For the participants in the study, family and communal solidarity was important to their ability to cope with the economic crisis. Laid-off workers were well-received back in their rural households; interviewees mentioned being able to borrow small amounts from relatives and friends to cover daily expenses; people could buy food and basic products on credit; and assistance from community institutions such as the local temple was available for the poorest. Some residents of Bangkok slums also benefited from NGO assistance. For example, the Mercy Center ran a school for children of informal workers, provided support to people living with HIV/AIDS, and offered health services for the community. A dramatic case of communal solidarity was observed in Bangkok's Klong Toey slum where a community savings cooperative used some of the group's money funds to bail out highly indebted members about to lose property used as collateral. By doing so they risked depleting the revolving funds and the savings of all members.

Social solidarity was also strong among cross-border migrants who provided support to each other, particularly against violence and harassment, but also financially through small loans. As for rural households, land seems to have been the ultimate safety net, allowing them to maintain production and consumption. Common property resources acted as a safety net for the landless, but people in the sample mentioned extensive contamination from pesticides and fertilizers of common ponds and public land, limiting the use of this strategy.

Formal Sources of Support

Government Response to the Crisis

The Thai government reacted swiftly to the economic contraction and to political unrest with two fiscal stimulus packages, the first approved in

January 2009, and the second in May. The first package focused on emergency response and aimed at increasing spending and stimulating internal demand by injecting B 116.7 billion into the economy in the form of cash transfers to low-income earners, tax cuts, and subsidies for education, transport, and utilities. Transfers included the one-time payment of $65 for low-income earners in the formal sector registered with the social security fund, and the Old-age Living Allowance of B 500 per month ($17) for citizens over 60 years not covered under any other retirement scheme. Funds for direct income support were expected to benefit 9 million people. Table 9.4 provides an overview of the first package.

Further initiatives included the introduction of the 15-Year Free Education with Quality program for formal and informal education and the extension of subsidies on water, electricity, and public transport, which had been established as a measure to help poorer households counter soaring food and oil prices in 2008. These government programs complemented ongoing contributory programs such as the social security fund (pension fund, compensation funds, and unemployment insurance) and programs financed from the national budget such as the universal health coverage.

Programs targeting growing job insecurity and stimulating production included a retraining scheme for workers at risk of losing their jobs, laid-off workers, and young graduates ready to enter the labor market. Tax cuts and credit at low fixed interest rates were made available for indebted

Table 9.4. January 2009 Stimulus Package

Areas and programs	Budget (B billion)
Increasing spending and stimulating demand	62.4
• B 200 direct cash transfer for low-income earners	18.9
• Extension of subsidies on water, electricity, and transport started during previous government	11.4
• Reduced prices on selected items for low-income earners	1
• Free 15-year education	19
• B 500 living allowance for senior citizens	9
• B 600 living allowance for village health volunteers	3
Developing small infrastructure (irrigation, village roads, health centers)	7.2
Increasing productivity and tackling unemployment (training)	6.9
Promoting tourism and country image abroad	1.3
Supporting SMEs and food industry	0.5
Establishing village funds	15.2

Source: Ministry of Finance in Mallikamas and Chirathivat 2011.

and cash-strapped companies for a year, if they retained their employees. Five key industries were targeted for assistance: automakers, textiles, electronics, food, and brand-name products. To support small and medium enterprises, the government increased the capital of the SME bank, but these enterprises were still having difficulties accessing credit and showed the lowest rate of recovery by early 2010. Apart from poor access to credit, SMEs and informal entrepreneurs faced other constraints, such as lack of access to markets and poor knowledge of consumer demand, which were not addressed in government programs. For example, workers in imitation gold ornaments in the sample complained that they could not effectively market their products because rents at markets and exhibition halls were too high and local police would not allow them to set their displays on the street; they were excluded from the gems and ornamental business associations due to their informal status; and they lacked information on their rights and the regulatory environment governing their industry.

The second stimulus package, known as Strong Thailand 2012, was announced in May 2009. It added B 1.43 trillion and focused mainly on creating job opportunities and ensuring the competitiveness of the country in the long run through large infrastructure development. Additional policies during this period included the transformation of the long-standing crop mortgage scheme to a price insurance scheme under which the government pays farmers the difference between market prices and guaranteed prices for key crops (rice, maize, tapioca, rubber) based on estimated production costs with a profit margin of 20 percent to 25 percent. More than 4 million farmers registered for the plan in 2009. Later in the year, the government began an innovative debt-refinancing scheme, targeting low-income earners struggling to pay back high interest rate informal loans. The program intended to help highly indebted people to transfer their informal loans, up to a ceiling of B 200,000, to state-owned banks offering better terms.

Workers' Perceptions of Selected Programs

The 15-year Free Education Program. The free education program subsidizes tuition fees, textbooks, learning materials, additional teaching activities paid to schools, and cash payments for uniforms paid directly to parents (table 9.5). During its first year, the program reached 12.3 million students, and according to a perception poll in 2009 (Suan Dusit University Bangkok Poll 2009), more than 60 percent in a sample of 1,238 beneficiary families said that the government's free education program had helped

Table 9.5. 15-Year Free Education with Quality Program (B per student)

Level	School tuition fees		Textbooks		Learning materials	Uniforms	Activities promoting quality improvements	
	Formal education	Informal education	Formal	Informal			Formal	Informal
Pre-school	1,700	—	200	—	100	300	215	—
Primary school	1,900	1,100	347.20–580.00	290	195	360	240	140
Lower secondary	3,500	2,300	560.00–739.20	360	210	450	440	290
Upper secondary	3,800	2,300	763.20–1,160.80	400	230	500	475	290
Vocational and technical education	4,900–11,900	4,240	1,000	500	230	900	475	530

Source: Bureau of International Cooperation 2009

Note: — = not available.

them to reduce their expenses. The poll also showed that prior to the program, almost 50 percent in the sample had used their savings to cover education-related expenditures, 27 percent had acquired loans from financial institutions, 14 percent sought urgent cash from informal financial sources, and 8.5 percent resorted to pawn shops.

Pawning jewelry and goods had been a common practice in slums, in particular at the beginning of a new school semester. Only a few respondents mentioned using this strategy for the school semester 2009–10, which could indicate either that most people had already depleted their resources and had nothing else to pawn and sell or that the subsidies were having a positive impact by reducing the necessity to pawn possessions to pay for school tuition fees. The subsidies, however, did not make school completely free, and initial findings from a subsequent assessment on impacts of the program in September 2010 indicate that parents still have a range of expenses to meet sending children to school (World Bank 2010b). Parents mentioned additional costs to cover at least two uniforms per year and extracurricular activities such as computer or language classes. These expenses might in part explain why dropouts were still reported in the slums in February 2010. People in the sample confirmed that the subsidy and additional support from charities allowed some households to keep their children in school, but the very poor may have still had difficulties in choosing whether to send their children to school, even at low cost, and sending them to work earning a minimal daily amount. That parents still face this choice suggests that a combination of instruments such as subsidies and direct and conditional cash transfers might increase the rates of success among the poorest.

Cash Transfers, Subsidies, and Microfinance. Respondents were satisfied with the monthly transfer to senior citizens under the first stimulus package, which reached more than 5 million people in 2009–10. Thailand is experiencing a rapid expansion of its older population, with the proportion of people 60 years old and above reaching 11 percent (about 7.2 million people) of the total population in 2007, and expected to reach 19.2 percent in 2015 (Fujioka and Thangphet 2009). Currently, most of the elderly are not covered by a pension scheme, which helps explain the high rate of poverty among this segment of society compared with the general population.

Many respondents also indicated having benefited from subsidies on water and electricity. One motorcycle taxi driver from a Bangkok slum indicated: "*Savings from free water and electricity are exactly the same as the costs of powder milk I have to buy for my child. It saves me a lot of money, and I hope the government could extend the support.*" Respondents living in rented apartments were less convinced of the positive impact of these subsidies on the poor and complained that in many cases landlords benefiting from the program kept on requesting their tenants to pay for the services. Furthermore, the subsidies did not help the poorest in rural areas or slum dwellers squatting on public lands that lack basic service infrastructure and are not connected to the grid or to water services.

The direct cash transfer program for low-income earners, known as Help the Nation, distributed a one-time payment of B 2,000 to workers earning below B 15,000 per month and making contributions to the social security fund. These transfers reached civil servants and workers in the formal sector but excluded the large majority of low-income informal workers not registered with the fund. Another program that according to respondents had only limited success reaching the poor was the promotion of microfinance channeled through the Village and Urban Revolving Funds (VRF), commonly known as village funds.[8] These credit funds, established in 2001, are active in all of Thailand's 77,000 villages, constituting one the largest microfinance program in the world and of extreme importance in the country's rural credit market (Menkhoff and Rungruxsirivorn 2011). A previous study suggests that the VRF has had a positive impact on welfare and that borrowers are disproportionately poor and agricultural (Boonperm, Haughton, and Khandker 2009). But people interviewed in 2010 indicated that choosing the village funds to boost microfinance in the context of the crisis greatly limited the success of the program in terms of reaching the most vulnerable. "*All these funds are supposed to be used to help the poor; but the rich always grab them first. The support does not reach the poor. The poor will continue to be poor,*" said a villager during the group discussions. Others complained of discriminatory attitudes toward the poor by the village fund committees in charge of approving the loans (table 9.6). People in the sample felt that they were left out because the committees believed that the poor would not be able to pay back their loans. Village funds are rated on efficiency criteria and are rewarded with extra money when high repayment targets are met, which may help explain the difficulties of poorer villagers in accessing funding.

Informal Debt Refinancing. The initial response to the debt-refinancing program was encouraging, with more than a million people registering

Table 9.6. Household Debt in 2009, Thai baht

Estimated households with debt	11.8 million
Only informal	900,000
Only formal	9.8 million
Mix of informal and formal	1.1 million

Source: NSO 2009.

for the program with debts averaging B 100,000. The results, however, are mixed. Less than half of the registered debtors were able to renegotiate their loans, and large numbers of borrowers did not join. According to respondents, two important requirements limited registration. First, the borrower needed to have one or more guarantors with a salary pay slip representing up to 10 percent of the loan amount, which was a challenge for people working in the informal economy with no links to higher income groups (Laodumrongchai et al. 2010).[9] The second requirement was to reveal the names of informal lenders when registering to carry on negotiations. Many informal moneylenders were opposed to having their names disclosed—possibly fearing taxes—and pressured their borrowers not to access the program. When the power relationships between borrowers and informal moneylenders became apparent, the government involved the police, which caused even more reluctance among moneylenders to be part of this program.

Conclusion

Between 2008 and 2009, Thailand suffered the combined effects of the global financial crisis and its own domestic political crisis. The financial crisis impacted growth through the fast decline in global demand for Thai exports, and political unrest added to the impact on domestic consumer confidence and internal demand. Macro-level effects were transmitted to people and communities mainly through a fall in demand for labor, which lowered wages and incomes. Workers in sectors linked to global trade initially experienced freezes in overtime, reductions in working hours, and eventually layoffs. In the informal sector, workers saw falling demand for their services and products, and they experienced growing competition from laid-off workers trying to work in the informal sector. Findings suggest that while the crises affected all workers in one way or another, informal workers and landless households dependent on remittances were hit hardest, had the most difficulties coping, and were taking longer to recover.

It was evident that Thailand had learned from the Asian Crisis of 1997 and a decade later exhibited a better developed social protection response. The government was quick in implementing countercyclical policies to avert the worst social impacts, restoring domestic demand and maintaining productivity in the short term and promoting Thailand's competitive edge for the future. Nevertheless, in spite of the stimulus packages, informal workers and landless households were still using extreme coping strategies, such as reducing their food intake for an extended period of time, exacerbating the vulnerability of individuals and communities. The challenges of targeting and better understanding the particular needs and circumstances of the poorest and most vulnerable remain, and addressing the inclusion of these groups will be critical as the country embarks on a process of reform of its social protection programs. (Indeed, in 2011, the government presented a proposal to expand the social protection fund to initially include 20 million informal workers and to progressively expand coverage to all 60 million informal workers.) Issues of equitable distribution, the social aspects of a healthy and educated society, and policies that address the sustainability of social spending in the longer term will be essential to attain and maintain the policy aims of a strong Thailand beyond 2012.

Notes

1. The areas are Bungkum, Klong Toey, Ram Intra, Romklaow, and Wangthonglang.
2. According to data from the Ayutthaya Provincial Labor and Welfare Protection Office, females represented 60 percent of the layoffs in that province in December 2008.
3. Agricultural employment increased by 11 percent between November and December 2008. Increases due to seasonality had averaged 6 percent in the previous five years. The capacity of the agricultural sector to pick up the slack of laid-off urban workers seemed to have weakened in 2009.
4. In 2007, there were approximately 450,000 home-based workers in Thailand. Around 80 percent of these workers are women, according to data from the National Statistics Office.
5. Thailand Ministry of Labor, 2008, cited in Chantavanich et al. 2009.
6. According to Human Rights Watch in 2010, migrants had restricted access to mobile phones, motorbikes, and cars in five provinces: Phang Nga, Phuket,

Ranong, Rayong, and Surat Thani. There were also severe restrictions on the rights of freedom of movement, association, assembly, and the right to property.

7. Thailand's unemployment rate has remained constant since 2006 at around 1.5 percent with a spike to 2.4 percent at the worst of the crisis in Q1 2009.

8. Village Funds received 8.7 billion Thai B from the Strong Thailand package.

9. Information collected by the World Bank and the Asian Research Centre for Migration (ARCM) during a third rapid assessment in 2010 with informal workers in Bangkok, Kong Toey, and Nakorn Rachasrima province. In *Thailand Economic Monitor, November 2010*, World Bank, Bangkok.

References

Boonperm J., Haughton J., and Khandker S. 2009. "Does the Village Fund Matter in Thailand?" Policy Research Working Paper 5011, World Bank Washington, DC.

Bureau of International Cooperation, Ministry of Education. 2009. http://planipolis.iiep.unesco.org/upload/Thailand/Thailand_free_education.pdf.

Chantavanich S., S. Laodumrongchai, M. Than, and A. Wong-a-thitikul. 2009. *Rapid Assessment on the Impacts of the Economic Downturn on Workers in Thailand*. Phase I, Bangkok: Asian Research Center for Migration, Chulalongkorn University.

Corner, L. 2010. *The Differential Impact on Women, Men and Children of Fiscal Responses to the Global Economic Crisis: Cambodia, Indonesia, Lao PDR and Vietnam*. UNICEF EAPRO, Bangkok.

Dercon, S., and J. Shapiro. 2007. *Moving On, Staying Behind, Getting Lost: Lessons on Poverty Mobility from Longitudinal Data*. Oxford: Global Poverty Research Group, Economic and Social Research Council.

Fujioka, R., and S. Thangphet. 2009. "Decent Work for Older Persons in Thailand," ILO Asia-Pacific Working Paper Series. Bangkok: International Labour Office Regional Office for Asia and the Pacific.

Human Rights Watch. 2010. *From the Tiger to the Crocodile: Abuse of Migrant Workers in Thailand*. New York: Human Rights Watch.

IMF (International Monetary Fund). 2010. *World Economic Outlook 2010*. Washington, DC: International Monetary Fund.

Laodumrongchai, S., W. Chaiyapa, C. Ariyasuntorn, and S. Chantavanich. 2010. *Rapid Assessment of the Impacts of the Global Economic Downturn on Workers in Thailand*. Phase II, Bangkok: Asian Research Centre for Migration.

Mallikamas, S., and S. Chirathivat. 2011. "Thailand's Economic Performance and Responses to the Global Financial Crisis." *Managing Economic Crisis in Southeast Asia*, ed. Saw Swee-Hock, chapter 5. Singapore: The Institute of Southeast Asian Studies (ISEAS).

Menkhoff, L. and O. Rungruxsirivorn. 2011. "Do Village Funds Improve Access to Finance? Evidence from Thailand." *World Development* 39: (1): 110–22.

NSO (National Statistics Office). 2007. *Survey on Informal Workers*. Bangkok: National Statistics Office.

———. 2009. *The 2009 Houshold Socio-Economic Survey*. Bangkok: NSO.

———. 2008. *Labor Force Survey, Whole Kingdom*. Bangkok: National Statistics Office.

Paitoonpong, S., and N. Akkarakul. 2009. "The Impact of the Economic Crisis on Women Workers in Thailand." *TDRI Quarterly Review*, December: 3–13.

Suan Dusit University Bangkok Poll. 2009. "Effects of Economic Crisis on Parents during School Term Opening." Suan Dusit University.

Tulaphan, P. 2008. *Economic Empowerment for Women in the Informal Economy in Thailand*. United Nations, Department of Economic and Social Affairs, Division for the Advancement of Women, EC/WSRWD/2008/EP.6.

UNDP (United Nations Development Programme). 2009. *Human Development Report, Overcoming Barriers: Human Mobility and Development*. New York: UNDP.

World Bank. 2009a. *Thailand Economic Monitor, April–June 2009*. Bangkok: World Bank. http://go.worldbank.org/129MKJ1L20.

———. 2009b. *World Development Indicators*. Washington, DC: World Bank.

———. 2010a. *East Asia and the Pacific Economic Update: Emerging Stronger from the Crisis*. Washington, DC: World Bank.

———. 2010b. *Thailand Economic Monitor, November 2010*. Bangkok: World Bank.

Country Studies

In addition to the eight countries covered as separate chapters in this book, field work reports from Ghana, the Philippines, Serbia, Ukraine, Vietnam, and Zambia helped inform the overview in chapter 1 and are listed below. Field work was also undertaken in Indonesia, Jamaica, and the Republic of Yemen but not reported in stand-alone documents.

Bangladesh

BRAC Development Institute. 2009. *Impact of Food, Fuel and Financial Crises in Bangladesh, Dhaka.* May.

Cambodia

Cambodia Development Research Institute. 2009. *Rapid Assessment of the Impacts of the Economic Crisis on Cambodian Households and Vulnerable Workers' Income, Consumption and Coping Strategies.* Second round. Phnom Penh. August.
———. 2009. *Rapid Assessment of Impacts of the Economic Crisis on Cambodian Households and Vulnerable Workers: Road to Recovery.* Third round. Phnom Penh. December.
Vuthy, T., and K. Sothorn. 2009. *Rapid Assessment of the Impacts of the Economic Crisis on Cambodian Households: Focus Group Discussions with Vulnerable Workers and Rural Households.* Phnom Penh: Cambodia Development Research Institute. July.

Central Africa Republic

Salmon, L. 2010. *Rapid Assessment of the Impacts of the Economic Crisis on Central African Republic Households and Vulnerable Workers: Income, Consumption and Coping Strategies.* First round. Bangui.

———. 2010. *Rapid Survey on the Effects of the International Financial Crisis on Poor and Vulnerable Households and Workers in the Central African Republic: Income, Consumption and Adaptation Strategies.* Second round. Bangui.

Ghana

Dogbe, T., and C. Marshall. 2009. *A Rapid Assessment of the Impact of the Global Economic Crisis in Ghana.* Kumasi: Participatory Development Associates, Ltd. July.

Kazakhstan

Sange Research Center. 2010. *Assessing the Social Impacts of the Financial Crisis in Kazakhstan.* Almaty. June–July.

Kenya

Lubaale, G. 2009. *Pilot Project on Qualitative Monitoring of the Impact of and Response to the Food, Fuel and Financial Crises. Kenya Country Report.* Nairobi: Mpereeza Associates. March.

Mongolia

Global Reach Center. 2009. *A Final Report for Study on the Crisis Implications for Household Livelihood.* Ulaanbaatar. May–June.

———. 2009. *Second Round Research on Monitoring the Impacts of the Economic Crisis in Mongolia.* Ulaanbaatar. August–September.

———. 2010. *Qualitative Monitoring of the Social Impacts of the Financial Crisis: Third Round Research on Household Livelihood in Selected Aimags.* Ulaanbaatar. March.

————. 2011. *Qualitative Monitoring of the Social Impacts of the Financial Crisis. Fourth Round Research on Household Livelihood in Selected Aimags.* Ulaanbaatar. January.

Philippines

Institute of Philippine Culture. 2009. *First Quarter Report, Qualitative Research on the Impacts of the Economic Crisis on the Vulnerable Sectors of the Philippines.* Manila.
————. 2010. *Second Quarter Monitoring Data, Philippines.* Manila.

Senegal

University Cheikh Anta Diop. 2010. *Economic Crisis Impact on Vulnerable Populations in Senegal. Dakar.*

Serbia

Ispos Strategic Marketing. 2009. *Crisis Rapid Assessment. Prepared for the Social Inclusion and Poverty Reduction Unit, Office of the Deputy Prime Minister for European Integration.* Belgrade: Serbia and World Bank. October.

Thailand

Chantavanich, S., M. Than, S. Laodumrongchai, and A. Wong-a-thitikul. 2009. *Rapid Assessment on the Impacts of the Economic Downturn on Workers in Thailand.* Asian Research Center for Migration. Bangkok. June.
Asian Research Center for Migration. 2011. *Second Round Rapid Assessment: The Impacts of the Global Economic Downturn on Workers in Thailand.* Bangkok. June.

Vietnam

World Bank, Oxfam GB, and CAF (VASS) (Centre for Analysis and Forecasting, Vietnamese Academy of Social Sciences). 2009. *Rapid Assessment on Social Impacts of Economic Crisis in Vietnam.* March.

ActionAid and Oxfam GB. 2009. *The Impacts of the Global Financial Crisis on Socioeconomic Groups in Vietnam: A Regular Monitoring Report.* Hanoi. July–August.

Ukraine

Center of Social Expertise. 2010. *Assessment of Consequences of Economic Crisis in Ukraine, First Round. Institute of Sociology of National Academy of Sciences of Ukraine.* Kiev.
———. 2010. *Assessing the Social Impacts of the Economic Crisis in Ukraine. Second Round. Institute of Sociology of National Academy of Sciences of Ukraine.* Kiev.

Zambia

Mulumbi, M. 2009. *Qualitative Monitoring of the Impact of and Response to the Food, Fuel and Financial Crises. Voices from the Crisis: Pilot Study of the Crisis Impact Using Qualitative Methods in Zambia.* Lusaka. February.

INDEX

Boxes, figures, notes, and tables are indicated by *b*, *f*, *n*, and *t*, respectively.

A

ActionAid International Kenya, 50, 167, 171
ADB (Asian Development Bank), 185, 200
agriculture. *See* rural households
AIDS. *See* HIV/AIDS
alcohol and drug abuse, 41–42, 150, 175–76, 178, 190
anatomy of effects and coping responses, 4, 15, 23–59. *See also under specific countries*
  adverse coping responses, 26–27
  asset-based responses, 26, 27–30, 29*t*, 33–34
  assistance-based responses, 26, 29*t*, 30
  behavior-based responses, 26, 27, 28*t*
  for children, 38–41. *See also* children
  community cohesion, 42–44, 182, 226–27
  conceptual framework for, 24–27, 25*f*
  covariate shocks, 26
  definition of coping mechanisms, 24–26
  direct versus second-order impacts, 26
  financing (formal, micro, or informal), use of, 44–46, 48, 50, 58
  idiosyncratic (household-specific) shocks, 26
  for individuals and families, 30–34
  for men, 36–38, 150–51, 177–78
  patterns of resilience and vulnerabilities, 3–4, 3*t*, 10–13
  policy implications of, 55–59

  social protection systems, formal and informal, 47–55. *See also* social protection systems
  types of coping responses, 27–30, 28–29*t*
  women, disproportionate effects of crisis on, 34–38. *See also* women
  for young people, 41–42. *See also* youth
Arab Spring, 64, 85–86
ARCM (Asian Research Centre for Migration), Chulalongkorn University, Bangkok, 234
Ariyasuntorn, Cheewin, xvii, 233
Asian Crisis of 1997, 239, 254
Asian Development Bank (ADB), 185, 200
Asian Research Centre for Migration (ARCM), Chulalongkorn University, Bangkok, 234
assets. *See* credit, debt, and assets
assistance-based coping responses, 26, 29*t*, 30. *See also* social protection systems
attribution, problem of, 13–15

B

Bangladesh, 61–89, 257
  anatomy of coping in, 75–82
  asset-based effects and coping responses in, 33
  attribution, problem of, 14
  children in
    education and child labor, 77–78
    feeding of, 76–77
    migration, impact of, 79–80
  community cohesion in, 44

domestic sector, impact of crisis on,
234, 235t
education in, 38–39, 246, 248, 249–51,
250t
export sector, impact of crisis on,
233, 236
food insecurity in, 243–45
income increases not matching rising
food prices in, 56
labor market in
agricultural employment, 245–46,
254n3
on cross-border migrants, 242–43
on factory workers, 237–38
government-run assistance programs,
248–49
on informal sector workers, 239–42,
240t
livelihood diversification, 246
producer networks, homeworkers
joining, 246–47
on rural households, 238–39
shifting sectors, 245–46
SMEs, 58, 236, 249
migrants, cross-border, 242–43, 247
political crisis of 2008 to 2011 in, 234b
qualitative research project in, 234–36
remittances in, 238
social protection systems in
government-run, 48, 49, 50, 247–53,
248t
informal safety nets, 247
NGOs and religious organizations,
50, 51, 247
women in, 34, 237, 240, 246
youth, effects of crisis on, 42
Than, Mya, xxi, 233
theft. See crime, increase in
tontines, in Central African Republic,
54, 138
Touba coffee, in Senegal, 223
transmission channels, 5f, 15–17, 17–18n3.
See also under specific countries
Turk, Carolyn, xxi, 23, 143

U

Ukraine
credit, use of, 44, 45
goverment-run social protection system
in, 47, 48

men, effects of crisis on, 37–38
noneconomic/emotional effects of
crisis in, 32
qualitative research in, 260
women, disproportionate effects of crisis
on, 34, 35
United Nations Development Programme
(UNDP), 134
urban areas, migration to. See migration

V

Vietnam
agricultural landowners, resilience of,
54–55
goverment-run social protection system
in, 50
informal social protection networks in,
53, 54
qualitative research in, 259–60
women, effects of crisis on, 36
youth, effects of crisis on, 41
Village and Urban Revolving Funds (VRF),
Thailand, 252
Voice of the Poor (Narayan, 2000), 17n2,
24
VRF (Village and Urban Revolving Funds),
Thailand, 252
Vuthy, Theng, xxi, 91

W

waste recycling trade
in Bangladesh, 67–68, 78
in Kenya, 175
WFP (World Food Programme) food-
for-work project, in Kenya, 166,
179–80
Wodon, Quentin, xxi, 117, 207
women
in Bangladesh. See under Bangladesh
in Central African Republic, 36, 135–36
children, women with, 34–35
disproportionate effects of crisis on,
34–38
domestic violence and, 36–37, 40, 178,
190, 191, 205
female-headed households, rise in, 37
in formal sector employment, 12, 34
increased labor force participation of,
35, 225–26
in Kazakhstan, 150–51